THE POLITICAL PHILOSOPHY OF PIERRE MANENT

THE POLITICAL PHILOSOPHY *of*

PIERRE MANENT

Political Form & Human Action

JOSEPH R. WOOD

The Catholic University of America Press
Washington, D.C.

Cataloging-in-Publication Data is available from the Library of Congress

ISBN: 978-0-8132-3890-6 | eISBN: 978-0-8132-3891-3

Book design by Burt&Burt
Interior set in Meta Serif Pro, Meta Pro, and Rift Soft

I shall, with divine aid, say such things as I consider necessary
concerning the origin, progress and merited ends of the two cities,
which, as I have already said, are implicated and
mixed with one another in this world.

ST. AUGUSTINE
City of God against the Pagans, Book X (conclusion)

An "ideal" society would be the graveyard of human greatness.
Chance will always rule history, because it is not possible to organize
the state in such a way that it does not matter who rules.

NICOLÁS GÓMEZ DÁVILA
("Don Colacho")

"For what can be imagined more beautiful than the sight
of a perfectly just city rejoicing in justice alone." . . . When reason and
revelation run together, why, then you have something, a great age.

MARK HELPRIN
Winter's Tale

TABLE OF CONTENTS

Acknowledgments
ix

Chapter One
PIERRE MANENT, BEING HUMAN, AND POLITICAL PHILOSOPHY
1

Chapter Two
MANENT'S PROJECT
23

Chapter Three
CITY AND EMPIRE
71

Chapter Four
NATION AND CHURCH
127

Chapter Five
THE MODERN STATE
169

Chapter Six
WHAT MANENT HAS TAUGHT US—SO FAR
229

Bibliography
251

Index
259

ACKNOWLEDGMENTS

THE PATIENCE AND SUPPORT OF MY WIFE, Merrie, and daughters, Eleanor and Anne, made my work on the book both possible and pleasurable, as did the enthusiasm of many friends and the superb faculty of the Catholic University of America School of Philosophy. My dissertation committee – Dr. V. Bradley Lewis, Dean John C. McCarthy, and Monsignor Robert Sokolowski -- provided essential guidance, and I am in the fortunate position of calling them good friends as well as teachers. Dr. Jude P. Dougherty and Father James V. Schall, S.J., both of blessed memory, were tremendously generous with their wise advice and kind encouragement. Dr. John Lenczowski of the Institute of World Politics opened the possibility of pursuing the PhD that led to this book. Mr. Leonard Leo and the Catholic Association; Mr. Montgomery Brown and the former Earhart Foundation; the School of Philosophy; and the taxpayers of the United States, who provide benefits to military veterans on an extraordinary scale, all offered generous material support. Dr. Russ Hittinger and Dr. Scott Roniger offered, and continue to offer, wonderful conversation on the matters at hand. Ambassador Francis Campbell and Dr. Renée Köhler-Ryan of the University of Notre Dame Australia supplied the time for additional research and revisions. I am grateful, and mindful of the debt I owe, to all mentioned here.

I particularly thank Professor Pierre Manent, whose body of work merits and will surely receive more and better exploration than what is found here, and who graciously shared much of his time with me. His friend and colleague, Dr. Daniel J. Mahoney, was also very helpful.

Finally, the prayers of many saints and angels must have been effective, as with all the help just acknowledged, a succession of minor miracles was necessary to bring this work from start to finish. Deo gratias.

THE POLITICAL PHILOSOPHY OF PIERRE MANENT

Chapter One

PIERRE MANENT, BEING HUMAN, AND POLITICAL PHILOSOPHY

La recherche que j'entreprends ici porte principalement sur les *formes politiques*, ces modalités de l'association humaine dont aucune science n'a fait son objet spécifique mais dont la succession ordonne le mouvement de l'histoire européenne.[1]

PIERRE MANENT

Parmi les philosophes politiques français de sa génération, Pierre Manent est sans doute l'un des plus lus et respectés, en France mais aussi en Europe et dans le monde.[2]

GIULIO DE LIGLIO, JEAN-VINCENT HOLEINDRE,
AND DANIEL J. MAHONEY

PIERRE MANENT IS GENERALLY ACKNOWLEDGED to be one of the finest political philosophers at work today. The central focus of his research, political form, is by his own admission a vague notion because no science of it exists despite its decisive importance in European history. Politics gives form to human life, and understanding political form—the broadest human association for the common good—is thus essential to understanding human life, to what man is and how he thrives; political form is essential to political philosophy and to a complete philosophy of man. Manent thus

---

1 Pierre Manent, *Les Métamorphoses de la cité: Essai sur la dynamique de l'Occident* (Paris: Flammarion, 2010), 27–28. "The research that I undertake here bears principally on political forms, those modalities of human association of which no science makes its specific object but whose succession orders European history." Translations from French are original unless stated otherwise.

2 Giulio De Liglio, Jean-Vincent Holeindre, and Daniel J. Mahoney, eds., *La politique et l'âme* (Paris: CNRS Éditions, 2014), 10. "Among the French political philosophers of his generation, Pierre Manent is without doubt one of the most respected, in France but also in Europe and the world."

seeks to develop a science of political form. Francis Slade highlights the importance of such a science:

> It is not sufficient for a philosopher to talk about political things to have political philosophy. What is said must have the formality of political philosophy. That formality consists in the presentation of political form. Political philosophy properly speaking manifests political form, setting it forth in distinctness. Political philosophy possesses, or should possess, what I have referred to as political specificity. . . . Clarity about political form is the defining mark of political philosophy properly speaking.[3]

Slade then quotes Manent from *Cours familier de philosophie politique*: "That there are a determinate number of political forms is one of the most important 'theoretical' propositions of political science. The human world insofar as it is political does not present an indefinite variability; it is articulated, it is ordered. . . . [F]rom the moment people live politically, they live in a political form, or in the transition from one form to another."[4]

Manent does not provide a strict definition of "form." Rather, throughout his work, he seems to accept a general notion of form as the definition or essence of something, or the visible shape of something. "Form" is broader than the Aristotelian "regime," or the constitution that decides who rules; different regimes can exist within the same form, as for example, different Greek cities or European nations (two examples of political form) were ruled by different rulers with different constitutions. Manent's work on political form seeks to identify the order of political forms as they have existed in the human world, in particular the European world, and thus to advance our knowledge of what is true of human things as that truth appears in human choice and action, especially in the political domain.

Manent's proposition is simple in statement and grand in elaboration: to understand man, we must understand politics, which is human action at its most intensive and visible; to understand politics, we must describe and understand political form. If Manent succeeds in providing a science of political form, at least for the available history of European politics, his contribution to philosophy will be highly significant. He would

---

3 Francis Slade, "Two Versions of Political Philosophy: Teleology and the Conceptual Genesis of the Modern State," in *Natural Moral Law in Contemporary Society*, ed. Holger Zaborowski (Washington, DC: The Catholic University of America Press, 2010), 237.

4 Slade, "Two Versions of Political Philosophy," 237.

reconnect politics to an objective nature in the way originally understood in the classical view and offer a way to understand the relationship between the individual human soul and human action in the particular person and the political community as a whole. Manent's project opens the way to the return to and advancement of a science of man as "the political animal" that modern philosophy has rejected at the risk of a damaging impoverishment of our understanding of who and what we are.

With that development, in turn, Manent would aid in restoring a proper grasp of the complementarity of reason and faith, philosophy and religion in their proper domains, and their relationship to political events, preserving the genuine freedom of human action. He would aid us in seeing the "what is" of the reality that shapes us and makes demands upon us in order for us to be truly human and to thrive—a reality whose plausibility and desirability have come under severe pressure in recent centuries. By elaborating a science of political form, Manent would describe our action and the nature within which our action takes place in formal and visible terms that would allow us to understand human and political action not merely in one historical moment or place, but in a broader and more enduring way. In so doing, he would extend Aristotle's science of regimes and human action through the subsequent two millennia of European history. Manent would restore politics to its ancient place as the science of man's greatest good and the science that governs the art of shaping souls "to be in good condition."[5] He would contribute not just to political philosophy and the philosophy of man, but to the philosophy of history in which man is the principle of action but not the measure of all things. He would restore all of those philosophies to metaphysical principles of "being" in an ontology of a constant nature, against the modern principles of anti-natural historicism.

MANENT'S EARLY LIFE AND EDUCATION

Manent was born in 1949 in Toulouse, France, to a family of leftist political leanings with a father who supported Soviet communism. He recalls as a boy being abruptly corrected by his father after expressing some friendliness toward the Americans who had arrived in his neighborhood, and he naturally adopted his father's views, including atheism. But by his late

---

5 Aristotle, *Nicomachean Ethics* 1.2.1094b3–11; Plato, *Gorgias*, trans. James H. Nichols Jr. (Ithaca, NY: Cornell University Press, 1998), 464b5.

teenage years, he had begun to move away from communism and had been introduced to Catholic Christianity in general, and to Thomism in particular, by Louis Jugnet, a teacher at his lycée. Jugnet opened Manent to a "simultaneous discovery of philosophy and religion."[6] During the tumultuous protest years of the late 1960s, Manent attended the École Normale Superieure (ENS) in Paris, an institution he describes, in an indication of a certain Aristotelian inclination, as displaying "no wonderment" and having little common life.[7] He describes philosophy as taught at ENS at the time as "industrial," a "process of taking apart systems and putting them back together again," in particular the systems of Descartes and Kant as well as their followers and intellectual descendants, wherein no "capacity for intelligence was really called for."[8] Manent found this approach unsatisfying and searched for alternatives, leading him to thinkers such as Raymond Aron.

Manent makes clear that he is a Catholic believer, though he does not expand fulsomely on his faith, to which his route was predominantly intellectual. As he learned of Catholicism while a young man, his "approach to religion was through speculative theology, and not through piety. This was a key factor in the path I took."[9] After arriving in Paris, he encountered the salon of Stanislas and Aniouta Fumet, a compartment of "a world prior to the University, a world in which literary life was at the heart of national life, where artistic and intellectual life were inseparable, and also where Catholicism was still ambitious and domineering."[10] The husband traveled in the circles of Claudel and Maritain and lived "amid poetry, music, and mysticism," while the wife inhabited a world that was "all about the play of grace and of freedom. God was perpetually and visibly active in Aniouta's world."[11] Manent found that world delightful and admirable, but it was not the world in which he would reside intellectually or professionally. His work, while influenced by Catholicism, would remain very much focused on the world of human action and politics.

---

6 Pierre Manent, *Seeing Things Politically: Interviews with Bénédicte Delorme-Montini*, trans. Ralph C. Hancock (South Bend, IN: St. Augustine's Press, 2015), 21. The biographical information here is drawn principally from part I of this book.

7 *Seeing Things Politically*, 23.

8 *Seeing Things Politically*, 24.

9 *Seeing Things Politically*, 21.

10 *Seeing Things Politically*, 64.

11 *Seeing Things Politically*, 64.

Over his four decades of work, Manent taught at Le Collège de France and L'École des Hautes Études en Sciences Sociales in Paris, where he was director of studies until his retirement in 2014. He was a founder and editor of the journal *Commentaire*. His work has often focused on European liberal political thinkers and, in more recent years, on the problems associated with the expanding power of the European Union and with the growth of Islam in France and Europe. As will be seen, and as is apparent in the opening quotation above, the notion of political form is fundamental throughout his work.

SITUATING MANENT INTELLECTUALLY IN UNDERSTANDING THE "WHAT IS" OF MAN

In a 1992 essay, Manent writes, "We cannot know ourselves without first understanding our situation."[12] To understand Manent's central project of investigating political form, then, it will be important first to situate him intellectually. His antipathy toward the standard "industrial philosophy" that he encountered at university is a first indication of where he does *not* situate himself. How should we understand Manent's vocation at the broadest level, before trying to understand his specific investigation into political form? From what sources does he take his bearings?

At the broadest level, Manent is a theoretical philosopher who seeks to understand "what is" rather than to prescribe solutions or invent systems. He will at times reject the label of "philosopher," as when he claims, again in 1992, that his inquiries over the previous twenty years "can appear . . . to belong to philosophy" yet do not.[13] But his rejection seems to refer to the kind of philosophy that he found at ENS: without wonderment, the process of constructing and deconstructing systems that required little intelligence. He is interested not in abstract systems of thought, but in the reality around him. "I want to understand—or rather I desire to understand. . . . Today the human ambition is to be a creator. . . . The human faculty that receives all the praise is the imagination. Now it

---

12 Pierre Manent, "The Truth, Perhaps," in *Modern Liberty and Its Discontents: Pierre Manent*, ed. and trans. Daniel J. Mahoney and Paul Seaton (Lanham, MD: Rowman & Littlefield, 1998), 33.

13 "The Truth, Perhaps," 33.

happens that I have no imagination . . . and I have no ambition to create. What I want instead is to understand."[14]

In particular, he desires to understand man, to know what it is to be human, to identify and inquire after what is properly human. In *The City of Man*, he asks, "What do we really mean when we use the word *man* today? Whom are we speaking of when we defend human rights or engage in the human sciences? Not only do we lack a clear answer to this question, we do not even know how to go about asking it."[15] In order to escape a condition wherein our "speech is obsessed with man . . . without inquiring who he is,"[16] Manent will turn to several enduring problems and tensions, such as the classical mind versus the modern, the classical citizen versus the modern individual within a state, and the relationship of the particular and the universal. He seeks to understand man by observing his deliberations and actions as he navigates these tensions in the concrete situations and circumstances that present themselves to men in particular times and places, in politics.

Politics will be the way in which the "what is" of man reveals itself to Manent. It is the privileged window or vantage point for understanding what it is to be human in concrete terms. We know man through his uniquely human activities of deliberation and action. These are the activities of politics: "Deliberation and action demand . . . judgment, a judgment that . . . must take account of all the various aspects of the phenomenon [under consideration] and thus must account as well as possible for what everybody can see; for we live and act in a common world, the world shaped by the words and deeds of human beings."[17] Thus, Manent limits his inquiry into "what is" to the observable activity of politics:

> My ambition is to understand human things, and more specifi-
> cally, to understand politics and political things. Not because I
> see political things as a subset of the human things that interest
> me, but because the political order is what truly gives human
> life its form. Political things are the cause of human order or

---

14 Manent, *Seeing Things Politically*, 1.

15 Pierre Manent, *The City of Man*, trans. Marc A. LePain (Princeton, NJ: Princeton University Press, 1998), 5.

16 *The City of Man*, 5.

17 Pierre Manent, *Beyond Radical Secularism: How France Should Respond to the Islamic Challenge*, trans. Ralph C. Hancock (South Bend, IN: St. Augustine's Press, 2016), 10.

disorder. . . . I seek to discern the true role of politics in the ordering of the human world.[18]

Politics is, in Manent's view, the bedrock science of the human and the
essential object of study for understanding the human world.

MANENT'S TRIANGLE OF POLITICS, PHILOSOPHY, AND RELIGION

Manent claims,

> I am inside a triangle: politics, philosophy, religion. I have never
> been able to settle on one of the poles. . . . Of course, I can say
> that the world draws upon these three great sources, that it turns
> on these great axes and therefore that, in keeping my distance
> in relation to these three points, I remain open to the diversity or
> complexity of the world. This is a flattering answer, but frankly it
> is not satisfying. The reason is that politics, religion, and philos-
> ophy represent three human attitudes, each of which requires
> complete devotion.[19]

He notes that to be what they wanted to be and truly were, the statesman
Churchill could not be a philosopher or a religious, Strauss and Socrates
could not be politicians or religious, and Thomas Aquinas, despite using
with great competence the tools of philosophy, could not be other than a
religious ("he has already given his soul to the Answer that precedes all
questions"[20]). Manent explains that each of the three vertices

> claims a complete devotion that I cannot or will not grant to any
> of them because the two others also appeal to me. I find a fragile
> equilibrium, or rather a productive disequilibrium, in this ques-
> tioning that I pursue concerning the very manner in which these
> three dimensions are articulated throughout Western history. . . .
> [B]y taking each of the three equally seriously, I attain a certain
> impartiality in understanding this history.[21]

---

18 Manent, *Seeing Things Politically*, 1–2.
19 *Seeing Things Politically*, 59.
20 *Seeing Things Politically*, 60.
21 *Seeing Things Politically*, 60.

With this suggestion, Manent introduces the vantage point from which he will view the three attitudes or sources that hold his interest: history, which is inside the triangle with him. The history that Manent seeks to understand reveals the "articulation"—that is to say, the reasoned speech—of philosophy, religion, and politics. The last of the three is, again, the most visible because it is the domain of the action that can be seen.

If Manent distanced himself from philosophy as it was practiced at ENS when he was a student, he likewise maintains a distance from religion even as he enters the Church:

> The more I came close to religion, the more I entered into it, the more on the other hand I had contact with the effects of religion that did not win me over, or that, in some respects, put me off. Even while Catholicism, in its doctrinal architecture, seemed to me to represent the crystal of every desired truth, I took note of its political incompetence and its effects in this domain that I would describe without hesitation as corrupting.[22]

Manent goes further: he claims that "piety leads us to expect a holiness from which one is, in general, naturally quite distant."[23] The religious and the natural domains are, for Manent, somewhat separated. He grants with Pascal that Catholic Christianity "has well understood mankind," but he finds that religion as a guide to our natural experience is untrustworthy;[24] that "for human nature to appear receptive to religious law, or at least capable of receiving it, it is sometimes necessary to pretend not to see things it is impossible to ignore";[25] and that a "work that brings together fidelity to human experience and commitment to a religious perspective is rare."[26]

Manent seems, then, to draw a very bright line between the domains of religion and human affairs as those affairs show up in politics. While this hard line softens later in his life as he turns from his work on political form to using that work in the understanding of contemporary political questions, he is concerned to preserve politics from the excessive intrusion of faith or theology in his investigation, though as will be seen such intrusion

---

22 *Seeing Things Politically*, 60.

23 *Seeing Things Politically*, 61.

24 *Seeing Things Politically*, 62.

25 *Seeing Things Politically*, 63.

26 *Seeing Things Politically*, 64. Manent claims that the Psalms comprise one such rarity. *Seeing Things Politically*, 63.

is part of the history he will study and an important consideration in what he will call the "movement" of political form. In his 1992 essay, he raises with apparent if tentative approval "the possibility that the political domain is really the generative principle of the human world."[27] This suggestion that men generate the world of human things in a domain of their own, on their own terms, is illustrated in Manent's more recent discussion of the Christian influence on political ideas such as equality and freedom. To those who find the basis of political equality in Christian teaching, he responds, "[W]hile Christianity has really done very little to reduce social or political inequalities (this was not and cannot be its purpose), it has, as much as it could, brought an end to the very radical separation that the Ancients imposed between the wise and everyone else.... [T]he hypothesis of a democratic secularization of Christian equality cannot be maintained, since the two ideas of equality are, as it were, unrelated."[28] This proposition also differentiates religion from philosophy, at least in their respective Christian and classical manifestations. Likewise, freedom is a subject on which Christianity has much to offer, in the realm of personal conscience. But in politics, its understanding of freedom is irrelevant: "Conscience is invisible; it opens up an invisible domain, but political life takes place in the visible world, and Christianity has nothing pertinent or specific to say concerning political life."[29] Manent thus maintains a strong separation among the vertices of his triangle. The vertices will prove to have substantial influence on each other, but in the form of tension more than complementarity, and that tension will play out in history as it results from and is visible in the actions of men. The interplay of philosophy, religion, and politics reveals itself as history, and Manent will focus on the political vertex of the triangle as the most visible and quintessentially human of the three while referring constantly to the other two.

THE TURN TO THE CLASSICAL

Manent's theoretical interest in what is, his distaste for what passes for philosophy in much of contemporary academe, and his mild repulsion at the pietism that seems to color the religious if and as they choose to operate politically in this world, all turn him toward classical political

---

27 Manent, "The Truth, Perhaps," 41.

28 Manent, *Seeing Things Politically*, 167.

29 *Seeing Things Politically*, 169.

philosophy as the basis for his examination of politics.[30] In a 1993 essay on Claude Lefort, he writes,

> Political philosophy, philosophy, and politics were "born in Greece." Plato, Aristotle, and Thucydides explored the public space with an amplitude and precision that even those least nostalgic for classical philosophy or for "ancient liberty" can hardly fail to admire. And if anything were lacking in the experience and thought of the Greeks, it seems that the long and singular history of Rome is there to supply it. . . . If we turn to modern political philosophy—as abundant, rich, and impressive as it is—to try to grasp the essentials of modern political life, we are struck by its singularly abstract character, which distinguishes it in so trenchant a fashion from classical political philosophy.[31]

Seventeen years later, he would describe his investigation as belonging

> to ancient political science, not because it is ancient but because it is political and it alone is wholly political; that is, wholly the science of the government of humans by humans. According to this science, the state of human things results principally from the deliberations and actions of humans, whereas modern political science . . . tends to make us the playthings of "causes" that "govern" us. The human world is governed by the way people govern themselves.[32]

Manent will situate himself in ancient political thought and align himself with its "aim to understand politics" in an endeavor "to attain a political science."[33] That science, as he believes classical thinkers would agree, is the science of human deliberative action. "There is a science of human things. That is what I believe, and there are very few who believe it. Our contemporaries think that there is obviously a science of nature. . . . But people take it as given that there exists no science of human things properly

---

30 This repulsion would seem to be mainly or entirely toward those who bring a disproportionately religious attitude to the domains of politics and philosophy. Manent's concern is not to reject religion (as will be clear below in the discussion of Strauss's influence) but to maintain the legitimacy of religion, politics, and philosophy on their own terms. This is necessary to sustain the integrity of each.

31 Manent, "Toward the Work and Toward the World: Claude Lefort's Machiavelli," in *Modern Liberty and Its Discontents*, 51.

32 Pierre Manent, *Metamorphoses of the City: On the Western Dynamic*, trans. Marc LePain (Cambridge, MA: Harvard University Press, 2013), 28.

33 Manent, *Seeing Things Politically*, 3.

speaking."[34] Manent will return to classical philosophy to ground his effort to reach a political science, a science of what is proper and natural to the human domain, a science whose existence contemporary philosophers would deny.

Manent's understanding of the classical link between deliberative human action and politics, a link centered on the reason that is unique to humans, becomes more apparent in his discussion of Jean-Jacques Rousseau in *Metamorphoses of the City*. Drawing on Rousseau's doubts that the rich and the poor could ever overcome or move beyond their positions and interests as rich and poor, Manent allows that these interests endure in politics on the part of each group, but he also allows the possibility that reason can and will lead to a recognition of a greater good. "[R]eason, however partisan its ordinary arguments may be, is more extended than the most extended imagination of the richest proprietor."[35] Reason permits the rich, in particular, to deliberate about something beyond their own interests. This possibility opens the way to politics, which is the actualization of reason as distinct from imagination:

> The most extended imagination has its center in the body itself, in the sentiment of the self, the sentiment of the existence of the human individual, whereas the least active reason, the one most constrained by the needs, the passions, the sentiment of the self, involves a decentering movement toward a point that exists only through it, the point of justice or the common good. Becoming a citizen and becoming a rational agent in this sense go together.[36]

If we are to be human, as rational agents, we will be political as well. What I have called here a "link" is in fact close to an identity. Our social nature becomes "the starting point of a vast and very complex, an unprecedented category of human movements, those that are proper to the citizen. And the city, or the public thing or the common good, is the object and the goal of these movements."[37]

Manent associates this "vast category of human movements" with the development of politics in the city, and thus with ancient political thought. His investigation, then, can also be seen as an effort to recover a science of this politics and its authentic human diversity, or heterogeneity.

---

34 *Seeing Things Politically*, 4.
35 Manent, *Metamorphoses*, 90.
36 *Metamorphoses*, 90.
37 *Metamorphoses*, 91.

> We need to recapture something of what democracy left behind
> in its march to supremacy. Modern democracy has successfully
> asserted and realized the homogeneity of human life, but it is
> now required to try to recover and salvage the intrinsic hetero-
> geneity of human experiences. The experience of the citizen is
> different from that of the artist, which in turn is different from
> that of the religious person, and so on. These decisive articula-
> tions of human life would be hopelessly blurred if the current
> conceit prevailed that every human being, as "creator of his or
> her own values," is at the same time an artist, a citizen, a reli-
> gious person—indeed, all these things and more. Against this
> conceit, political philosophers should undertake to bring to light
> again the heterogeneity of human life.[38]

We will return momentarily to the tension between ancient and modern
political thought and form that Manent implies here, and return again
later to his critique of the modern democratic state. At this point, it is
important to emphasize that as he turns to ancient thought in his political
investigation, he locates there the possibility of a diversity or heterogeneity in the domain of human action, the science of which is lost, and
which contemporary philosophy should seek to recover. This diversity is
what results when human reason is activated in politics. It exists, in the
particular case of Europe, in a double indeterminacy: the indeterminacy
both of the Christianity that demands a human response to the propositions and claims of the Church (which response each person determines
in his own reason), and to the indeterminacy of choice of political form,
or the form of the organization for the common good:

> The production of common things always holds a part of
> mystery. The diversity of common things produced by humanity
> is the object of wonder and admiration. The diversity of common
> things produced throughout European history is particularly
> surprising and admirable. I have sought the conditions of this
> incomparable fecundity in the need to articulate the indetermi-
> nacy of the political regime and form along with the indetermi-
> nacy of the response to be given to the Christian proposition of
> an alliance between human freedom and divine benevolence.
> Each form of common life in Europe was a way of resolving this

---

38 Pierre Manent, "The Return of Political Philosophy," in *The Great Lie: Classic and Recent Appraisals of Ideology and Totalitarianism*, ed. F. Flagg Taylor IV (Wilmington, DE: ISI Books, 2011), 590.

> double indeterminacy by in a way linking the concretization of
> a way of governing oneself with the concretization of a certain
> relation to the Christian proposition.[39]

The choice of political form in response to the indeterminate condition that precedes and opens the way to that choice—there is no predetermined political form for Europe—as seen over the course of European history, becomes for Manent the broadest and best way to explore human deliberative and reasoned action in the domain of human things, the domain of politics. That choice takes place in the context of a relationship of tension between the political and the other domain that demands a human response, religion. Philosophy, where it resigns itself to the barren construction and deconstruction of "systems," has little to offer in the articulation of the interplay among the three vertices. Where philosophy seeks to understand what is, it plays its proper role in that articulation.

ANCIENT POLITICAL THOUGHT

Manent's understanding of ancient and modern political thought will be discussed extensively throughout this book. It will be helpful here to sketch out the ancient political thought that serves as the basis for his understanding of European political development.

That classical thought begins with Plato and Aristotle, and as noted above, their understanding of politics is entirely in relation to the human soul, the "what is" of man. Especially in his dialogues the *Republic*, *Statesman*, and *Laws*, Plato introduces the possibility of comparing and contrasting different regimes, or different ways that cities are governed with respect to the citizens and their souls. Very explicitly and schematically in *Statesman*, he describes and names rule by the one, the few, and the many.[40] One who rules according to expert knowledge of governance is a king, a name that applies as well to a single ruler who may lack such expertise but at least imitates it through adherence to laws and customs. The one who rules without expertise or regard to laws is tyrannical. The regime of the few who rule according to law and customs is an aristocracy, and its lawless counterpart is oligarchy. The name "democracy" would apply to rule by the many both according to law and in disregard of it, though both in the *Statesman* and in the *Republic*, Plato suggests that he

---

39 Manent, *Beyond Radical Secularism*, 86.
40 Plato, *Statesman* 292d–297d.

has little confidence in the possibility of a good democracy, as the masses would be unable to understand the expertise of politics and inclined away from law and custom.

Plato's student Aristotle expands and refines this regime analysis in his *Politics*, a book that treats collective and political life as a companion to the *Nicomachean Ethics* and its explanation of the moral and intellectual virtues of individuals. Aristotle's treatment is grounded both in a series of natural relationships beginning with the family and culminating in the city (each with its own end according to nature), and in the claim that man is by nature—in his very essence as human—a political animal who must, again by nature, seek his own particular good and a collective good in a common operation with others. Aristotle's regime discussion looks at various actual cities and describes them, their strengths and weaknesses, in great depth. As such, he is the first to combine an effort to examine rigorously actual political events and conditions as well as the philosophy of political life, and in the latter endeavor he does not spare his teacher Plato from criticism. Manent will ground his own work in a similar twofold approach, beginning with and broadening Aristotle's interest in the Greek polis to the political forms that have appeared in Europe, from the city forward.

TWO PATHS OF INQUIRY

To understand the "what is" of politics, Manent will undertake a historical investigation that has two intertwined paths. Both paths observe what is visible to us in the political domain, and both begin with his interest in the transition from ancient to modern political thought and the tension between the two. The first path is the recollection of the major developments and changes in the history of European political form that, as noted above, gives human life its form. The West is uniquely marked by a movement that is evident in the change of political form: "There are great civilizations apart from the West, and many things take place there, but they have not known movement, historical movement. . . . There is in the West a singular principle of movement and that is what characterizes it above all. The principle of Western movement is politics."[41] If, as described above, man is the principle of politics, and politics is the principle of the unique and extraordinary movement of the West, then ultimately man is the principle of that movement. The political history that demarcates the

---

41 Manent, *Metamorphoses*, 4.

movement of Europe is understood and evaluated along the second path, that of the history of political thought.

With regard to this first path, Manent turns first to experience rather than metaphysical speculation or modern philosophical system-building to understand what he was seeking. He writes in 1992 that instead of looking to modern philosophers such as Marx or Nietzsche or Heidegger to illuminate how modernity arose, "It was more urgent to reconstruct an exact chronology [of the transition from ancient to modern]. My first task then was to reconstruct its exact chronology, the precise articulation of the modern movement of becoming modern, being conscious of it, and willing to be modern. This required a work of history and the historian."[42] He writes in *The City of Man*, "Only a historical inquiry in the most basic sense of the term can lead us to the moment and the context in which the historical point of view and the consciousness of being modern first came to light and were articulated."[43] Almost two decades later, Manent will thus describe the concern of perhaps his greatest work, *Metamorphoses of the City*, as "to lay bare the illuminating power of a carefully considered history of political forms."[44]

Manent is careful, though, to distinguish between "history" and "historicism," or history and History. The term "history" refers to the study of what is as it presents itself in politics. Historicism, or History, is a modern understanding of reality and man's place in it that Manent rejects as he returns to ancient political science. He places the modern notion of man as a historical being in opposition to the classical understanding of man as natural and subject to law:

> Modern man lives in History; he understands and defines himself as a "historical being." Taken seriously as it ought to be, this definition signifies that a new element has been discovered that envelops and dominates the traditional articulations of human experience. To recognize this new element and to think and act in accord with it—with History and not any longer with Nature or Law—is the duty and privilege of modern man inasmuch as he is modern.[45]

---

42 Manent, "The Truth, Perhaps," 34–35.

43 Manent, *City of Man*, 12.

44 Manent, *Metamorphoses*, 9.

45 Manent, *City of Man*, 203–4.

This modern appreciation of man as Historical "displaces man's relations to nature and law. . . . In this enterprise, the nature of man is his principal enemy."[46] Manent turns to history to locate, in the movement of European political form, this transition to the modern "enthronement" of History or historicism. Political history will be Manent's means for understanding the turn to the modern. "What is central to this [political history of the last three centuries], what makes it precisely a history with a meaning (and which gives the different historicisms their *almost* irresistible plausibility), is the rational and really irresistible connection of its phases," its movement of political form from absolutism to democracy.[47] It is telling that Manent regards historicism as "almost plausible": he is observing the same movement of form as historicists or as modern thinkers who see themselves as Historical, yet he will not see in that movement the triumph of History over a view of man based in nature and law. In this investigation of history, Manent reveals himself again to be a theoretical philosopher of man, studying man through the events of history behind which man, political man in his deliberative action and in his universal human nature subject to law, is the principle.

The second path for Manent, closely related to the first, is the study of the political thought that articulates the causes and motives for changes in European political form.

> When I try to give an account of the passage from one political form to another, with the help of ancient and modern historians, of philosophical and literary works, and of religious and theological texts, under what rubric shall I place this inquiry. This inquiry is subject to no disciplinary protocol, and yet, it does not proceed at random, or at least I hope not. . . . Let's say that, since I aim to understand politics, if I practice the discipline, then it is political science.[48]

Manent sees as relevant to his political science an extraordinary range of thought, from history to literature to theology to philosophy. His effort focuses on political thought, informed by other aspects of intellectual history. Again driven by his interest in the turn to the modern, he writes,

---

46 *City of Man*, 204.
47 Manent, "The Truth, Perhaps," 39.
48 Manent, *Seeing Things Politically*, 3.

> The modern age is characterized by a strange interpenetration between the concept and event, between intellectual and political history. Because of this, it was necessary to elaborate exactly the conceptual content of modern politics. And it was reading the political philosophers, from Machiavelli to Montesquieu, from Rousseau to Tocqueville, that brought me the most light. This point does not entail the adoption of any methodological approach.[49]

Rather, simply reading these texts offers us the "what is" of the ideas of political history that Manent is seeking along this second path of historical inquiry. They "provide us a convincing phenomenology of the political and moral life of the last three centuries."[50] Manent's allusion to a phenomenological approach will be discussed briefly below. But it is clear from a survey of his work—especially his detailed exposition of major liberal thinkers, *Les Liberaux*; his volumes on Tocqueville and Montaigne; and his *Intellectual History of Liberalism*—that much of the burden of his work is in this examination of political thinkers, which issues in his analysis of the political thought that spurs or describes the movement of political form. He is careful not to oversimplify—"movements of thought never have a simple chronology"—even as he draws from a broad range of Western political thinkers of the last three centuries.[51]

We have now situated Manent as a theoretical philosopher, interested in what is true of man as revealed in the deliberative action of politics, which shows itself most completely at the broadest political level: the choice of political form. Aware of and interested in philosophy, Catholic Christianity, and politics, he is a practitioner of none of the three exclusively, instead drawing on each of the three for the truth they offer while not committing exclusively or even primarily to any of the three vertices. He is observing the political and intellectual history that appears as the visible outcomes in human action of the tensions among the three vertices. He consciously adopts the ancient view of political science whereby man has a nature according to which he is political: "The source of European development is the desire or the need for a political order that is at least somewhat reasonable, somewhat coherent. The cause of history is man's

---

49 Manent, "The Truth, Perhaps," 36.
50 "The Truth, Perhaps," 36.
51 Manent, *Seeing Things Politically*, 89.

political nature."[52] Manent is *in* history but not *of* it; he is *in* faith, politics, and philosophy, and *of* all three, for that is where the human is to be found. He does not claim that this makes for a neat approach, solving the conflicts and smoothing the angles of the triangle or devising a system that imposes order on the history within. He does insist that this messy condition is the human one, where man is the principle of what is and what takes place in politics and human action.

A BRIEF COMPARISON: MANENT AND ALASDAIR MACINTYRE

To begin the investigation of Manent's work on political form, it will be helpful to briefly compare his approach to that of another well-known philosopher with an interest in what it is to be human, how politics figures into that question, and in particular the relationship between the human person and political form. Alasdair MacIntyre shares many aspects of Manent's thinking, in particular a sense that ancient and medieval philosophy have much to teach on the question of being human and a skepticism of what modernity has wrought with the advancement of liberal principles. Both share Aristotle's axioms that man is a rational, political, and social animal. But there are differences between the two as well.

In his original political philosophy, Aristotle began by looking around at the Greek cities of his day. In his own looking around, MacIntyre notices several features of contemporary politics. The first is "compartmentalization imposed by structures. . . . As individuals move between home, school, workplace, the activities of leisure, the arenas of politics, bureaucratized encounters with government, and church or synagogue or mosque, they find themselves cast in different roles and required to express different and even sometimes incompatible attitudes."[53] This compartmentalization characterizes both politics and political philosophy. "Each has become a specialized and professionalized area of responsibility, with its own specific idioms and genres, its own forms of apprenticeship, its own methods of protecting itself from anything that would put the form of its activities seriously in question."[54] The result is that philosophical

---

52 *Seeing Things Politically*, 116.

53 Alasdair MacIntyre, "Politics, Philosophy and the Common Good," in *The MacIntyre Reader*, ed. Kelvin Knight (Notre Dame, IN: University of Notre Dame Press, 1998), 235–36.

54 "Politics, Philosophy and the Common Good," 236.

reflection no longer informs politics. It is incapable, as Manent argues, of thinking about what it is to be human; thus, it has nothing to offer in the conversation of what politics is or should be.

Beyond this "unphilosophical nature of [contemporary] politics and with it the exclusion from politics of philosophical questions concerning politics," MacIntyre also sees the "closely related exclusion from political debate . . . of substantive issues concerning ways of life; and the fact that the activities of government are such that they are not in their effects neutral between ways of life, but undermine some and promote others."[55] This critique of the false notion of a morally neutral modern state parallels that of Manent, as we will see later.

MacIntyre here distinguishes politics as one of several domains in which the human person exists and acts. His scope of human action thus goes beyond the political form that Manent sees as the central and privileged arena of human action, a difference to which we will return in chapter 6. MacIntyre goes on to conclude that the Enlightenment (and specifically Kantian) hope for a rational politics of independent moral reasoners has instead deteriorated into a set of "small-scale academic publics—scientific, historical, literary" that conduct isolated and self-referential rational inquiry into their own interests, "with no practical effect on the conduct of political life." Instead, contemporary public political life is one in which "rational inquiry is excluded."[56] Man's rational nature, displayed in a search for a common good in a political community, is thereby unfulfilled in contemporary politics. While Manent calls for attention to a politics of the genuine heterogeneity of human action, MacIntyre sees in the modern state "a social order whose institutional heterogeneity and diversity of interests is such that no place is left any longer for a politics of the common good."[57] An ersatz diversity of division supersedes a genuine diversity of human choice expressed in an often contentious but very human search for the common good.

Both MacIntyre and Manent share a focus on the polis, the political community or form that is the target of Aristotelian investigation. As we will see in chapter 3, Manent considers the city the only political form that can be clearly defined. He turns to Leo Strauss and Aristotle to provide the definition: the polis "is 'that complete association which corresponds

55 "Politics, Philosophy and the Common Good," 236.
56 "Politics, Philosophy and the Common Good," 239.
57 "Politics, Philosophy and the Common Good," 239.

to the natural range of man's power of knowing and of loving.' In such a definition the *ought* is included in the *is*. But let us also listen to the best analyst of the ancient city: 'the best defining principle for a city is this: the greatest number of members with a view to self-sufficiency of life that is readily surveyable.'"[58] Manent assesses the form of the city by its limits, its size that is within the ready, immediate comprehension of the senses. MacIntyre, in his own definition of the polis, describes it as "a kind of community in which each individual's achievement of his or her own good is inseparable both from achieving the shared goods of practices and from contributing to the common good of the community as a whole."[59] He will agree with Aristotle and Manent that such a city is necessarily small and limited in size and population. This tight integration of the political part—the individual citizen—and the whole—the polis—is very different from other forms such as liberal democracy (which, for Manent, will lie somewhere between the Christian nation and the modern state, perhaps tending toward the latter). Manent (with Strauss and Aristotle) and MacIntyre supply three complementary definitions of the city that together give us a good understanding of that form.

MacIntyre, however, is concerned with the city as the political community where, to use Manent's phrase, the "ought" is included in the "is." For MacIntyre, this political form is normative as that which enables the human person to thrive as rational and social-political, in which the full range of human associations including home, work, leisure, education, religious practice, and political choice all are possible in accord with human nature: a "polis is always, potentially or actually, a society of rational enquiry, of self-scrutiny."[60] For Manent, the city is the original political form, one whose presence lingers in all subsequent forms (which, as we will see, are in some sense metamorphoses of this first form). But, though it holds a special place, it is not the only normative form. It is the beginning of political development, and indeed of human rationality in community, that follows pre-political forms such as tribe (cited by Manent) and *Volk* (cited by MacIntyre) that are also prerational or nonrational. For both Manent and MacIntyre, the city is critical to political philosophy and

---

58 Pierre Manent, *Democracy without Nations? The Fate of Self-Government in Europe*, trans. Paul Seaton (Wilmington, DE: ISI Books, 2007), 91. Manent quotes Leo Strauss, *Natural Right and History* (1953; repr. Chicago: University of Chicago Press, 1974), 254n2 and Aristotle, *Politics*, 1326b, trans. Carnes Lord (Chicago: University of Chicago Press, 1985), 205, respectively.

59 MacIntyre, "Politics, Philosophy and the Common Good," 240–41.

60 "Politics, Philosophy and the Common Good," 241.

history. MacIntyre focuses on the polis as the form where human thriving is possible. Manent sees it as the start of political history and development (of political motion) that is assessed and evaluated in political philosophy.

This distinction, though, does not relegate MacIntyre to a hypothetical or speculative inquiry, nor Manent to a historical narrative. Both thinkers agree that a study of philosophy as well as actual historical events is essential to reaching any true conclusions about politics. As we have seen, Manent began his approach with a development of the events of political history. MacIntyre claims that "philosophical inquiry, in ethics as elsewhere, is defective insofar as it is not historical."[61]

With this context to help place Manent's work among the broader scholarship of the day regarding what it is to be human and to be political, we can proceed to a fuller understanding of the task he has undertaken.

---

61 Alasdair MacIntyre, "An Interview with Giovanni Borradori," in *The MacIntyre Reader*, ed. Kelvin Knight (Notre Dame, IN: University of Notre Dame Press, 1998), 261.

Chapter Two

MANENT'S PROJECT

AS A PHILOSOPHER OF MAN AND OF HUMAN ACTION, Manent covers a broad range of questions as they surface in politics, especially questions that inquire about the tensions among the three vertices of philosophy, religion, and politics. Two particular questions or sets of questions animate his work over time. The first and broader is the meaning of "modern" in European intellectual history, what this term means in general and in its particular political usage. The second is the theologico-political question, or the relationship between secular and religious authorities. The tensions between the premodern and modern, and between the civil and Church authorities, drive the development of political form in Europe in a movement that is apparent in intellectual and political history.

To understand how Manent approaches these questions and his work on political form, it will be useful to identify key influences on his thought. "Influence" here is taken to mean not just a thinker whom Manent has studied, but a thinker whose way of thinking, fundamental premises, and body of work helped shape Manent's own approach and work. Four such influences, two ancient and two contemporary, seem particularly important: Aristotle, St. Augustine, Raymond Aron, and Leo Strauss. Manent is continually in conversation with Aristotle and Augustine, a conversation he was led into by Aron and Strauss even as he enters into conversation with them as well. With an understanding of the two beginning and guiding questions and the influences that shape Manent's response to them, we can turn to an initial examination of his work specifically on political form.

A FIRST BEGINNING QUESTION: THE MODERN DIFFERENCE

We have already seen Manent's interest in the modern, especially modern man as a "historical being," as a significant concern that led him to sympathize with classical thinkers in his work on a science of political forms. His understanding of the modern political form will be examined extensively in later chapters. Here, as essential underpinning to those examinations, it will be useful to discuss further how Manent sees the contrast and tension between the premodern or classical view and the modern view, and how that difference developed. How did modern man come to see "the nature of man as his principal enemy"?

Looking back on his work, Manent asks,

> How shall I formulate this project that has continually engaged me, which I have never left behind and which I have pursued ceaselessly, for better or worse? . . . [W]hat has kept me going is "the question of the modern difference." It is characteristic of the moderns that they declare themselves moderns and will to be moderns. . . . *At a certain time, something happened.* At a certain time, Europeans decided to do something new, something absolutely unprecedented, . . . which they called modern and by which they distinguished themselves from everything previous. The very idea of the modern thus refers to a proposition, to a project.[1]

In opening his *Metamorphoses of the City*, Manent stakes this work on this question of the modern and its ambiguous meaning: "We have been modern now for several centuries. We are modern and we want to be modern."[2] But the identifiable steps in the modern project, such as those of 1789, 1917, 1968, and 1989—here he traces the results of his first path of investigation into the political events of history—prove only to be "deceptive stages on a road that leads we know not where."[3] Manent studies "this phase, this period, this moment . . . when something decisive happens, but something that still remains enigmatic today," and the enigma will defy a full explanation despite methodical explorations of the political,

---

1 Manent, *Seeing Things Politically*, 86.

2 Manent, *Metamorphoses*, 1.

3 *Metamorphoses*, 1.

religious, and technological aspects of the project.[4] The modern remains an enigma that draws Manent throughout his work.

Manent asserts that "the modern centuries have this quality of being dominated by the hope and by the fear of a radical transformation of the human condition—a hope and a fear, moreover, which can be shared by the mind or heart of the same person."[5] In his 1992 essay, Manent phrases differently the question of how this union of hope and fear divides the modern character, the elusive question of how man came to see his own nature as his enemy:

> We cannot know ourselves without first understanding our situation. And we cannot achieve either without first recognizing ourselves as "moderns." We must affirm the "modern difference" in order to identify ourselves: it is part of our self-understanding. . . . In what way and to what extent does being a "modern" man differ from being simply a "man"? In a certain way all of *modern* philosophy is a commentary on this difference. But where did the difference originate?[6]

Manent locates the source of the difference in the field of philosophy, which "during the course of the seventeenth and eighteenth centuries, elaborated the project of reforming European religion, politics, and society in accordance with reason or philosophy itself. To be modern, in its simplest and at the same time most august definition, is to live according to reason."[7] Manent claims, then, that one of the vertices of the triangle within which he views history attempted to bring religion and politics under its own method and terms, those of reason without reference to faith or nature. The apotheosis of this philosophical appropriation in the political domain comes with Hegel's *Philosophy of Right*. But subsequent philosophers—notable exemplars were Kierkegaard, Marx, Nietzsche, and Heidegger—"revolt against the rational order of Enlightenment in the name of faith or of action, of creation or of thinking."[8] Philosophers within the modern era thus turn on themselves, and political thinkers reject the political order described by the philosophers of reason. Political philosophy "will have no systematic expression, or even a truly coherent one"

---

4 Manent, *Seeing Things Politically*, 86–87.

5 *Seeing Things Politically*, 86.

6 Manent, "The Truth, Perhaps," 33.

7 "The Truth, Perhaps," 34.

8 "The Truth, Perhaps," 34.

after the early nineteenth century.[9] We are left with a paradox: "Today the rational [political] order reigns from Los Angeles to Vladivostock. One is left with a major difficulty, however: the docile inhabitant of this 'rational' order thinks in the same way as do its enemies. He thinks, for example, that man 'creates his values. . . .' The rational order harbors and foments the negation of reason."[10] Modern man thus draws conflicting fundamental premises from the vertex of philosophy: reason is supreme, and reason is wrong or inadequate. Philosophy for modern man destroys the vertices of faith and politics (in the latter case, a politics that other modern philosophers had themselves constructed), then destroys itself or at least positions its diametric opposite in an unresolved competition with itself. The modern difference means that man lives both "according to reason [and] according to the denial of reason."[11]

In *The City of Man*, Manent offers an extensive treatment of the question of how this modern difference developed, his "most rigorous analysis of these modern notions of . . . society, history, the rights of man. [This] is the most complete and systematic form of what I might call my critical analysis of the intellectual framework of the moderns."[12] In the intertwined history of politics and political thought, the modern difference began in a particular time and place, in the seventeenth century on both sides of the English Channel in England and France, particularly the latter.[13] "The quarrel of the Ancients and the Moderns emerges in France near the end of the seventeenth century. But . . . Joubert wisely set 1715 as the end of the ancient world."[14] That same year marked the death of King Louis XIV. In particular, Manent sees the work of Montesquieu in the years just after that death as a key source of the modern difference and of the origin of the modern understanding of history. Again, Manent identifies a movement in Montesquieu's *Spirit of the Laws* "between the two poles of Ancient and Modern. The one is the ancient world of republican 'virtue,' the other is the England of 'commerce' and 'liberty.' Between the ancient and the modern there is the present of the French monarchy."[15] In

---

9 "The Truth, Perhaps," 34.

10 "The Truth, Perhaps," 34. Presumably, Manent is surveying the world from Los Angeles moving east, rather than taking the most direct route to Vladivostock.

11 "The Truth, Perhaps," 34.

12 Manent, *Seeing Things Politically*, 90.

13 Manent, *City of Man*, 11.

14 *City of Man*, 11.

15 *City of Man*, 12.

addition to these three possibilities, Montesquieu adds a fourth, despotism, bringing to completion a system of political classification of form that Manent asserts "exhausts all the modalities of being. His [Montesquieu's] is a philosophical ambition, to grasp all the forms of the human world."[16] Manent interprets Montesquieu based again on the tenet that men are political animals and that the most distinctly human action is political action. But Montesquieu then does something that is difficult to explain: he leaves England, the object of his consideration, out of the formal scheme he has developed. Manent treats this apparent lapse on Montesquieu's part as manifesting his move to the modern,

> which can be summed up in the opposition between "seeking" and "finding." For the first time in the history of philosophy, a philosopher invites us to cease "seeking." . . . He opposes two attitudes, two approaches: one, "seeking," is the search for a principle or foundation that resides in the nature of things or man; the other, "finding," consists in turning to good account what fate brings our way and what, it appears, could not have been.[17]

The attitude of finding becomes the historicism to which, as seen above, Manent will be opposed. That attitude does not accept the possibility of truth as inherent in nature and sought or seen in the events of history; truth, in modern historicism, is found in the unfolding of history. This unfolding is an "'effectual truth,' . . . a new kind of reality that the ancient philosophers . . . were not able to find—it is a 'historical fact.'"[18] Such facts are devoid of any relationship to a natural principle. Thus, Montesquieu's approach aims "to weaken decisively the authority of the Ancients, of the idea of the 'best regime,' the idea of virtue, in order to replace it with the authority of the present moment, of the modern experience, summed up in the notions of 'commerce' and 'liberty.'"[19] Those notions will be central to the form of the modern state.

Montesquieu's modern move from seeking to finding carries important consequences, and it is an important episode—the first episode in modern thought—along Manent's path of the study of political thinking. Manent ties Montesquieu's overturning of the ancient understanding of

---

16 *City of Man*, 12.
17 *City of Man*, 14.
18 *City of Man*, 15.
19 *City of Man*, 15.

virtue to his new understanding of the distinction between the particular
and the universal. Montesquieu claims that the Greeks saw virtue as the
principle of government and that their form of government was self-rule,
or democracy. He essentially equates the ancient principle of virtue that
marks the best regime, with virtue understood as a universal found in
nature, to the particular form of the city of Athens, where democracy
was in fact an opportune form of rule for some and a target of criticism
for others, but never a universal principle of liberty. With that equation
of the general—virtue—with the particular—the democratic regime of
Athens—Montesquieu

> shows . . . his more attentive reader that Greek political and
> moral philosophy, guided and so to speak held together by the
> notion of virtue, has nothing pertinent to say to those who do
> not *live* under the popular government of a Greek city. . . . His
> procedure is first to particularize and democratize the idea of
> virtue then to turn this "democratic" virtue into the type of all
> virtue, political as well as moral or religious.[20]

With this, Manent claims, the Aristotelian understanding of the gap or
distance between the particular and the general is compressed. "Previously, the human world was interpreted according to the immovable
distance between the particular whose existence one could measure
and the essence whose general character one could contemplate."[21] The
task of the human mind was to seek the truth of both, understanding the
distinction between the two. With Montesquieu's new notion of particular
and general, "the distance is abolished, immobility gives way to mobility,
and the new notion, neither general nor particular or sometimes both,
circulates freely within the world."[22] This freedom proves enormously
empowering to the human mind, which is liberated from the ancient
constraints of nature as reflected in the old particular and general. The
new notion of them collapses from two poles into two "moments," and
this new understanding, "covering the two moments and drawing power
from their combined forces, becomes, as it were, a magical instrument.
In whatever point the mind applies it, the mind finds itself capable of
producing . . . at once the particular and the general, that is to say the

20 *City of Man*, 19–20.
21 *City of Man*, 20.
22 *City of Man*, 21.

human world in its entirety."[23] "What is" is no longer given in nature; it is what the human mind determines it to be at any instant as history unfolds. "The mind finds itself in a position of causal sovereignty. It can explain the world at will. The condition of the human mind was to be caught in the tension between the particular and the general. The new idea allows it to see itself or to consider itself outside and above this tension."[24] And, if the tension between particular and general is an essential element of the nature of things in the ancient view, Montesquieu's effort to resolve that tension marks the beginning of his metaphysical break with the ancient understanding of nature and man's place in it.

Armed with this apparent resolution of the quandary of the particular and the general, modern man will look back on ancient notions of virtue and law as unnecessary detractions from, rather than the ways to, a good life. "Virtue is now no more than an unnatural obedience to a repressive rule."[25] But an immediate reaction to Montesquieu's approach comes from Rousseau. Manent claims that Rousseau rejects Montesquieu's effort to establish a "modern experience":

> By a singular reversal, the repressive and unnatural character of virtue that Montesquieu had deliberately suggested in order to steer his readers away from it, was emphatically proclaimed by Rousseau to the great acclaim of his readers. The fiction [Montesquieu's account of virtue] that was intended to keep the prestige of the past and the authority of Antiquity at a distance came [in Rousseau's use of it] to violently challenge the authority of the modern experience it sought to establish. The interpretive principle that was meant to close an epoch of history became the active principle capable of opening another period that was no longer "modern" but "revolutionary."[26]

Yet Rousseau's reaction brings not a restoration of the classical account of virtue as natural but rather a competing version of the modern, which shares the central feature of Montesquieu's view, "the cruel character of civic virtue. . . . Rousseau himself does not love the virtue he celebrates or he only loves it without his natural goodness enabling him to practice a virtue that is contrary to nature. . . . Both Montesquieu and Rousseau

23 *City of Man*, 21.
24 *City of Man*, 21.
25 *City of Man*, 29.
26 *City of Man*, 30.

equally perceive the ambivalence of the law and its cruelty."[27] Montesquieu and Rousseau sustain a positive rhetorical image of ancient virtue but deprive it of any real force other than as a repressive notion to be left behind or a source of revolutionary fervor.

The consequence of Montesquieu's break, once one brings in the reaction of Rousseau, is a new understanding of virtue and law different in crucial aspects from the ancient view represented in both pagan Greek and Christian thinking. Those ancient traditions are not identical, of course, but "the Christian and Greek ideas of virtue overlap a good deal. For both the philosophers and the Christians, virtue is the subjection of the passions to reason, of the soul's lower to its higher parts, an ordering and an order wrought by the soul."[28] Modern man will find this shared pagan and Christian notion of virtue to be uncomfortable, limiting, and more trouble than it is worth. He will be uninterested in this ordering and order: "The new virtue and new law entail the denial of individual nature, without it being clear whether this negation brings with it any higher or lower state for the man who practices virtue. This incertitude is the decisive element in the new determination. Unable to find or to conceive any place in the degrees of Being, the new virtue and law will be forever eluding the old ontology."[29]

In this discussion, Manent demonstrates his interest in the "what is" of the science of man at its broadest level: what it is to be human. He seeks in his path of study of the history of political thought the changed understanding of what man is from the ancient to the modern. In the ancient conception, law opposed nature but in so doing brought nature to its full self. Man sought the good or excellent, in himself and in his regime. This seeking was his motive for action. Modern man, on the other hand,

> discovers that in the knotted tissue of human life with its goods and evils there runs a seam that joins and disjoins two possibilities in life. One of these seeks an uncertain good exposed to corruption and the other . . . seeks to escape the evils of which it has first taken careful stock. In opposition to and in the

---

27 *City of Man*, 30.

28 *City of Man*, 31.

29 *City of Man*, 32. In the original French, "ontology" at the close of this citation is capitalized: *la vieille Ontologie*. This suggests a status for the old Ontology as a science that ranks with or corresponds to its subject, "Being" itself. This detail may point to Manent's eventual hope to return to a science of politics like ancient political science, or Political Science properly understood, which would depend on the ancient Ontology. Pierre Manent, *La cité de l'homme* (Paris: Flammarion, 1997), 47.

place of the desire to seek the good to attain it and so to perfect oneself arises the urgent need to flee from evil in order to be safe and free.[30]

These two attitudes are incompatible, and the result as well as the cause of the irreconcilable conflict is the modern attitude toward law. With human action now oriented to the demands of flight from the twin evils of what would make him uncomfortable or unfree, modern man flees as well from that friend of ancient man, the law. The flight becomes one without constraint: "Nothing substantial, be it law, good, cause, or purpose, either holds [modern man's] attention or holds back his advance any longer. He has become a runner and will go on running until the end of the world."[31] In Aristotelian terms, man has become all potential without the possibility of rest or end.

The political consequences of this new understanding of man will be explored more fully in the discussion of the modern state. Here, in considering Manent's view on how the modern change in the understanding of the nature of man plays out in political action, it is important to note that the first consequence is the escape from the traditional relationships of family and city, which now "appear as closed as a monk's cell."[32] This flight from the law and from the constraints of what had been thought to be man's fundamental natural relationships "is proper to modern man and sums up his whole experience."[33] Moreover, modern man is aware of this difference and "experiences within himself the succession and incompatibility of two moral attitudes, two directions of attention and intention."[34] The modern experience is to be conscious of both the ancient attitude and the modern difference. "Once this consciousness is formulated explicitly and objectively, it comes to see that the two distinct humanities [ancient and modern], incompatible and successive, are bound and borne by neither nature nor law, but by the mother and sum of all successions, which is History."[35] History is now the replacement for Being as it had been understood in nature and law, and historicism can replace ontology. This

30 Manent, *City of Man*, 47.
31 *City of Man*, 48.
32 *City of Man*, 48.
33 *City of Man*, 48.
34 *City of Man*, 48.
35 *City of Man*, 48.

is the crux of the tension between the ancient and modern conceptions of man.

A SECOND BEGINNING QUESTION: THE THEOLOGICO-POLITICAL PROBLEM

Manent's second guiding question explores the theologico-political problem, closely related to the question of the modern difference. In *An Intellectual History of Liberalism*, he explains this problem:

> [B]y its very existence and distinctive vocation, [the Church] posed an immense political problem to the European peoples. This point must be stressed: the political development of Europe is understandable only as the history of answers to problems posed by the Church, which was a human association of a completely new kind. Each institutional response created in its turn new problems and called for the invention of new responses. The key to European development is what might be called, in scholarly terms, the *theologico-political problem*.[36]

If political form is Manent's vehicle for understanding European political development, the tension between the Church, which Manent identifies as a political form (if an unusual one) itself, and the other forms that arise in Europe is essential to his inquiry. The "playing out" of this tension will be described more fully later. Here, the nature of the question and how it fits within Manent's broader inquiry requires explanation.

Manent lays the foundation for this question in his 1992 essay, "The Truth, Perhaps," in a way that shows its direct relation to the question of the modern difference:

> One of two things must be true. One possibility is that Christian revelation is true. If this is true, the essential fact remains that the soul's relationship is with the true God. Then democracy, assuming that it derives from Christianity, is only a consequence, perhaps a happy one, but more likely an ambiguous one as are all human things. In any case it is subordinate to the truth of Christianity itself. Or the Christian religion is false.

---

36 Pierre Manent, *An Intellectual History of Liberalism*, trans. Rebecca Balinski (Princeton, NJ: Princeton University Press, 1995), 4.

> Then, far from democracy being its result or consequence, it is
> the Christian religion that would be the first, imperfect, and
> alienated experience of democracy. Religion, then, would not
> explain democracy since democracy explains itself.[37]

Manent refers here specifically to democracy, but the question arises
also with the political forms that precede modern democracy. Much of
Manent's subsequent effort will be the explanation of the importance of
this tension between the possible truth of Christian claims and the desire
of men to liberate themselves from those claims.

This tension provides the context for modern man's flight from
nature and law discussed above. In Christian thinking, God is supernatural, a status that is a problem for modern thinkers.

> [I]n order to liberate himself from the "supernatural," modern
> man cannot rest content with becoming "pagan" again. It is not
> enough to affirm or reaffirm nature. . . . If nature is good, even
> very good, the supernatural is necessarily better, because it is
> infinitely good. If the earthly city provides natural goods, the
> heavenly city, which the church prefigures, dispenses supernat-
> ural goods that are incomparably superior to the former. Thus,
> between these two cities, the contest is unequal as long as the
> earthly city remains "natural." Therefore, if the critique of the
> supernatural is going to achieve its political ends (i.e., if it aims
> to exclude in advance any possibility of being trumped), it must
> entail a critique of nature. The critique of Christian revelation
> implies the critique of pagan politics and philosophy.[38]

Manent attributes a political purpose to the modern rejection of the
supernatural, which in turn demands a rejection of the natural. This
rejection might give us pause. One could respond to Manent that on his
account, the moderns might well have been content with an Aristotelian
notion of the natural city. Such a city did not just provide natural goods,
as Manent suggests here; it did not exist merely to survive or live, but to
live well: "A city is the community of families and villages in a complete
and self-sufficient life. This, we assert, is living happily and finely. The
political community must be regarded, therefore, as being for the sake

---

37 Manent, "The Truth, Perhaps," 40.
38 "The Truth, Perhaps," 41.

of noble actions, not for the sake of living together."[39] Why would such a natural city not accommodate the modern project as fitting within a modern understanding of living well?

As we have seen, nature and law, while in one sense opposed to one another in the ancient view, also complemented one another in that law allowed for the fulfillment of nature. That natural fulfillment amounts to the realization of the telos of the city, and of the people within it. But this notion of a telos within the being of the political association is itself a constraint given by nature, as we do not choose such a political telos for ourselves. Modern man must thus reject it as well in order to complete his liberation; in this sense, Manent attributes to the modern project a very radical critique of the pagan idea of nature. The idea of an end or telos in nature must be jettisoned entirely: "In order for nature and law to be free from one another, the understanding of nature changed; henceforth, it would not concern itself with ends; it would be a nature without finality. This new nature entailed and presupposed a new law, detached from human nature and sovereign and artificial to the extent that it leaves nature altogether free to be itself and nothing but itself, without any modification."[40] But this newly liberated nature, and the consequent liberation of man from the need for law, turns out to be insufficient for modern purposes: "[T]he experience of modern democracy, the appearance of man characterized by an unprecedented taming of his nature, suggests that this experience was not confirmed by experience. . . . The law which authorizes produces no fewer effects than the law which prohibits. . . . In this sense, authorization is too authoritarian."[41] Modern man must seek further liberation, indeed incessant liberation, to pursue his project,

---

39 Aristotle, *Aristotle's Politics*, Translated by Carnes Lord, 2nd ed. (Chicago: University of Chicago Press, 2013), 3.9.1280b40–1281a3.

40 Manent, *City of Man*, 181. Manent's language and explanation of the modern move in politics here parallel the jettisoning of final cause as a concern for physical sciences signaled by Descartes in *Meditations on First Philosophy*, Meditation IV, 55: "I consider the customary search for final causes to be totally useless in physics; there is considerable rashness in thinking myself capable of investigating the ‹impenetrable› purposes of God." In *The Philosophical Writings of Descartes*, trans. John Cottingham, Robert Stoothoff, and Dugald Murdoch (Cambridge: Cambridge University Press, 1984). The apparent motives of the modern political thinkers are different from those claimed by Descartes: in Manent's understanding, the former see God or nature as a constraint, while the latter simply believes (or claims to believe) that divine ends exceed our capacity to grasp in the way we might understand physical phenomena by rational investigation and experimentation, and we should avoid exceeding our own capacity in order to avoid error. In both cases, however, the disregard for final cause or telos seems to open a never-ending quest.

41 Manent, *City of Man*, 181.

which Manent describes as the "movement that never arrives at its term, its resting place."[42]

How did Christianity specifically produce this modern drive for motion and provoke the crusade for liberation from law and nature in search of a politics free from their oppression? To understand this, it is essential to follow a different but closely related intellectual path to modernity from the one beginning with Montesquieu. Manent's explanation begins in an overlapping pair of critiques, that of pagan politics by Christianity, and that of Christianity by political philosophers, beginning notably with Niccolo Machiavelli. Manent claims that the disruption created by Christianity draws a response from political thinkers from Machiavelli forward. Manent traces in political philosophy the "democratic vector," the roots of Europe's political development toward democracy in the events of history, to the political thought of Machiavelli and Thomas Hobbes, and on to Alexis de Tocqueville.[43]

> A critique of pagan politics and philosophy is already contained in Christian revelation, more precisely in the critique of paganism this revelation introduced. The locus classicus of this critique is the one leveled by Saint Augustine in *The City of God*. The Machiavellian critique of Christianity, the origin of the modern vector, constantly intersects with the Augustinian critique of paganism and of sinful humanity, sometimes overlapping with it, or at least superimposing itself on it. I believe that this web merits being disentangled with care: this double critique delineates and produces the dialectical circle from which the modern moral and political development cannot extricate itself. It is the source of the perpetual movement and apparently endless radicalization of democracy.[44]

The Augustinian critique will prove essential to Manent's investigation, as will be discussed below in the development of St. Augustine as an influence on Manent. The Machiavellian critique of Christianity, the beginning of the modern or democratic vector, is clarified in Manent's more recent work. In *Seeing Things Politically*, after noting that the idea that Christianity drives European development comes from many sources and in many forms, he offers his own elaboration:

42 Manent, *Metamorphoses*, 4.
43 Manent, "The Truth, Perhaps," 41.
44 "The Truth, Perhaps," 42.

> [T]he essence of the Christian proposition understood as an historical factor is that it introduces something deeply troubling, a problem that proved insurmountable, in the practical framework, the arrangement of human virtues and motives. It addresses humanity with demands of unprecedented radicality. In particular, it presents a demand that endangers the natural framework of motives and virtues, that is, the political association. It endangers the political framework of human life by requiring human beings to love their enemies. One must ask how this exorbitant requirement could ever have been put forward, understood and propagated, but in any case, it represented a radical modification of the relationship between the political order and the religious order. Up until the irruption of the Christian proposition, the religious association was not distinguished from the political association; the gods were only an institution of the city. . . . With the Christian Church, religion becomes entirely distinct from the political order; it leaves behind the radical dependence that tied it to the political order in order to attain an essential independence.[45]

Manent knows that Christians continued to hate their neighbors; nature did not change, and "the structure of virtues and motives remained what it is by nature."[46] The Church would be closely involved in politics, concerned as it was for the salvation of souls for whom politics had direct implications. But the bright line between religion and politics was established, at least in Europe, with the arrival of Christianity. Thus the division between two vertices of Manent's triangle, religion and politics—both of which modern philosophy had attempted, in self-contradicting ways, to supersede or subdue—arrives and brings with it the tension, again closely related to the ancient-modern tension, that will propel the motion of European development. This is, indeed, the central focus of Manent's major work, *Metamorphoses of the City*, and it clarifies his reason for claiming, as seen above, that his work will yield insight by seeking "the illuminating power of a carefully considered history of political forms":

> The history of the West unfolds in the tension between the civic operation, such as the Greek city gave birth to and that the republican or "Roman" tradition endeavored to preserve and

---

45 Manent, *Seeing Things Politically*, 205.
46 *Seeing Things Politically*, 205.

> spread, and the Christian Word that, in proposing a new city
> where actions and words would attain an unprecedented unity
> and where one would live *in conformity with the Word*, opened a
> disparity between actions and words in political society that was
> impossible to master. In promising a perfect equation between
> action and word in the city of God, the Christian proposition
> opened an insurmountable disparity between actions and words
> in human cities. . . . [T]he practical solution of a confessional
> stamp was found in the nation, administered by a secular State,
> and governed by a representative government. But this solution
> had neither the energetic simplicity of the [ancient] civic form
> nor the ambitious exactitude of the ecclesial form, and the West
> would not cease to search for a "solution" that would at last be
> complete and that would unite the energy of the civic operation
> and the exactitude of the religious proposition.[47]

Thus we have a second kind of restlessness that plays a driving role in European history: in addition to the restlessness of modern man who seeks to oppose his own nature and flee from its constraints as well as those of law, there is a restlessness to resolve the tension between secular and ecclesial authority. These aspects of restlessness and the importance of the "two-cities" understanding suggest again that St. Augustine will be a major influence and source for Manent, as will be discussed below.

In his later work, *Beyond Radical Secularism*, Manent posits the theologico-political problem and its implications even more forcefully:

> From the time the inhabitants of our continent received the
> Christian proposition and began to pay attention to it, they found
> themselves confronted with a two-fold task: they had to govern
> themselves, and they had to respond to the Christian proposition
> of a "new life," henceforth accessible to every person of good
> will, which consisted in participation in the very life of God in
> Three Persons. Both halves of this task were characterized by a
> high degree of indeterminacy. The task of self-government was
> made uncertain not only by the question of political regime
> (monarchical, aristocratic, or republican), but also by that of
> the political form (city, empire, or an unprecedented form to
> be invented). The task of responding to the Christian proposi-
> tion did not come down to a choice between acceptance and

---

47 Manent, *Metamorphoses*, 9–10.

refusal, since the countless heresies combatted by the Church represented so many ways of half-accepting or refusing this proposition. Given such great political as well as religious indeterminacy, so much greater was the breadth of indeterminacy that affected the articulation of the two, the difficulty of conjoining the religious and the political determination. . . . Never was history more *open*, and Europeans have already been mistaken several times in declaring it over and done. This was, then, the starting point and the principle of European history: *to govern oneself in a certain relation to the Christian proposition.*[48]

We thus have European man confronting his own twofold restlessness, but in a position to choose and act in response to that restlessness because the outcomes of the propositions of politics and faith are not determined. Both vertices of religion and politics remain open to continued questioning, resistance, choice, and change. There is a motion, as noted above, not "of" history as a spirit bringing itself into existence or fullness, but "in" history, which fascinates Manent. He sees, in this playing out of human freedom in the face of political and religious indeterminacy, a tremendous, genuine diversity of human action. His history is one of freedom for man, who in motion exercises his freedom seen and revealed in his choices of political regime and form.

INFLUENCES ON MANENT: ARISTOTLE

Crystal Cordell Paris has noted that "no work, no article devoted to Aristotle figures in the abundant bibliography of Pierre Manent; we insist still that Aristotelian philosophy inspires entire sides of Manentian thought."[49] We have already seen several references to Aristotelian features of Manent's thinking as well as Manent's claim that he seeks a "political science" as a "science of human things." We have seen as well that Manent makes a deliberate choice to return to a classical view of nature, especially human nature, at least partly in response to the "industrial philosophy" he had found at ENS. Further, Manent's two-path approach—studying both

---

48 Manent, *Beyond Radical Secularism*, 62–63.

49 Crystal Cordell Paris, "L'inspiration aristotélicienne dans la pensée de Pierre Manent. Les phénomènes, la chose commune, l'action," in De Ligio, Holeindre, and Mahoney, *La politique et l'âme*, 189. "Aucun ouvrage, aucun article consacré à Aristote ne figure pas dans la bibliographie abondante de Pierre Manent; nous soutenons cependant que la philosophie aristotélicienne inspire des pans entiers de la pensée manentienne."

political thought and political events—mirrors Aristotle's approach, seen in both the *Nicomachean Ethics* and the *Politics*, of evaluating different opinions in light of actual experience, in order that logos will match what is observable and seen or revealed by looking around. Like Aristotle, Manent seeks not to focus narrowly on one domain of study but rather to cross fields—philosophy, theology, political events—as such broad observation tells us more about the "what is" of man.

Manent's study of political form, both in his understanding of the political nature of man and in his belief that human action in politics best reveals the "what is" of human nature, is rooted in Aristotle's thinking. Manent is clear on this: "The author who for me has the most authority on these questions, that is, Aristotle, treats the questions that interest me under the rubric of political science."[50] To explain his project more fully, Manent describes two great cycles of political science in the West: ancient and modern.

> For the Greeks, experience came before theory. . . . When [Plato and Aristotle] analyzed the city, it was at the end of its development. It was possible to sum it up. . . . Among the moderns, political science comes, as I have said, before and after experience. Liberal political science, taken as a whole that goes from Hobbes or Locke to Tocqueville, is at once a constructive project and an evaluative description. Since this project is incomplete, since we always intend to "democratize democracy," our experience also seems to be incomplete.[51]

Manent seems to refer here in the modern cycle to the never-ending, never-concluding nature of the modern project, propelled by modern man's restlessness in the constant flight from nature and law. But, as will be seen more fully in the discussion of the political form of the modern state, he believes we are closer to the end of that form than many may think, and that we can therefore conduct more evaluation than at first seems likely. This is his project in its grandest sense:

> I think that we can, and therefore that we must, be more ambitious. We are probably as advanced in the modern democratic cycle as the Greeks were in the democratic cycle of the city at the time of Aristotle, and certainly more advanced than they

---

50 Manent, *Seeing Things Politically*, 3.
51 *Seeing Things Politically*, 8.

were at the time of Plato. We have no excuse for not trying with all our strength to understand, and thus to evaluate, where we stand. . . . If I let myself get carried away in invoking what would be the extreme limit of my ambition . . . I would say that I would like to be capable of replacing the two great political cycles of the West, including, of course, the very long period that separates and joins them, in a *histoire raisonnée* based upon this single hypothesis: man is a political animal. To lay out our whole *history* starting from our political *nature*—that is what I would like to show and to make comprehensible.[52]

Of course, that man is a political animal by nature is the fundamental premise presented by Aristotle in Book I of the *Politics*.[53] Aristotle reached his conclusion based on his observation and evaluation of the Greek city and the regimes manifest in that form. Manent proposes as his own project to explain all of the history of European political form on the basis of the same principle. He will bring the events of the modern era back to and under the same guiding principle as the ancient. This is both a re-embrace of the classical view of man and a rejection of the modern flight from nature.

Such an effort is possible because there is a continuity between the thinking of Aristotle and the truth of "what is" today: the constant of human nature. The man of Aristotle's politics who comes together in the natural relationships of family, household, village, and city, is the same man, by nature, who finds that nature to be his enemy and embarks upon the flight away from it in the modern age. Manent identifies the tension between the ancient and modern views of nature, law, and man not in any real difference between ancient and modern man but in whether the same man seeks to live in accord with that nature (generally through the virtues) or to deny it. As we have seen, he claims that man becomes rational as and when he becomes political. It is that move, rather than a move to the modern and especially to modern democratic politics, that represents the real moment of human transformation:

> For over three centuries "moderns" and "antimoderns" have made the European scene echo their disputes. In previous works I have given great attention to these disputes, elaborating an interpretation that made "modern democracy" the goal and heart of European development. The search for which I here

52 *Seeing Things Politically*, 8–9.
53 Aristotle, *Politics* 1.2.1253a2.

provide the elements distances itself from this perspective that was "Tocquevillean" in more than one sense. The defect that I see in this procedure today, a defect from which Tocqueville himself is not immune, is to exaggerate the political and human transformation, the "anthropological transformation" that the progress of modern democracy brings with it. It appeared to me more and more clearly that the formation of the Greek city represented a much more substantial anthropological transformation . . . than the modern democratic revolution, which moreover was in some sense built upon the Greek one. I saw it more and more clearly unfolding starting from the prodigious innovation that was the first *production of the common*. . . . I saw more and more clearly the forms of our common life unfolding from the first and master form as so many reverberations of this original conflagration, as so many metamorphoses of this primordial form.[54]

Aristotle claims that "he who first founded [a city-community] is responsible for the greatest of goods," for the city responds to the truth that "there is in everyone by nature an impulse toward this sort of community."[55] Manent will agree and will base his examination of all political forms on this first form studied by Aristotle, and the human good it makes possible.

Manent's intellectual debt to Aristotle extends to the essential nature of human action in itself. He relies on an Aristotelian framework to understand action as the result of deliberation guided by virtue and intrinsic to the nature of man, which is his ultimate concern.

But it is when we act that we experience the world's resistance and, at the same time, that we resist the world. It is this negotiation with the world that the cardinal virtues administer. It is through them that the influence of the world and our influence on the world come together. And it is only in a community of deliberation and of action that this coming together, which is always precarious, can happen. Thus, today as in the past, and today much more than in the past, the question of actions to be done lies before us, and political or practical science is always, or is now again, the first of the human sciences.[56]

54 Manent, *Metamorphoses*, 13–14.

55 Aristotle, *Politics* 1.3.1253a30.

56 Manent, *Seeing Things Politically*, 211. The phrases "resist the world" and "negotiation with the world" to describe true human action resemble at least prima facie the phrase "crease the world," used by Robert Sokolowski and discussed further in the conclusion.

Manent mounts here a vigorous defense of the eternal truth of the Aristotelian understanding of human action, manifest most excellently in political action and gauged by the virtues. He is consistent in this view and its importance in politics:

> If we do not give up on life, we must act. In order to act, we must have confidence in the possibility of the good. . . . It seems to me, in any case, that if we do not succeed in turning once more with confidence towards the possibility of the Good, or at least in tracing this movement of the heart, we will not recover the desire to govern ourselves and the confidence in our own powers that alone can nourish this desire. The idea of acting for the common good has lost its meaning for us. We [now, after the modern difference] do whatever we do, not because it is useful, honest or noble, but because it is necessary, because *we cannot do otherwise*. . . . [W]e have organized ourselves in order to have less and less need of free will, in order to have less and less need to carry out a complete action, that is, one oriented by the idea of a good desirable in itself, since we no longer want to act except as driven by necessity.[57]

This Aristotelian notion of a human science of acting for the good, he will claim, is a key aspect of what is lost in the modern difference. These lines are among the most personal and passionate passages in all of Manent's writing. One senses the urgency he attaches to the project of bringing the ancient and modern cycles, the sum total of political thought and action, under the Aristotelian understanding of man as a political animal. The intellectual stakes of attaining this grasp of "what is" are high; the practical stakes, in this case closely related, are the recovery of the correct idea of what it is to be human. Aristotle shapes Manent's work in central ways: Manent's essential premise and conclusion are that Aristotle was right all along.

INFLUENCES ON MANENT: ST. AUGUSTINE

As in the case of Aristotle, situating Manent intellectually and understanding his guiding questions have already brought references to St. Augustine. If Aristotle serves as an anchor for the philosophical vertex

---

57 Manent, *Beyond Radical Secularism*, 71–72.

in Manent's philosophy-religion-politics triangle, Augustine provides the anchor for religion and, in particular, for both the Christian critique of pagan philosophy and for the "Christianization" of the understanding of nature and law found in Aristotle. Manent will at times criticize Augustine's critique of the pagan,[58] but certain essentials of Augustine's thought appear to help Manent decisively in his investigation.

Almost all of Manent's works contain some reference to Aristotle; this is not the case for Augustine. Augustine appears in the 1992 essay, "The Truth, Perhaps," by way of his critique of paganism that intertwines with Machiavelli's critique of Christianity—a weaving that Manent says deserves to be understood but leaves for some future occasion. In *An Intellectual History of Liberalism*, Augustine is mentioned twice, both times obliquely: once as one of the few in Western Christendom who, prior to the rediscovery of Aristotle in the Latin West, had some understanding of ancient thought,[59] the other as a parenthetical reference to his definition of grace as "the power of the good that orders what it gives."[60] Manent asserts that the abandonment of this notion of grace as "the power of the body politic . . . [means] that man can understand himself only by creating himself."[61] This is a reformulation of the modern difference, based on the modern renunciation of "thinking about human life in terms of its good or end"[62] and the flight from nature. Manent thereby implies a close relationship between the Aristotelian teleological notion of a nature to human life and politics and Augustinian ideas of grace. This suggests that Augustine's thinking is compatible with the major influence of Aristotle on Manent in important ways.

Further, Augustinian thought often lurks in the background of Manent's most important claims. For example, in a 1993 essay, he critiques the liberal state in these words:

> It is the fact that the liberal state, in its first project, or primary purpose, wants to institutionalize the sovereignty of the human will. Recognizing only free and equal individuals, it has no

---

58 See for example Pierre Manent, "Between Athens and Jerusalem," *First Things*, no. 220 (February 2012): 37. In that article, Manent argues that Augustine failed to preserve a "living relationship" between Christianity and the Jews, or between Christianity and philosophy.

59 Manent, *Intellectual History of Liberalism*, 10.

60 *Intellectual History of Liberalism*, 114.

61 *Intellectual History of Liberalism*, 114.

62 *Intellectual History of Liberalism*, 114.

legitimacy except that founded on their will: the institutions
of this state have for their raison d'être the manifesting of this
will through suffrage, then the putting of this will into action
by a representative government. Such a project . . . by positing
that the political body has for its only rule or law the will of the
individuals who compose it, . . . deprives the law of God of all
political authority or validity, whether the latter is conceived as
explicitly revealed or solely inscribed in the nature of man. It
refuses all authority to that which has by definition, naturally or
supernaturally, the highest authority. . . . One might add, if there
is a God, the human will cannot be "autonomous, or "sovereign": to affirm this "autonomy" or "sovereignty" is to deny the
existence of God.[63]

Intentionally or not, this comment faithfully reflects Augustine's discussion of eternal and temporal law in book I of *On Free Choice of the Will*:

[L]et us call a law "temporal" if, although it is just, it can rightly
be changed in the course of time. . . . Then consider the law
that is called the highest reason, which must always be obeyed,
and by which the wicked deserve misery and the good deserve a
happy life, and by which the law that we agreed to call "temporal" is rightly enacted and rightly changed. Can anyone of sense
deny that this law is unchangeable and eternal? . . . [N]othing is
just and legitimate in the temporal law except that which human
beings have derived from the eternal law.[64]

Manent's critique of the liberal state involves, in Augustinian terms, the
exclusion of eternal law from the process of determining temporal law, or
a choice of man's will over or aside from God's will in politics (and in all
else), or a rejection of nature as decided and created by God. For Augustine, this will amount to a fundamentally flawed order of love, a preference
for the goods of the temporal realm over the eternal good of God—in effect,
the denial of God's existence and authority that Manent sees in the modern
insistence on human autonomy.

　　As a matter of political thought, Augustine does not offer a regime
analysis like that of Aristotle, though in *City of God* as well as his Letter

---

63 Pierre Manent, "Christianity and Democracy: Some Remarks on the Political History
of Religion, or, on the Religious History of Modern Politics," in *Modern Liberty and Its
Discontents*, 99.

64 Augustine, *On Free Choice of the Will*, trans. Thomas Williams (Indianapolis, IN: Hackett
Publishing, 1993), 1.7.

to Marcellinus he critiques extensively the Roman Empire in defense of Christianity against the charge that the new faith had fatally weakened the empire. Indeed, Augustine argues that all regimes are instituted by God, and an analysis of their relative merits exceeds Augustine's capacity:

> [L]et us not attribute the power to grant kingdoms and empires to any save the true God. He gives happiness in the kingdom of Heaven only to the godly. Earthly kingdoms, however He gives to the godly and ungodly alike, as it may please Him, Whose good pleasure is never unjust. But although I have in some measure spoken of those things which it has pleased Him to make clear to me, it is a task too great and too far surpassing my powers to search out the secrets of human affairs and by clear inspection to give judgment as to the merits of kingdoms.[65]

Augustine emphasizes, rather, the orientation of any government and its people toward the telos of human life, or toward something else, reflected in what that people chooses to love: "[L]et us say that a 'people' is . . . an assembled multitude, not of animals but of rational creatures, and is united by a common agreement to what it loves. . . . Clearly the better the objects of this agreement [about what to love], the better the people; and the worse the objects, the worse the people."[66] Augustine provides a Christian expression of the Aristotelian happiness that is man's telos, while leaving open possibilities for human action in the political domain that are evaluated only by their final loves; he avoids using Christianity to determine man's best choice of political form. This combination of Aristotelian and Augustinian thinking, held together by a classical understanding of nature and law, provides a combination on which Manent can rest much of his thought.

In Manent's *The City of Man*, one finds in the index references to, inter alia, Aristotle, Churchill, Freud, Hamlet, Hegel, Homer, Kant, Marx, Milton, Napoleon, Thomas Aquinas, and Satan—a remarkably full range of figures associated with each of the vertices of the philosophy-religion-politics triangle. Augustine is not on the list. Yet, as the title suggests, the entire book is a tribute of sorts to Augustine's *City of God*, in which Manent will provide the intellectual history that led to the form of the modern state, the quintessential "earthly city" (Augustine's more frequent title for the

---

65 Augustine, *City of God against the Pagans*, trans. R. W. Dyson (Cambridge: Cambridge University Press, 1998), 5.21.

66 *City of God* 19.24.

city of man) that opposes the City of God. In *City of God*, Augustine posits two cities, the City of God—the saints in eternal heaven and those who, in temporal life, have chosen that city and seek it—and the city of man whose denizens have chosen to love temporal goods to the exclusion of divine good, with the cities intermixed until the end of time: "I shall treat as fully as I can of the origin and progress and merited ends of the two cities— that is, of the earthly and heavenly—which . . . are in this present world mixed together and, in a certain sense, entangled with one another."[67] This "two-city" framework becomes central to Manent's work, and it will be helpful to understand some of the implications of Augustine's thought for Manent's use of the framework.

Without naming Augustine, Manent cites him once in *The City of Man* to establish this dichotomy of cities and their inhabitants by cutting to the essential difference between Machiavelli and Augustine, the former representing the modern and the latter establishing the Christian claims regarding the good. Manent first cites Machiavelli, in a synoptic reference to *The Prince*: "In the eyes of the citizen, what value is there to the morti- fication of the Christian, when what matters is not to fall on one's knees but to mount one's horse, and the sins one ought to expiate or rather correct are not the sins one commits against chastity and truth, but mili- tary and political errors?"[68] He then cites Augustine, again without naming him except in the footnote, in a synoptic reference to *The City of God*: "In the eyes of the Christian, what value is there to the political and military endeavors of the citizen, when he believes that, victory or defeat, whatever the regime, this world is a vale of tears ravaged by sin and that states are nothing more and better than vast bands of robbers?"[69] The result is a clash of two incompatible understandings of the good: "To each of the two protagonists, the sacrifices the other calls for are vain."[70] The two cities have competing and, short of the end of time, irreconcilable views of the true good, eternal or temporal. This conflict between Augustine and Machiavelli epitomizes the theologico-political question.

Manent leans heavily on Augustine, then, for an understanding of the theological side of the theologico-political question as well as for a representative of the classical view of man and nature, as assimilated

---

67 *City of God* 19.1.
68 Manent, *City of Man*, 27.
69 *City of Man*, 27.
70 *City of Man*, 27.

by Christianity, from which the modern will turn away. As seen above, Manent finds in the modern project a "movement that never arrives at its term, its resting place." He identifies in modern man two related kinds of restlessness: a flight from the constraints of nature and law, and a churning toward a political arrangement that will resolve the theologico-political question. Yet he sees also in the modern a turn from the "seeking" of the ancient philosophers, who sought the principles of our nature, to the "finding" advocated by Montesquieu with the abandonment of the classical understanding of the place of virtue as a principle of man. Perhaps the most famous single sentence in all of Augustine's work is from the opening chapter of his *Confessions*: "You stir man to take pleasure in praising you, because you have made us for yourself, and our heart is restless until it rests in you."[71] This statement is a Christian extension of Aristotle's opening in the *Metaphysics*: "All men naturally desire knowledge,"[72] and as Aristotle conveys in both *Metaphysics* and *Nicomachean Ethics*, we desire the knowledge of the highest, divine things as the principle of "what is." The modern project abandons the classical search, the restlessness prompted by our nature, in favor of a "finding" that denies nature and its inconvenient constraints without understanding any final principle toward which it is nevertheless impelled to fly. Augustine, on the theological vertex of Manent's triangle and in line with Aristotle on the philosophical vertex, finds the principle of man's seeking in God, much as Manent seeks to understand politics (and philosophy) under the principle of Aristotle's political nature of man.

That political or social nature, and the need for human action, are also accommodated in *City of God*. Augustine writes, "The philosophers also consider that the life of the wise man is a social one; and this is a view of which we much more readily approve. . . . [H]ow could the City of God have first arisen and progressed along its way, and how could it achieve its proper end, if the life of the saints were not social?"[73] Man is created social by nature. But in the city of man, "Who, however, could manage to number and weigh the great ills which abound in human society and the woes of the mortal condition?"[74] From the trials of marriage and family to

---

71 Augustine, *Confessions*, trans. Henry Chadwick (Oxford: Oxford University Press, 1991), 1.1.1.

72 Aristotle, *Metaphysics*, trans. Hugh Tredennick (Cambridge, MA: Harvard University Press, 1933), 1.1.980a22.

73 Augustine, *City of God* 19.5.

74 *City of God* 19.5.

war, the social condition of the city of man is dark: "Have not these trials everywhere filled up human affairs? Do they not many times arise even between friends whose love is honourable? Do we not know that human affairs are everywhere full of such undoubted evils: of injuries, suspicions, hostilities and war? And even peace is an uncertain good, since we do not know the hearts of those with whom we wish to maintain peace."[75] But within this sad state there is still room for, and need for, human action. Augustine ponders the case of the well-intentioned judge who must torture a defendant to determine his guilt or innocence. Some defendants might confess wrongly to crimes they did not commit in order to be executed and escape further torture, a prime example of the evils of the city of man. After the execution,

> the judge still does not know whether he has slain a guilty man or an innocent one, even after torturing him to avoid ignorantly slaying the innocent. In this case, he has tortured an innocent man in order to discover the truth, and has killed him while still not knowing it. Given that social life is surrounded by such darkness, will the wise man take his seat on the judge's bench, or will he not venture to do so? Clearly, he will take his seat; for the claims of human society, which he thinks it wicked to abandon, constrain him and draw him to this duty.... The wise judge does not [torture the innocent] through a wish to do harm. Rather, he does so because, on the one hand, ignorance is unavoidable, and, on the other, judgment is also unavoidable because human society compels it.[76]

Likewise, "the wise man . . . will wage just wars" while deploring the necessity for such wars as well as the "iniquity of the opposing side" that creates the necessity for the just war.[77] Augustine's two-city framework yields a domain for human action that must, as far as possible, love the eternal while valuing whatever temporal goods are rightly ordered to that eternal. It is a domain where philosophy, manifest in the wise man who agrees to serve as judge or general despite the dark possibilities he will confront, has a role to play on its own merits in discerning duty and, within the limits of the city of man, justice. In this domain, the telos is the Christian notion of love and knowledge of God, and God as creator is the

---

75 *City of God* 19.5.
76 *City of God* 19.6.
77 *City of God* 19.7.

principle of the nature of man, but the principle of what unfolds in the movement of politics is, as Manent claims, man freely choosing his action as a political animal.

Manent objects strongly to efforts to order the earthly city as if it were the City of God. We have seen that he believes Christianity has "nothing pertinent" to say regarding earthly political arrangements and that the Church is generally incompetent and corrupting in the political domain. But he believes especially that Christian efforts to order the earthly city according to the principles of the City of God have proven deleterious:

> Of course, the point of Christianity is not to order the cities of this world, but to build the city of God; this much is clear. . . . I think that it is legitimate to criticize it when its action on behalf of the other world, or directed toward the other world, brings about effects in this world that spoil the very humanity that it intends to perfect and lead to salvation. I am thus inclined to say that that for which I blame Christianity, or in any case the Catholic Church, is its excessive mistrust and sometimes plain enmity where manifestations of human pride are concerned, that is to say, in the modern period, where liberal and national movements are concerned. Or I might say, adversely or symmetrically, that what I hold against the Church is the preference it has too often shown toward authoritarian regimes which, as Aristotle said of tyrants, do not tolerate virile virtues in citizens.[78]

In other words, Manent, like Augustine, rejects the possibility of creating the City of God on earth, even with the Church's efforts. But he, like Augustine, sees possibilities for excellence in human action in the political domain, however marked by choices and actions of strife and evil that domain is. Perhaps Manent would find Augustine's estimation of the limits of human action too confining and pessimistic, but this is a matter of degree, and his conclusion is similar: "Of course, neither Athens, nor Jerusalem, nor the Christian Church wholly or visibly brings about the fulfillment of humanity: something always goes wrong!"[79]

Augustine's thought would thus appeal to Manent because he does not traverse Manent's lines between the vertices of religion, philosophy, and politics is a way that would deny the proper domain of any of the three. The three domains are not hermetically sealed; they affect one

---

78 Manent, *Seeing Things Politically*, 169–70.
79 *Seeing Things Politically*, 176.

another as parts in a whole. As already noted, the City of God and the earthly city are intertwined, producing the tension that is the basis for Manent's theologico-political question. The good of those who choose the earthly city is decidedly inferior to the eternal good of the City of God, but it is a good nonetheless:

> But the earthly city will not be everlasting; for when it is condemned to that punishment which is its end, it will no longer be a city. But it has its good in this world, and it rejoices to partake of it with such joy as things of this kind can confer. And because this is not the kind of good that brings no distress to those who love it, the earthly city is often divided against itself by lawsuits, wars, and strife, and by victories which either bring death or are themselves short-lived.[80]

Augustine's understanding of the good that is possible in this world is, further, compatible with the classical understanding of the role of virtue. In *On Free Choice of the Will*, Augustine explains that a good will, one that loves the eternal, will produce in its bearer prudence, justice, fortitude, and temperance.[81] These virtues permit, as for Aristotle, a happy life. Included in Augustine's notion of happiness is, first and foremost, love of the divine, the end of the citizens of the City of God. But this happiness, for those of the City of God traveling through the earthly city, also includes the goods protected by temporal law: the health and beauty of the body, the freedom to be without other human masters, family, the city, and property.[82] These temporal goods, which must always be subordinate to the eternal, provide the objects for human choice and action within the domain for human action. In *City of God*, Augustine focuses on the peace of the earthly city as a good:

> A people estranged from god, therefore, must be wretched; yet even such a people as this loves a peace of its own, which is not to be despised. It will not, indeed, possess it in the end, because it does not make good use of it before the end. For the time being, however, it is advantageous to us also that this people should have such peace in this life; for while the two cities are intermingled, we also make use of the peace of Babylon. . . . It is for this

---

80 Augustine, *City of God* 15.4.

81 Augustine, *On Free Choice of the Will* 1.13.

82 *On Free Choice of the Will* 1.15.

> reason, therefore, that the apostle admonishes the Church to
> pray for kings and for all that are in authority, [praying for] the
> temporal peace which is for the time being shared by the good
> and the wicked alike.[83]

Properly understood, politics orders these temporal goods according to nature and to a common good or, to use the phrase Manent often chooses, the "common thing." In that ordering, we should see the extraordinary diversity or heterogeneity of human action that modernity has lost and that Manent's project of political science seeks to recover. Augustine thus provides Manent with a two-city framework that can help explain the "what is" of man and politics, grounded in a teleological and natural understanding like that of Aristotle, that will provide a vital basis for Manent's examination of the movement of history and political form. That examination is seen most completely in *Metamorphoses of the City* and will require a more thorough exposition later; for now, we can understand how Augustine influences Manent's situation in his religion-philosophy-politics triangle and his fundamental outlook. Manent finds in Augustine a thinker whose view of the nature of man and of politics is in key ways compatible with Aristotle, and whose thought regarding the two cities is borne out in political history. That is not to say that Manent sees a seamless whole in the work of the two; much of Manent's work deals with the apparent contradiction between Aristotelian magnanimity and Christian humility, a central driving force in the movement of European political form. But the essentials of Manent's view are found in these two thinkers.

A NOTE ON CICERO AND ST. THOMAS AQUINAS

Before discussing two contemporary influences on Manent, Raymond Aron and Leo Strauss, it will be helpful to touch on two other premodern sources, Cicero and St. Thomas Aquinas, who have not been included here as influences. Like Augustine, Cicero figures in much of Manent's work, especially *Metamorphoses of the City*. Also like Augustine, Cicero is unnamed in the index of *The City of Man*. But Manent is unequivocal regarding Cicero's importance:

---

83 Augustine, *City of God* 19.26.

> [I]f not for the ages, then at least for many centuries, it is Cicero
> who gathered most intelligently and wisely all the usable
> elements of the pagan political tradition and transformed them,
> but still without being able to give them an operational form.
> He will be the source and the resource of political thought for
> as many as fifteen centuries. He is a major point of reference for
> Augustine as well as for St. Thomas. He is truly the source. And
> his authority, in what we call the Christian centuries, is more or
> less equal to that of the Church fathers.[84]

Both as an influence on the history of political thought that forms one track
of Manent's investigation, and as a political actor himself (unlike Aristotle,
and unlike Augustine except in the latter's exercise of his ecclesial func-
tions), Cicero looms large. Manent credits him with subjecting "classical
Greek philosophy to a profound transformation" in at least three ways:
the introduction of the idea of the magistrate as a public person with a
representative function; the definition of the purpose of the political order
as the protection of property; and the insistence on both a common nature
to all persons and a particular nature to each person, which demand that
all persons follow both.[85] These are important contributions to political
thought in the West, and to the eventual development of the modern
difference.

Cicero also transforms Greek thought, in particular Aristotle's
thought, in another way. Where Aristotle held the highest life for man to
be the contemplative life (though it is such a divine life that few if any can
live it) with the life of virtuous action in politics the second-best life (and
the life more available to men), Cicero argues that the best life is one in
politics, while he leaves open the possibility that the contemplative life
can be good:

> [W]e must decide that the most important activities, those most
> indicative of a great spirit, are performed by the men who direct
> the affairs of nations; for such public activities have the widest
> scope and touch the lives of the most people. But even in the
> life of retirement there are and there have been many high-
> souled men who have been engaged in important enterprises
> yet kept themselves within the limits of their own affairs; or,
> taking a middle course between philosophers on the one hand

---

84 Manent, *Seeing Things Politically*, 114.
85 *Seeing Things Politically*, 113.

and statesmen on the other, they were content with managing their own property.[86]

In this development, Cicero established politics as a vertex in Manent's triangle on an equal footing with the other two, and he populates that vertex himself. His understanding of the place of virtue in the political life—and his political activity made him an exemplar of such a life—incorporates prudence, justice, fortitude, and temperance, and thus accepts in broad outline the Aristotelian explanation of virtue grounded in nature in the *Nicomachean Ethics*.[87]

But Cicero's work is ultimately more an important object of study for Manent than an influence on Manent's fundamental view as a scholar and thinker. Cicero accepts the classical worldview, which Manent consciously adopts, and he influences but does not propose the two-city framework that Augustine makes available to Manent. But these are second-order effects: "His role of mediator [of Greek philosophy to Rome] excludes any true philosophic originality."[88] His significance in Manent's project should not be underestimated, but his role in shaping Manent intellectually is less than that of Aristotle or Augustine.

St. Thomas Aquinas is a curious figure in Manent's work. One might expect to find in Thomas's blend of Aristotelian and Christian thinking a body of thought that would appeal directly to Manent. His exposure to Thomas in lycée was, as already noted, an important step in his intellectual and spiritual progress. At one point, Manent describes himself as having been torn between "the equilibrium and the beautiful architecture of Thomism and Strauss's austere demand that I choose between philosophy and religion"[89] but finally as having stayed outside both camps. Manent will incorporate Thomas where it is useful in his consideration of philosophy and political thought, as in *The City of Man* where he cites Thomas, without naming him but referring to him as among "the most authoritative theologians," as a foil to Kant.[90]

But Manent finds Thomas's political and philosophical thought lacking in several major respects. Earlier, we saw that he views Thomas as

---

86 Cicero, *De Officiis*, trans. Walter Miller (Cambridge, MA: Harvard University Press, 1913), 1.26.

87 *De Officiis* 1.5.15.

88 Manent, *Metamorphoses*, 172.

89 Manent, *Seeing Things Politically*, 46.

90 Manent, *City of Man*, 203.

a thinker whose commitment to the theological answer, as a religious who capably uses philosophical tools, nevertheless means that Thomas's applicability or efficacy in the political and philosophical spheres is limited (Cicero may be vulnerable to the same criticism, fluctuating between the philosophical and political vertices). One result of this limitation is that Manent judges Thomas's effort to synthesize the pagan virtue of humility and the Jewish-Christian virtue of humility to be "essentially unstable and fragile . . . [with] elements that are as disparate as philosophy and revelation, . . . only held together by its author's architectonic genius, later reinforced by the approval given to it by some institution as, in the case of Thomism, the Catholic Church, the institution par excellence."[91] Therein lies a sharp example of a violation of Manent's division of the two vertices of religion and philosophy.

Manent defines the "Ciceronian moment" as the extended period of centuries after Cicero until the development of the nation-state. During these centuries, Europe experienced "paradoxically the absence or the indeterminacy of the political order. . . . The political order is indeterminate because it has not found its political form. . . . The only political teaching that remains relevant is Cicero's, with [its] strengths and limits."[92] As a political thinker, Thomas is irrelevant.

> Moreover, if we look at the histories of political philosophy, it is clear that there is the great grouping of the ancients, and then there is that of the moderns, and then there is a long period between the two that we do not know what to do with. . . . [T]he thought of medieval authors is divided essentially between a part that extends ancient thought or that derives from it and a part that announces or prepares modern thought.[93]

Again, Thomas has nothing of special importance to offer Manent. He sees the Thomist tradition as deficient for grasping the "what is" of politics:

> [T]heir Aristotle is an Aristotle almost completely detached from his political context and his political concerns; their Aristotle sometimes has little to do with the real Aristotle. . . . The Aristotle that the Thomist tradition deploys is usually one who is merely preparing his political analysis proper. Thus, there are whole

91 *City of Man*, 33.
92 Manent, *Seeing Things Politically*, 114.
93 *Seeing Things Politically*, 115.

> stretches of politics that are ignored. . . . I would say that the
> Thomists have moralized and depoliticized Aristotle.[94]

Thomas, then, despite being an obvious candidate as a major influence
on Manent, turns out to be of lesser significance in Manent's political
thought. Manent is, rather, an Aristotelian Augustinian in his fundamental
outlook.

RAYMOND ARON
AND LEO STRAUSS

Raymond Aron and Leo Strauss were early and consistent influences
on Manent's thinking, and in his own mind they are closely linked; they
will thus be treated together. Manent has written extensively on their
influence, simplifying the task of understanding how they helped shape
his work.

The same lycée teacher who introduced Manent to Thomist thought,
Louis Jugnet, also suggested that, when he arrived at ENS, he should
immediately contact Raymond Aron—a piece of advice Manent describes
as "the ultimate benefit I attribute to him."[95] This is the first example of
how Manent is handed from teacher to teacher in his intellectual journey,
a succession that Manent says provides "a reassuring sense of continuity
and coherence."[96] Manent approached Aron with a desire "to return to the
[political] things themselves . . . or the beginnings of a move toward political philosophy."[97] He immediately admired Aron with a special fondness:
"It is difficult to speak of such a relationship. I would have to say there was
an element of passion and love. I was carried away with admiration for
Aron when I met him."[98] Aron did much to orient Manent's basic approach
to the world:

> Before teaching me through his books, Aron educated me first
> of all, and I would say especially, by his very person, that is by
> his way of holding himself in the world and of practicing his
> humanity in the world. By his very being he made it clear that

94 *Seeing Things Politically*, 46.
95 *Seeing Things Politically*, 22.
96 *Seeing Things Politically*, 35.
97 *Seeing Things Politically*, 35.
98 *Seeing Things Politically*, 35.

only a long education of the intellect and of the faculty of judgment makes it possible to find one's way with some certainty in
political life. In this way, he delivered us from the contempt or
disdain for politics that comes so naturally to intellectuals, even
or especially to those who are "politicized." By the way that he
gathered and synthesized the information he needed for all the
subjects he treated, he demonstrated that, in politics too, there
is something to be known. . . . Aron knew what he was talking
about [concerning politics], and by this very fact he educated his
reader or his listener because he showed that there was something to be known, and therefore that political judgment, far
from being derived simply from our values or our choices, from
our "project," is based on the patient analysis of the political
things themselves.[99]

Aron thus affirmed for Manent the possibility of a science of human things,
of a political nature and order that could be studied. This confidence was
an essential first step that, more than any particular idea of Aron's, would
permit Manent to proceed in developing his own project.

Aron's seminar was, like Aron himself, a point of intellectual revelation for Manent. Manent was teaching at a lycée at the time he first met the
seminar, and if given a choice between a mandatory lycée faculty meeting
and Aron's seminar, he unhesitatingly chose the latter.

In Aron's seminar, I thus met people who had their own interests, who were involved in a work or a project they could offer
to me, and who had knowledge to transmit to me. This was a
gathering of strong intellectual personalities who deferred to
and admired Aron, yet still maintained their intellectual independence, even in relation to Aron. . . . It suffices to name Jean-
Claude Casanova, Alain Besançon, and Jean Baechler, just to
mention those who remain my closest friends. . . . This was therefore a gathering of independent minds, each having its own view
of things. A second feature of these intellectual personalities was
that they were unclassifiable by academic discipline. . . . [This
reflects] a more general phenomenon that is proper to France:
namely, the existence of these intellectual figures not tied to any
discipline.[100]

99 *Seeing Things Politically*, 37.
100 *Seeing Things Politically*, 67–68.

Aron was an intellectual leader who did not seek disciples. In addition to affirming for Manent the possibility of a science of "what is," he affirmed as well that intellectual independence is a good to be cultivated. Manent can thus situate himself among the three vertices of religion, philosophy, and politics, and among their representatives, with no need to commit to one vertex; instead he seeks to see things whole. He is able to study, learn from, and admire those who exert a major influence on him (as well as those whose thought is more an object of study than a key influence) while nevertheless criticizing their limitations or mistakes. He is also liberated by those in Aron's seminar, and by a particular French tolerance for intellectual "generalists," to draw on all fields of study to pursue his project, without concern for a comfortable but constraining spot within an academic discipline. Daniel J. Mahoney writes,

> Manent admires Aron because he is the model of the man of political reason. He refused to acquiesce in the ideological distortion of reality. He knew that liberalism has enemies and that the liberal regime had to be protected against both its immoderate friends and its ideological enemies. Aron knew that the progress associated with liberal institutions and practices would not put an end to the need for political judgment or civic virtue. Aron was a political scientist who equitably judged the human world, upholding liberal principles but refusing to neatly fit human and social needs and passions into some doctrinal straitjacket. [But Aron's and Manent's] philosophical standpoints, as well as their evaluations of liberal democracy, are, in some important respects, quite distinct. Aron was a conservative-minded liberal while Manent is a conservative who opposes any "reactionary" rejection of modern democracy. The practical conclusions of the conservative liberal and the liberal conservative are often indistinguishable, but in their deepest bearings they belong to distinct, if overlapping, spiritual families. . . . But despite these differences, the liberal Aron was, for Manent, in some important sense a premodern orator and educator. Through his scholarship and journalism, he helped preserve the political contents of the moral life.[101]

101 Daniel J. Mahoney, "Modern Liberty and Its Discontents: An Introduction to the Political Reflection of Pierre Manent," in Manent, *Modern Liberty and Its Discontents*, 18.

Mahoney here confirms that Manent found in Aron's thinking an affirmation of a classically understood natural moral and political order that demanded study and also demanded human action, as political action. Manent's view of the failures of the modern state develops in some ways as a foil to Aron's confidence in liberal principles, but both views are based on a shared notion that a political and moral "what is" should be the basis of politics. Manent himself admires Aron's example of political virtue:

> This is why the principal virtue of political order, *prudence*, inseparable from *moderation*, is discredited to the extent that it is: it alone allows one to unite conservation to innovation and to creation; it alone guarantees the salutary influence of reason and protects us from the temptation of petrifying social life by imposing by means of violence "rational society," in fact, the enemy of all reason as of all humanity. In this century, Raymond Aron is an exemplary representative of this cardinal virtue. Without making himself the preacher of moderation, . . . he illustrates it in each one of his words and deeds. . . . This is why Raymond Aron, intransigent adversary of communism, intransigent defender of liberal institutions, was never a doctrinaire liberal. . . . He never succumbed to the temptation . . . of ideology. His analyses prolong and shed light upon the problems with which the political actors, citizens or statesmen are actually confronted in the city.[102]

Aron is, again, the example of the virtuous man of politics for Manent: "Aron situated himself within the political," as distinct from Strauss within the philosophical or Maritain within the religious.[103] But, like Cicero, Aron was informed by philosophy:

> It seems to me that the role that the political Aron has in relation to Aron the philosopher, the Kantian Aron, is analogous to that which the political Cicero had with Cicero the philosopher; the orator knows that the stars exist, but most often he leaves it to the others to describe the movement of the constellations; or, if he ventures there himself sometimes, his voice betrays a saddened irony. His own task is to introduce a bit of order and

102 Pierre Manent, "Raymond Aron—Political Educator," in *Political Reason in the Age of Ideology: Essays in Honor of Raymond Aron*, ed. Bryan-Paul Frost and Daniel J. Mahoney (New Brunswick, NJ: Transaction Publishers, 2007), 29.
103 Manent, *Seeing Things Politically*, 59.

clarity into the sublunar world: to do this one must forget the stars as much as one remembers them.[104]

Aron's progress from his study of philosophy in Germany to journalist and speaker on contemporary issues is a clear case of a man forced to choose between two vertices of Manent's triangle and who, in choosing, demonstrates the bright line between the two:

> [I]n the later career of Raymond Aron, philosophy in the more restricted and academic sense of the term gets relegated to the background. Events, institutions, societies must be confronted and understood on their own terms and not on the basis of a philosophy of history, which, exceeding the limits of reason, would eliminate their contingency and dissolve their individual-ity. To understand events on their own terms is to understand the intentions and deeds of historic actors. . . . There is a density and intelligibility inherent in historical events that the interpreter, philosopher or historian cannot reduce to a set of historic or sociological "laws" without annulling precisely this particular density and intelligibility.[105]

Manent sees in Aron a mentor in the study of the history of political events—one of Manent's two paths of inquiry, alongside the study of political thought—without historicism and without ideology, those illicit transgressions of the boundary between philosophy and politics. "This is why historical narrative, such as the finished model that Thucydides left us, holds an irreducible validity and dignity for Aron."[106] And for Manent.

---

104 "Raymond Aron," 27. Manent may be referring here to book VI in Cicero's *De Re Publica,* where Paulus reminds Scipio that in order to join those in the heavens, he must first live well on earth and "love the justice and duty, which are indeed strictly due to parents and kinsmen, but most of all to the fatherland [*patria*]." Cicero, *De Re Publica*, trans. Clinton Walker Keyes (Cambridge, MA: Harvard University Press, 1928), 6.8.16. It is also easy to imagine in this starry metaphor traces of both the allegory of the cave in Plato's *Republic*— when the philosopher who has climbed to wisdom and can see things as they are returns to govern the city—and of Aristotle's political life of virtue—with its occasional instances of contemplation of the divine things in the *Nicomachean Ethics*—both of which may have directly or indirectly influenced Cicero. But while in his *Metaphysics*, book XII, Aristotle is content to let the astronomers determine the precise number of prime movers, he does not seem to suggest that interest in the heavenly and divine beings must be rejected or minimized in order to study earthly phenomena such as biology, poetry, or politics.

105 Manent, "Raymond Aron," 19.

106 "Raymond Aron," 19.

Aron was the next teacher to pass Manent on to his subsequent major influence, Leo Strauss. Aron understood that Manent was looking for more than Aron himself had to offer:

> Aron turned me definitively toward political things as the site where human life finds its proper tension and reveals its stakes. At the same time, . . . I was looking for a reference point beyond politics. Perhaps my interest in theology played a role in this, but, in any case, even within the philosophical domain, I felt the need for a criterion of politics, a reference beyond politics that might supply a criterion of politics. Aron understood my preoccupation, but such questions had no urgency for him. He spoke commonly of "regulative ideas": "Yes, of course, we need regulative ideas, in Kant's sense, to orient us in the political world," but actually he got along fine without them. . . . But Aron was the least Kantian thinker there is; he sought no horizon beyond politics, no "kingdom of ends," no "pure morality." He inhabited the immanence of human things without anxiety; . . . what must regulate human things is apparent in the very immanence of political life. . . . Aron was the perfect gentleman who experienced no need of transcendence.[107]

Such blissful equanimity in the domain of human action escaped Manent. Aron proposed as a possible remedy that Manent read Strauss, in whose Platonism Aron thought Manent might find a better guide for his purposes. Manent would continue as Aron's research assistant (though Aron needed no such assistant, according to Manent, making this an ideal post) and colleague for many years, and Manent credits Aron's generosity for a suggestion that he knew might distance his student and friend from his immediate and direct influence.[108] "Aron's influence was, therefore, doubly decisive for me: in teaching me how to approach political things"—an approach that included a sense for a nature of political things and of men, as well as independent thought shaped by diverse disciplines—"and in leading me to Strauss."[109]

Strauss's influence on Manent as he developed his own project of political science was profound, not least in inducing Manent to consider

---

107 Manent, *Seeing Things Politically*, 38–39.
108 *Seeing Things Politically*, 39, 85.
109 *Seeing Things Politically*, 40.

the meaning of the modern difference and to turn consciously to the ancient view of politics, nature, and reason.

> [W]here purely speculative thought is concerned, Leo Strauss has had the greatest influence on me. He is the author with whom I have debated most intensely.... Strauss rediscovered the Ancients. What does it mean to "rediscover the Ancients"? This means, first, that he discovered an alternative to the Moderns because he had good reason to doubt the wisdom of the Moderns. The axis of Western higher education aims, or tends, to make us spectators in the triumphal march of modern philosophy since Descartes or Bacon.... This triumphal march of modern philosophy leads up to the crowning moment, the symphonic orchestra, the great systems: Hegel and German Idealism. In the face of this great orchestra of modern philosophy, we hear Strauss's discordant voice, at first almost inaudible—a very sober and reticent voice.... But this music of Strauss's is such that, once it has got into your system, you are profoundly taken by it. All the forms of prestige under which we live are subverted to the point that we find ourselves asking this radical question: does this huge deployment of modern political philosophy, with the huge institutional machinery that we have built in large part according to plans laid down by this philosophy—do these not finally have the effect of separating us from nature, and in the first instance from our own nature?[110]

Manent was open to Strauss's broad and deep influence because of his own "sensitivity to the pathologies of modern democratic society, a certain anti-modern sensibility.... Strauss ... sought most vigorously to find the root of the modern project and to bring it to light as a political project."[111] In that light, some see in the title of Manent's *The City of Man* a reference to Strauss's *The City and Man* (though, like Augustine, Strauss's name does not appear in Manent's index to *The City of Man*). *The City and Man* explored the political basis of the ancient city through Plato, Aristotle, and Thucydides, while *The City of Man* undertook to expose the intellectual bases for the modern state. In the introduction to his volume, Strauss writes, "But in our age it is much less urgent to show that political philosophy is the indispensable handmaid of theology than to show

---

110 *Seeing Things Politically*, 40.
111 *Seeing Things Politically*, 41.

that political philosophy is the rightful queen of the social sciences, the sciences of man and of human affairs."[112] He continues, "The return to classical political philosophy is both necessary and tentative or experimental."[113] Strauss separates the philosophical domain from the religious and stands the human domain on its own, visible in politics and political thought, in order to better understand modernity and modern political events. Like Aron and Manent (and Lefort, noted above), he finds in Thucydides a helpful example of political narrative. He provides the inspiration for Manent's turn to ancient political thought to better grasp the "what is" of man and human action and the reasons for the modern departure from that "what is." The parallels between Manent's project and Strauss's are apparent.

Strauss's inquiry thus becomes the first of Manent's beginning questions, the question of the modern difference, and Manent learned from Strauss that this project must be dealt with as a human endeavor: "Strauss brings to light an alternative history in which the modern project is no longer the superhuman realization of reason but an altogether human project that begins with Machiavelli and by which Europe commits itself to the huge enterprise of 'acquiring the world' in order to achieve the mastery of the human condition—a mastery that may coincide with the greatest alienation or loss of self."[114] But Strauss, unlike Manent, will devote little time to tracing this history in much of modern philosophy after Rousseau:

> But why did Strauss choose to study this [modern disposition of returning to the ancients while at the same time emphasizing their limits] in the thought of Rousseau and not Nietzsche or Heidegger? . . . Why did Strauss stop at the French Revolution? Why did Strauss not devote any of his most important works to any of the greatest writers after the French Revolution? . . . [Because] the conditions of political philosophy are "radically modified" by the French Revolution. With this, for the first time in its history, philosophy accepts a revelation, even if it is the revelation of reason: for the first time, it [philosophy] leaves its own element [of reason], and, Strauss suggests, it will not succeed in reentering it.[115]

---

112 Leo Strauss, *The City and Man* (Chicago, IL: University of Chicago Press, 1964), 1.

113 Strauss, *Seeing Things Politically*, 11.

114 Manent, *Seeing Things Politically*, 41.

115 Pierre Manent, "Strauss et Nietzsche," *Revue de Metaphysique et de Morale* 94, no. 3 (1989), 338.

This fundamental insight of Strauss regarding philosophy's turn away from reason—a grand historical transgression of the line between philosophy and religion, both for Strauss and for Manent—and with it the onset of the modern flight from nature and law, provide part of the mystery of the modern for Manent. Recalling Manent's claim that the modern had a specific time and place of beginning in eighteenth-century France and England, this point is foundational to his understanding of the paths of political thought and of political events. In *An Intellectual History of Liberalism*, he writes,

> After the Revolution, the men of the nineteenth century no longer lived merely in civil society or the state, they lived in a third element that received various names, usually "society" or "history." Regardless of what it was called, this element had the greatest authority. . . . Its authority did not lie in nature, but in "history," in the historical evolution. It is true that, from the seventeenth century on and especially in the eighteenth century, Europeans had felt that a process independent of political events was changing the state of social man, thanks to progress in the sciences, art, and commerce. But this process was perceived as a technical improvement of man's social nature. Man did not cease to live in nature. . . . That something entirely different was at stake in the nineteenth century is revealed by the most cursory comparison of the writings of Montesquieu and Benjamin Constant.[116]

Of Strauss's contributions to Manent's thought, this interest in the modern difference is of premier importance. Manent will seek to understand that difference in part by examining the political forms that preceded and followed it.

Mais pourquoi Strauss choisit-il d'étudier ce dispositif chez Rousseau, et non pas chez Nietzsche ou Heidegger? . . . [P]ourquoi Strauss s'arrête-t-il à la Révolution française? Pourquoi Strauss n'a-t-il consacré aucun de ses plus importants écrits à aucun des plus grands auteurs postérieurs à la Révolution française? . . . Les conditions de la philosophie politique sont «radicalement modifiées» par la Révolution française. Avec celle-ci, pour la première fois dans son histoire, la philosophie accepte une révélation, même si c'est une révélation de la raison; pour la première fois, elle sort de son élément, et, suggère Strauss, elle ne parviendra pas à y rentrer.

116 *Intellectual History of Liberalism*, 81.

In a less direct way, Strauss is also helpful with Manent's second beginning question, the theologico-political question, by challenging Manent's early Thomist assumptions:

> Strauss nourished my torment over many long years . . . particularly for the following reason. . . . I had discovered philosophy and religion together . . . from a Thomist point of view, within the serenity of the great Thomist edifice in which, in a way that is obviously very satisfying, reason's conclusions come together harmoniously with faith's propositions, or at least prepare them. Strauss, on the contrary, emphasizes that philosophy and religion are two incompatible ways of life, and that one must, therefore, choose: either/or.[117]

Strauss tells Manent that the Thomist synthesis is impressive but risks losing the essential in both philosophical and theological thought. That point sticks with Manent; we have seen his separation of the three vertices of his triangle, and Strauss's philosophical-theological separation contributes to his interest in the theologico-political question.

But here Manent begins to distance himself from Strauss and from American Straussians. He sees the weaknesses of Thomist political thinking but is himself a believer, and thus unwilling to align himself exclusively with the philosophical vertex as Strauss does, though he acknowledges Strauss's "clear advantage" in political thought.[118] This is what Manent means by his self-assessment as a dissatisfied half-Thomist, half-Straussian. Moreover, Strauss's understanding of the philosopher type, who lacks *thumos*, perplexes Manent:

> I have never been able to understand the figure Strauss sketches of a philosopher who would fulfill his being by completely abandoning all interest in human things, who would leave all human interests behind. I find more humanity in religion, in the religious person, than in the philosopher [who rises] above all human things, for whom justice becomes a secondary consideration and for whom human bonds are of no real interest.[119]

The importance of love and its correct ordering in both the individual soul and the political community that is central in Augustine seems to prevail

---

117 Manent, *Seeing Things Politically*, 45.

118 *Seeing Things Politically*, 47.

119 *Seeing Things Politically*, 49.

here over the impersonal philosophical elevation of Strauss's philosopher. Manent continues, "[T]his human type [the philosopher] who so interests us [is] deprived of the very part of the soul that makes human beings interesting! I will say a little flatly: philosophers would not have been able to discern and distinguish the role of *thumos* in human life if their soul had remained prey to *thumos*, if they had not entirely overcome it."[120] Manent can thus profit from Strauss's approach to ancient philosophy and to the sources of the modern difference without accepting Strauss's view of the philosopher's disdain for the human.

Further, Manent encounters Straussian thinking in the person of Allan Bloom, a regular visitor to Paris who loved France's particularity and was himself very different from the so-distant-from-the-human philosopher described by Strauss, in everything from his "wit and wry humor" to his love for "fine and expensive things" to his love for children.[121] Bloom made Strauss personal for Manent, as Aron had been and continued to be. Intellectually, he made the classical notion of the philosophical ordering of the soul "concrete and relevant for me."[122] This was an important development for Manent, as it brought close the truth that, unlike the modern industrial philosophy he had encountered at ENS, "philosophy in its original meaning entirely escapes the artifice of systematic, conceptual constructions and finally consists in finding the right disposition in which to hold oneself in the world, or in relation to the world."[123] Manent rejects as unconvincing the superhuman philosopher of Strauss's construction; there thus remains in Manent's picture of "what is" a place for the religious man, and for love. But he finds the Socratic natural tradition of the understanding of the soul, pursued by Strauss and Bloom, "to be the most convincing and dazzling part of the 'science of man' that it is possible for us to know. . . . I have tried to make good use of this in my effort to understand political things."[124]

Aristotle, Augustine, Aron, and Strauss comprise the major influences that shape Manent's exploration of political things as they are. Manent believes that ideas produce effects, and the ideas of these four thinkers guide his examination of both ideas and effects. Their influence

---

120 *Seeing Things Politically*, 57.
121 *Seeing Things Politically*, 51.
122 *Seeing Things Politically*, 58.
123 *Seeing Things Politically*, 58.
124 *Seeing Things Politically*, 59.

will be evident throughout the remainder of this inquiry into political form in Manent's work.

A BRIEF NOTE ON PHENOMENOLOGY

Manent would not generally be counted among the school of those who study and write on phenomenology. But Crystal Cordell Paris believes that phenomenology is a pillar in Manent's thinking, because "it constitutes an effort to preserve our access to human things or to 'phenomena' in their true-to-life reality and in their completeness."[125] There is reason to believe that Manent finds phenomenology to be, at a general level, a useful way of thinking about political things as they are. First, he is interested in Heidegger as well as other thinkers such as Lefort who were influenced by phenomenology. Further, Manent himself uses the terms "phenomenon" and "phenomenology" throughout his work. Examples include the following:

> Thus Lefort, drawing part of his inspiration from the phenomenological tradition, brings to our attention the bodily character of the political, or the political character of the body. This close relationship, although coming to the surface of speech in common expressions like "political body" or "body politic," has long been obscured in our democratic dispensation.[126]

> The modern age is characterized by a strange interpenetration between the concept and event, between intellectual and political history. Because of this, it was necessary first of all to elaborate exactly the conceptual content of modern politics. And it was reading the political philosophers . . . that brought me the most light. This point does not entail the adoption of any methodological approach. . . . If this procedure imposed itself on me, it was simply because read attentively, with the passionate attention paid to them by Strauss, the texts of these philosophers

---

125 "L'inspiration aristotélicienne," 191. "[Phénoménologie] constitue un effort pour préserver notre accès aux choses humaine ou aux «phénomènes» dans leur réalité vécue et dans leur intégralité."
126 Manent, "Return of Political Philosophy," 587.

provide us a convincing phenomenology of the political and moral life of the last three centuries.[127]

[In Aristotle's *Politics*] the bringing to light of the elements of the city, the critical and impartial analysis of the claims of the different parties, the exploration of the problem of justice, of the relations between liberty, nature, and law: the phenomenology of political life is presented without either prejudice or lacuna.[128]

Such explicit mentions of phenomenology are abundant, as are examples of an implicit acknowledgement of phenomenology such as this:

Contrary to what is commonly believed, and this brings us back to Aron, the capacity to perceive what is happening right in front of us, to be sensitive, as Péguy said, to the bite of the present, is something rare to possess and difficult to acquire.[129]

What I am trying to describe are the possibilities of life that are deployed or that become visible in the West.[130]

All of these comments suggest that Manent has in mind a phenomeno-logical frame of reference as he travels his two paths of investigation of political thought and political events. A complete examination of this topic is beyond the scope and competence of this book. But it is worth noting that at least one scholar of phenomenology has found Manent's work interesting from that perspective:

But if political life is a crown of speech, it also perfects it and makes it more exact. It provides the setting in which speech is most itself. Pierre Manent writes, "It is not the word that produces community, but community that produces and sustains the word. If there are all sorts of communities and, therefore, all sorts of words, all the words nonetheless find the place for their

---

127 "The Truth, Perhaps," 36.
128 "Christianity and Democracy," 101–2.
129 *Seeing Things Politically*, 140.
130 *Seeing Things Politically*, 184.

pronunciation (*le site de leur respiration*) in the political association, the city."[131]

Manent claims that politics is human action at its best, and Sokolowski
adds phenomenologically that part of that action is speech, which is
revealed to be "most itself" in politics.

POLITICAL FORM

With this understanding of Manent's inquiry and influences, we can turn
to the question of political form. Manent identifies several political forms.
The earliest to develop was the "*band*, a group of twenty to twenty-five
hunter-gatherers that constituted the fundamental collective organization
of Paleolithic men."[132] This first form became a "*tribe* when demographic
pressure became too strong, the occasions for conflict more numerous,
and broader protection was needed than the band was able to provide.
The tribe is the collective form that assured this protection. It is defined
by a twofold permanent movement of fission or division, when danger is
distant; and fusion or coagulation when it is near."[133] Manent suggests that
these early forms confirm that "there is no indefinite political form. The
tribe, the most supple political organization, was already perfectly defined
thousands of years ago."[134] While Manent agrees that these early forms
differ radically from later forms in their lack of a public-private distinction
and of an advanced institutionalization of political activity, his point here
is that even in man's distant past, his activity was ordered in definable
organizational forms.

Manent then identifies the political forms that will be of main
interest to his project: city, empire, the Catholic Church, nation or nation-
state, and modern state. We will take each form in turn. While this division
will allow Manent's material to be handled in digestible quantities, it is
important to keep in mind that while he insists on clear definitions of

---

131 Robert Sokolowski, *Phenomenology of the Human Person* (Cambridge: Cambridge
University Press, 2008), 269. The Manent citation is from *La raison des nations: Réflexions
sur la démocratie en Europe* (Paris: Gallimard, 2006), 43–44.

132 Pierre Manent, *A World beyond Politics? A Defense of the Nation-State*, trans. Marc Le
Pain (Princeton, NJ: Princeton University Press, 2006), 44. There is some inconsistency
between Manent's discussion here and his later claim that the city is the first political form
that emerged from a pre-political condition.

133 *A World beyond Politics?*, 44.

134 *A World beyond Politics?*, 44.

each form, the scheme is not the kind of the system-building of industrial philosophy he encountered as he began his time at ENS. Rather, the definitions allow for rigorous analysis of each form in itself, for a comparison with other forms, and for consideration of the dynamic movement from form to form over time. Manent's approach discerns the order in the apparently messy march of political events and thought.

Chapter Three

CITY AND EMPIRE

MANENT'S INQUIRY INTO THE MODERN DIFFERENCE and the theologico-political question examines political form as the phenomenon that best reveals the "what is" of the reality that corresponds to those questions. He opens the way to a fuller account of human action and the science of the human. "A political form—the nation, the city—is not a light overcoat that one can put on or take off at will and still remain what one is. It is the Whole within which all elements of our life come together and take on meaning."[1] Political form, then, is fundamental to human life and action. It is the sphere where Aristotle's claim for the city—that it exists to live well, nobly, or finely—is fulfilled or not. "But then, in defining man as a political animal, classical philosophy saw the city as a Whole where man finds all the goods proper to his humanity."[2] Manent broadens Aristotle's claim for the city to all of the forms he examines. Those forms or Wholes that Manent describes (and capitalizes for emphasis) comprise an essential feature of the being of their human citizens.

Manent's project on political form is rarely schematic. The forms are understood in comparison or contrast to one another, and they are seen in the movement from a pre-political condition to an articulated form, or in the tension between one form and another, or in the movement from one form to another, so that elements of one form may be present in another. Nevertheless, as we saw Francis Slade insist in chapter 1, political associations are necessarily identifiable by their form. They are the result of rational, political choices whose outcome is a form.

In this chapter, we will first examine Manent's efforts to define and describe the forms of city and empire. We will then explore Manent's understanding of the nature of the city as the original political form, whose

---

1 Manent, *Democracy without Nations?*, 4.
2 Manent, *City of Man*, 79.

influence endures through all subsequent forms. Manent's account of the emergence of the city as drawn from the poetry of Homer and as rooted in war will follow. We next explain Manent's fundamental treatment of the "civic operation" and the "common thing" as the characteristic political activities of the city (and of any natural, or at least not anti-natural, political form). Finally, we will turn to the empire form to see how, in the case of Rome, it emerged from the city and profoundly influenced the subsequent movement and development of political form in Europe.

CITY AND EMPIRE: A START

The first two political forms of significant interest to Manent are the city and the empire. These are the forms that were "characteristic of Greek and Roman antiquity."[3] Aristotle's political science deals with the former; Augustine's *City of God* deals with political communities in general and, especially, with the Roman empire and the Christian critique thereof. Manent devotes great attention to both forms, which he describes as natural, each appealing or responding to some part of man's political nature. The actual, realized examples of these forms that interest Manent are Athens, Rome, and Rome again.

Manent claims that "there is an ancient world—let us say the Greco-Roman world—in which we can distinguish two main forms of human association, the city and the empire."[4] Understanding these forms will permit us to explain the history of the ancient world.

> Here we must add immediately that the city is the new form of the ancients, the form . . . produced by the Greeks, while the empire obviously refers first to non-Greek empires, the Asiatic empires. The invention of the city, moreover takes on a revolutionary and positive meaning: Greeks are free, Asiatic peoples are slaves. The history of the ancient world is, at bottom, the history of the interplay between these two political forms. It is either the story of war between these two political forms, Greek cities against the Persian Empire, or it is that of the passage from one of these forms to the others, that is, from city to empire.[5]

---

3 Manent, *Democracy without Nations?*, 91.
4 Manent, *Seeing Things Politically*, 108.
5 *Seeing Things Politically*, 108.

Such a passage will turn out to be a rare exception. But this ancient historical movement will also be the source of all European political motion.

The city is the form "for which we can give a complete, and thus a completely satisfactory definition." To define the city, Manent turns to Strauss and Aristotle:

> The city is particularly susceptible to being defined because it is constituted by its *fines*, by its limits. In Leo Strauss's felicitous formulation, "the *polis* is that complete association which corresponds to the natural range of man's power of knowing and of loving." In such a definition the *ought* is included in the *is*. But let us also listen to the best analyst of the ancient city: "the best defining principle for a city is this: the greatest number of members with a view to self-sufficiency of life that is readily surveyable." We need to keep in mind this defining trait of the city: the city is readily surveyable, it is *eusunoptos*.[6]

The city is a form, a whole, that is natural, complete, and limited; its "ought," or what it should be and do, is included in Strauss's definition of what it is. In contrast, the empire is natural but by definition unlimited and, in that sense, never really complete; it is therefore less natural.

> The empire is less easy to define because in contrast to the city its defining trait is its limitlessness. Far from being *eusunoptos*, it extends well beyond the horizon. To be grasped it requires the imagination which it stirs and even inflames. You could retort that with all this indeterminacy, the empire implies a clear definition inasmuch as the notion points toward an all-encompassing gathering of all peoples under one rule—ultimately, the gathering of the whole human race, all humankind, under the same rule. The objection is valid, except for the fact that this gathering of all men, contrary to the civic association, is an imagined gathering: the most extended empires in history have left out large segments of humanity. Thus, practically speaking, the notion of empire is a performative one; it involves the impulse and efforts to attain the greatest possible extension of a domination.[7]

---

6 Manent, *Democracy without Nations?*, 91. See Aristotle, *Politics* 7.4.1326b7–10. Strauss's definition appears in his *Natural Right and History* (Chicago, IL: University of Chicago Press, 1953), 254n2.

7 *Democracy without Nations?*, 91–92. Manent sometimes refers to the United States as an empire. Walter McDougall provides an anecdote that ties that characterization to Manent's point about empire: "Three Americans [of the 1880s] are toasting their nation in

The city is identifiable by its limits, which can be seen and sensed. The empire is identifiable by its motive for performance or action, its desire for universal domination, which is a function of the imagination and the will. City and empire,

> far from being contingent, displayed a very marked character of intelligibility, and . . . one could say they were on the whole "natural." The city is the smallest human association capable of self-government, of autarchy. Empire, on the other hand, is the most extensive possible assembling under a single sovereign. Thus we have two conceptions of humanity, two ways of crystallizing the fact of being human—a group small enough and large enough to govern itself, and the assembling of the whole of humanity, or at least the greatest possible number, under a single power. The pagan order, the ancient order, is an order that rests on these two great political forms and their interrelations. This pagan order is the "natural" order of human things, to the degree that these two modes of human association developed spontaneously, that is, in the absence of any prior idea or conception.[8]

Both self-government of the particular, smaller city and the empire's defining motive of the universal, are natural to man, as they follow the Aristotelian principle that man is a political animal; city and empire seek to provide an association under that principle. Both develop without an idea that precedes and guides their establishment. But as empire moves beyond a surveyable or sensible scope, it also becomes impossible to realize in the scale of its ambition: "Aiming ultimately to gather the entire human race, which is humanly impossible, it tends beyond humanity. Only a super-human ruler would be able to govern the human race. The emperor has to have a godly or divine nature."[9] Manent does not say

---

the presence of their foreign hosts." The first raises his glass to the United States bounded by British America (Canada), the Gulf of Mexico, the Atlantic Ocean, and the Pacific Ocean. The second proposes the United States bounded by the North Pole, the South Pole, the rising of the sun in the east, and the setting of the sun in the west. "But the third carried the day: 'I give you the United States—bounded on the north by the Aurora Borealis, on the south by the precession of equinoxes, on the east by the primeval chaos, and on the west by the Day of Judgment!'" This would seem to trump even the British Empire, on which the sun never set. Walter McDougall, *Promised Land, Crusader State: The American Encounter with the World since 1776* (New York: Houghton Mifflin, 1997), 97–98.

8 Manent, *Seeing Things Politically*, 109.

9 Manent, *Democracy without Nations?*, 92.

so, but in this case the theologico-political question would be resolved by the merger of the divine and human ruler. The city is realizable for humans; the empire seeks an association that cannot be finally realized, thus we might see in it the first indications of the perpetual restlessness, the constant incompleteness, that Manent associates with modern man. Empire is both less definable and less suitable to the realities of human nature in its need for the political community, than city.

As noted above, Manent claims that men become rational as and when they become political. This has implications for political form:

> Aristotle in some way equates rational animal and political animal, an animal living in a polis, that is, in a determined political form. Of course, those human beings who do not live in cities properly speaking but in tribes or empires also belong to the species, although they are without doubt less accomplished since the framework for the deployment of their *logos* is less favorable. But in all cases, speech and reason develop in a community that is real, and thus distinct, that can be seen, named, and, so to speak, touched.[10]

City and empire both permit the appearance of rational man as political animal, and empire remains sensible—it can be touched though its limitlessness means it must also be imagined—but in some lesser degree than the surveyable city, whose limits are visible. As forms, city and empire are thus different modes of becoming human and acting meaningfully.

A concise definition of empire, such as the one that Strauss gave for the city, eludes Manent.

> Empires are able and likely to be found in all parts of the world and all civilizations. In China, in Africa, in Central America, in ancient and modern Europe—one could go on and on. This is not the case with the city, . . . [which] has fully developed only in the European domain broadly understood—that is, from the Greek *poleis* through the cities of northern Italy and northern Europe to the *townships* of New England.[11]

Empire can be described by reference to example, but to the extent it can be defined, at least in the West, the definition is as an alternative to or

---

10 Manent, *Metamorphoses*, 135. Manent does not provide a specific citation in Aristotle for this claim, but it is evident in the discussion in *Politics* 1.1.1252a1–19.

11 Manent, *Democracy Beyond Nations?*, 92.

formal development of what was a city, or in contrast to the city and its limits.

> One could maintain that there are two main political forms, the city and the empire [the tribe is only semipolitical]. . . . The city is all things considered the purest political form, insofar as it has no other *raison d'etre* than to produce the association, or the community, whose material and moral resources are sufficient to allow citizens to lead "the good life." For this very reason it is the purest expression of human pride, in which human beings, by governing themselves, experience and freely enact their humanity.[12]

Manent notes the city's pride; that feature of pagan politics and humanity will be the principal point of contention with Christianity as presented in Augustine's critique of paganism. Manent then goes on to establish the contrast with empire, where pride is present but manifests itself differently.

> The moral character of empire is more uncertain, even suspect, insofar as the pride of domination flourishes there in an expansive movement that has no natural limits, even though, in the best case, the extent of the empire tends to coincide with a given area of civilization. To be sure, the city can be quite insolent and aggressive, as was Athens, but it retains a sense of its limits and of the limits of human things: it retains self-awareness because it governs itself. Empire can be very well and very humanely governed, as was the Roman Empire under the Antonines, but it is subject to a principle of boundlessness that prevents or hinders the mind's self-reflection.[13]

Empire is identifiable by a pride in domination, as opposed to the city's pride in the possibility of human action and self-governance within the limits that make excellence in such action possible. Likewise, and closely related, the city is characterized by self-reflection and self-awareness, which the empire lacks in the same measure. Manent thus sees the city as more amenable to philosophical deliberation—the use of the reason that, in Manent's view, arises at the same time that men become political—than the empire, and that capacity ensures the city's superiority as a form for human action and politics.

---

12 *Beyond Radical Secularism*, 59.
13 *Beyond Radical Secularism*, 59.

Manent's claim that the city is characterized by self-awareness is acute. Presumably, this self-awareness marks the citizens of the polis as well as the city itself, as a whole. Athenians were aware of their status as Athenians, both individually and collectively. In empire, this awareness becomes distended as the imagination extends beyond surveyable limit; with it, presumably the rationality that arises with politics becomes distended as well. Philosophy would thus, like pride, be at its most pure in the city form. The pride of the citizens of the polis thus attaches to philosophy, the contemplation of the highest truths; both philosophy and politics reflect human action at its best. Empire sacrifices philosophy in pursuit of extension, and thus sacrifices some measure of humanity as well.

Empires also turn out to be weaker than cities, as "their expanding domination . . . tends naturally to make good government difficult, in particular the government of the parts furthest from the center. This is therefore a political form that is relatively weak, or exposed to devastating weaknesses."[14] He cites the example of the success of the Arab conquests of the Byzantine and Persian empires; the long rivalry of the latter two empires, particularly on their peripheries, substantially reduced their military effectiveness against the Arabs. This aspect of empires makes them more subject to territorial changes, which would presumably make a good or fully human empire-wide politics yet more unlikely than in a city. Moreover, these examples demonstrate that "it is not enough to say 'empire,' because there are several kinds of empire."[15] The empire that will most concern Manent, of course, is the Roman Empire that was the basis for the West, the empire that emerged from the city of the corrupted Roman republic. "Under the Western Empire, there was always the city as a living, even if almost smothered principle; beneath the *princeps* or *imperator*, there was always the *populus romanus*."[16] Unlike other empires, which did not begin with or retain a city as their starting and enduring principle, Rome-the-empire remains Rome-the-city after it changes form and becomes empire: "Rome presents us with a different kind of case, since, in the case of Rome, it is the city itself that gives birth to the empire, the city itself that experienced this extension, that applied this almost

14 *Beyond Radical Secularism*, 59–60.
15 *Beyond Radical Secularism*, 64.
16 *Beyond Radical Secularism*, 64.

unbelievable effort to transform itself from a small city into a world empire."[17] At least in the case of Rome, the forms of city and empire are not altogether mutually exclusive and cannot be easily schematized; empire emerges from city while retaining some aspect of that city. The definition of the city will remain relevant to the Roman empire even after it takes on its imperial "performative" principle; the further implications of this Roman uniqueness are explored below.

With these definitions or quasi-definitions, characteristics, and contrasts of city and empire established, we can focus on the first form, the city. It will be essential to keep in mind that while city and empire are certainly distinct, because the latter grows from the former at least in the case of Rome, there is not an absolute or abstract distinction between the two; and, again at least in the case of Rome, the city's original principle remains active if subdued, supplemented, and covered by the principle or motive of domination. When we think of empire in the context of Western political development, we should always keep in mind city as well, because the two remain related and, in a sense, intertwined: understanding empire demands an understanding of city. In no case of political form does Manent identify quantitative measures or highly specific criteria to identify a form. He will point out characteristics, and there is always a degree of "know it when you see it" judgment involved. That judgment develops from Manent's survey of historical events and actual political associations that preceded his examination of political thinking. He observes the forms as they have appeared in history, in particular in the way they have appeared in Europe, then turns to political thought to help understand the movement or change of political form.

THE CITY AS ORIGINAL FORM

As would be expected from Manent's conscious adoption of the classical view of man and politics, he returns to that view to understand the city as it appeared in ancient Greece and Rome, and he relies on Aristotle and Strauss as his thinking on political form develops over much of his work. The city is "the starting point of any political reflection. . . . It is the original home of European and Western politics, which has derived its very name from polis, the Greek word for the self-governing city."[18]

---

17 Manent, *Seeing Things Politically*, 109.
18 Manent, *A World beyond Politics?*, 44.

From French revolutionaries to Benjamin Constant to student protestors in 1968, political thinkers and actors in later centuries turned to ancient cities—Athens, Sparta, Rome—as the basis for comparison with all future political forms and practices; again, understanding this form is central to grasping its successors. "The ancient city is not just a memory, a shining image, a prestigious reference. It is rooted in a founding experience, in the discovery of what men can and must do to attain justice and happiness," the ancient concerns of how to achieve the good life as individuals and as political communities.[19] "For the Greek philosophers the city is the form of political life par excellence. According to them, the citizens' life 'in the city' is the only way of life that is fully 'according to nature.' This is the meaning of Aristotle's famous phrase, 'man is a political animal'—political, that is, made to live in a city."[20] The city, then, is the foundational and highest formal example of the political principle under which Manent proposes to organize his science of man. He reverts often to Strauss's definition:

> But why, or in what way, is the city especially natural? It is so because it corresponds to the human ability to know and to love. The power to know: the citizens know one another because in the first place they see one another. They know one another at least "by sight" since the city is finite. The assembly makes decisions after public deliberations and thus all the political structures of the city are so to speak visible. The city is "synoptic." The power to love is linked to the power to know, since the citizen identifies easily with a community that is so immediately present and familiar to him. One can notice how the natural character of the city makes itself visible in that male and sometimes even female citizens go naked in the gymnasium. This nudity distinguishes Greeks from Barbarians.[21]

The ancient city was "synoptic" or "surveyable." This feature made it highly personal and permitted Aristotle's notion of political concord, or love or friendship as depicted in the *Nicomachean Ethics*, in and for a place and for citizens who existed concretely and registered in the senses, rather than in the imagination of what lies beyond the city's physical limits.[22] Moreover, the citizens participate in the external conflicts of their city as

---

19 *A World beyond Politics?*, 44.
20 *A World beyond Politics?*, 45. See Aristotle, *Politics* 1.2.1252b27–1253a3.
21 Manent, *A World beyond Politics?*, 45.
22 See Aristotle, *Nicomachean Ethics* 8.9.1159b25–8.11.1161b10, 9.6.1167a21–b16.

soldiers and "in sovereign deliberations and magistracies" as direct partic-
ipants in the effort to resolve or mitigate the internal divisions marked
principally by "the internal war between rich and poor."[23] "In sum, the
city knows only face-to-face encounters. There is no voting booth! Nor is
there any filter, only a sort of permanent incandescence."[24] The citizens
act directly as legislators or warriors, with no intermediary representatives
as "filters" between themselves and political action; there is an "incandescence" or heat from the city's external wars with other cities and its
internal conflicts. Manent's description of the city is consistent with Aristotle. "The truth of the city is liberty and war, inseparably."[25] This provides
a key contrast with empire: "The city signified war and liberty; the empire
signified peace—the *pax romana* (war was pushed to the distant frontier)
—and property, or private right. Ancient politics, whether Greek or Roman,
was thus deployed between the limits and concentration of civic life in the
city and its extension and dilution in the empire."[26] We always understand
the city more completely by contrasting it with its successor form, and
in particular we must understand Rome, which as discussed below was
anomalous as a city that did not, like the Greek cities, disappear after its
initial form of city decayed but rather transformed into an empire. Manent
reaches an understanding of these forms in his path of evaluating the
political events that occur within the forms and in the change from one
form to another, or as the forms pass out of political history.

In *Metamorphoses of the City*, Manent refines his earlier reliance on
Strauss and adopts a more original approach, while remaining consistent
with his Aristotelian roots. He identifies two essential aspects of the city
not in what the city is, but in what it does.

> To the question, what is a city? It is tempting to reply equally or
> indifferently that it is a "big family" or a "little world." These
> are the illusions that are inseparable from the city. In reality,
> the city cruelly or imperiously subordinates the family and the
> world. It takes young men from their families living, and brings
> them back dead. It declares the world, the unknown beyond the
> walls of the city, enemy territory where one does not venture
> unarmed.[27]

---

23 Manent, *A World beyond Politics?*, 45.

24 *A World beyond Politics?*, 45.

25 *A World beyond Politics?*, 46.

26 *A World beyond Politics?*, 48.

27 Manent, *Metamorphoses*, 27.

Manent begins his greatest work on the city, asking about the "what is" of the city, not with an apodictic definition—though no doubt with Strauss's definition in mind—but with two acts that characterize the city, the subordination of the family to its needs and the demarcation of the boundary between the city, where the political concord that Aristotle speaks of might exist, and the world where only varying degrees of enmity are possible. Aristotle links the degree of possible concord in a regime to the degree of justice in that regime, noting that "in the deviation-forms [of regimes: tyranny, oligarchy, democracy], as justice hardly exists, so too does friendship [hardly exist]."[28] In that sense, a regime where justice is lacking resembles the world beyond the limits of the good city, the world Manent describes as "enemy territory." For Aristotle, the presence or absence of justice is a component of the definition of the regime: a king or aristocracy is by definition good and just, while a tyrant or oligarchy is by definition deviant and unjust (Aristotle allows for a greater degree of concord in deviant democracies, due to the equality of the citizens). Manent, though, at least at this stage, is not interested in the city form's goodness or deviancy; implicitly, he accepts that the form can be either, depending on the character of its regime, accepting as well Aristotle's explanation of the various specific regimes available, as will be discussed below.

From the two defining acts of the city, its subordination of the family and its demarcation of the broader world, Manent extracts three "natures" or natural aspects of the city: First, it has a "tragic nature, as it appears in its conflicting rapport with the family, the families from which it issues. This is the city according to its birth, the city inasmuch as it is born and as it signifies a second birth for its members. *Birth* is one of the meanings of the notion of nature."[29] Next, it carries a "philosophic nature, in the measure that it arouses and constrains the desire to accede to the world without borders, the pure world that is beyond the city. This is the city according to its ultimate end, or the end that is beyond it. *Finality* is one of the meanings of the notion of nature."[30] The city with its limits evokes

---

28 Aristotle, *Nicomachean Ethics* 8.11.1161a30.

29 Manent, *Metamorphoses*, 27. Manent here seems to suggest a kind of spiritual second birth or rebirth in politics by means of citizenship, or coming to accept one's status as a member of the political association, that must follow one's first birth into the natural family; such rebirth might be analogous to the Christian notion of the need to be "born again" in the spiritual domain, or to tribal "coming of age" rituals that might combine political and religious elements.

30 *Metamorphoses*, 27. The French verb *accéder*, translated here as "accede," can have the sense of being able to enter into or having access to something, which seems to be the sense Manent intends here.

a philosophical desire to know "what is" beyond those limits, what is ultimate or final for the city and beyond it. Third, the city has within itself a natural movement of the political: "Between birth and end, there is the city according to its own life, forgetful of its pre-political birth as well as of its metaphysical end, the city according to its *political* life, according to the *movement* of its political life—of internal struggle and external war— . . . that leads it naturally to death. What has in itself the principle of its *movement* is natural."[31] The city, then, commits two acts and has three natural aspects. Those natures are, in turn, explored not from different perspectives but by three different "articulations of the human world once this world is grasped and determined by the political form, the form of the city."[32] Sophocles and the Greek tragedians turn their attention to, and articulate, the city's tragic aspect; Plato and Aristotle articulate the final or philosophical nature; and those two as well as Thucydides express the political aspect. In understanding the two basic acts of the city and its three natures, Manent will find the basis of his work on political form: "If we understand the city according to its limits, we place ourselves in a position to understand the possibility, perhaps the necessity, of the other political forms. More precisely, by keeping before us both the ancient science of the city and its limits as well as the later experience of other political forms, we open for ourselves the possibility of a more complete science."[33] This is the science Manent is looking for, not a synthesis of ancient and modern science but the ancient one, "because it and it alone is wholly political," enlarged to accommodate the understanding of later political forms as they manifest human action, under the single principle that man is a political animal. Understanding the city and its limits is the key to that science, to a more complete science of man and action, as the "human world is formed by the way people govern themselves: it is in the city, in the city-form, that people came to know this."[34]

31 *Metamorphoses*, 27.
32 *Metamorphoses*, 28.
33 *Metamorphoses*, 28.
34 *Metamorphoses*, 28.

THE SOURCES OF THE CITY
IN POETRY AND WAR

In *Metamorphoses of the City*, as Manent begins his treatment of the political form of the city, we are afforded a notable example of his use of literary sources to see what has transpired in political history: he engages the first of the city's three aspects, the tragic aspect, in its poetic birth. "Poetry here is meant to include epic and tragedy, since comedy does not give us the birth of the city but an image of its life and perhaps of its decline."[35] This first political form, the first of Manent's modes of being political and thus rational and human, has its deepest source not in a systematic or contrived political philosophy that preceded its realization, but in the pre-politics of the drama that describes what happened as the city form came into existence.

This discussion of the poetic sources of the city is one of the few cases where Manent focuses largely on one form with only limited reference to other forms for comparison or contrast. Even here, he devotes considerable attention to contrasting the city with the modern state. But this account of the emergence of the first city, the first political form, from a pre-political condition is unique in Manent's work for its focus on one form in itself: the original form. Manent seems to imply that the emergence of the form is as or more important than its definition, and that the city is best seen and understood in its emergence or in the movement that produced it.

Manent turns to Aristotle's *Poetics* to analyze the Greek poetry that would have such profound political implications. "Epic and tragedy have in common that they 'imitate noble actions' (*Poetics*, 1448b25), that they are 'an imitation of people who are to be taken seriously' (1449b10)."[36] Manent does not note it here, but such people would be those whose opinions would be worth considering as Aristotle surveys various *doxa* regarding ethics and politics; they would also be those capable of participating in the city's end of living nobly or well. Homer's works fit both the epic and the tragic categories: "In effect, epic is the matrix of tragedy in that Homer is the father of 'serious' poetry (1448b34), the author of two epic poems that not only furnished the matter or inspiration of numerous tragedies, but that moreover are in themselves 'dramatic interpretations' (1448b35–36)."[37] In general, Aristotle describes the "difference between

---

35 *Metamorphoses*, 29.
36 *Metamorphoses*, 29.
37 *Metamorphoses*, 29.

epic and tragedy [as lying] in epic 'having its verse unmixed with any other and being narrative in character' (1449b11), whereas tragedy presents characters actually engaged in 'action' (1449b26)."[38] Manent's interest in Aristotle's analysis would not seem to be abstract or idle; rather it stems from his interest in the science of human things, or human action, and Aristotle brings drama into this science. Aristotle treats tragedy as the generally superior form of poetry because "the tragic fable is more unified and visible; thus it is more 'concentrated' than the epic narrative. In matters of art as in those of nature, there is a certain 'dimension' that makes them susceptible of being encompassed 'in a single view [*eusunopton einai*]' (1451a4 and also 1459a330)."[39] Tragedy, then, mirrors in some sense what Manent describes elsewhere, explained above as the synoptic or surveyable aspect of the city with its limits and concentrated action, while epic resembles the more extended form of empire. There is a parallel between Manent's descriptions of the two ancient political forms and his interpretation of Aristotle's analysis of poetic forms. But in the case of Homer, the two forms merge: "Homeric epic is, so to speak, as concentrated, as 'synoptic,' as a tragedy. The *Odyssey* and the *Iliad* are constructed around a unified action [*peri mian praxin*]' (1451a28)."[40] The action in Homer renders the two poetic forms indistinguishable; that action takes place at a time before the emergence of the city, when the two ancient political forms were yet to manifest themselves, at least in the Greek world.

The world of noble action that Homer describes gives us "access to the birth of the Greek city [in] gathering oral traditions around the year 725 B.C." The state of Greek life at this point was "clearly prior to or different from civic life as such. The first to hear the Homeric poems as we know them were probably citizens of the Greek cities of Ionia, but the narrative that enchanted them spoke of a life very different from their own."[41] Homer was the narrator of that earlier experience, and he thus serves as the educator of the Greek cities about their origins. The awareness of that earlier life turns out to be profoundly important for Western political development:

---

38 *Metamorphoses*, 29.
39 *Metamorphoses*, 29–30.
40 *Metamorphoses*, 30.
41 *Metamorphoses*, 30.

Whatever the uncertainties weighing on Homeric chronology and the history of Greece before the development of the cities or at their beginnings, there is no doubt that the *Iliad* and the *Odyssey* constitute the spiritual basis of that development. I have many times emphasized how Greek civic experience formed the original experience of Europe, or at least one of the two constitutive experiences of the European spirit; it is in any case the original *political* experience of Europe, which includes reflection on this experience itself. To speak of Homer as educator of the city means that there was an experience prior to the experience, an origin prior to the origin. Before there was the city there was the educator of the city.[42]

This passage brings out several points. First, the original source of the city's spirit that Manent most emphasizes is the poet as educator. The city's citizens had to be told about themselves, about their pre-civic roots, and to reflect on those roots in order to be the citizens, the human agents, that they would be in the city of noble, rational action. Second, Manent again confirms that, as in the rebirth of the citizen into awareness of his status as participant in a particular political community—an Athenian or Spartan—this poetic education causes a spiritual and political transformation, a fundamental change in his self-understanding and in his capacity to act as a result of this education. Third, this essential educative transformation into a civic actor is the most fundamental basis of European political development, a transcendent step in human history. It explains why, as noted above in a citation from *A World beyond Politics?*, all subsequent European political thinkers of all stripes would refer, consciously or not, to the original city. It is in this sense that the city "is the condition for the production or the matrix of a new form of life, political life, in which men govern themselves and know that they govern themselves. This form of life can take diverse forms, for there are different ways of self-government. The city opens the possibility of a self-government that actualizes or concretizes itself according to a particular mode, according to a particular *regime*."[43] It is poetry that points the way from the pre-political form of the tribe to the political form of the city with its diverse possibilities for self-rule and action.

---

42 *Metamorphoses*, 30.
43 *Metamorphoses*, 18.

Manent notes the Socratic criticism of Homer and Hesiod in the *Republic* and claims that we have difficulty taking these passages seriously, first because it is shocking that Socrates "should presume to correct Homer," and second because as moderns we are skeptical that Homer and Hesiod as two mere individual men could, with poetry, author Greek religion.[44] But Manent cites Eric Voegelin approvingly in pointing to two essential insights provided by these Socratic critiques of Homer and Hesiod. First, the Greeks knew that "the order of their gods was of recent origin and could not be traced" to a time before the epic poets. These gods were divine in some sense, but not demonstrably eternal or creating. Second, "they were convinced that the myth had not grown anonymously over a long period of time, but had been crafted by definite persons, the poets."[45] Manent draws out the implications of these insights:

> All of this is very important, not only for what it teaches us about Homer and about Greece, but also because this eminent example alerts us to the fact that there is no collective intellectual or spiritual invention, but that it is individual human beings who are the primary cause of human works, even if the record has not left us distinct particulars of dates and places of birth and death, biography, physiognomy, and so on. Let us not be as obtuse as Polyphemus who, when he was asked, "Who is doing that?" answered that it was "Nobody!" That is just what we say when to the question of who fashioned the Iliad or Homeric religion, we answer that it was Mycenaean or Pelasgian or Aegean civilization, it was this or that collective name. That Homer and Hesiod elaborated the theology of the Greeks encourages us to dedicate ourselves to our own task, which is to attempt to understand what they did.[46]

This is perhaps Manent's clearest rejection, based on the earliest Western sources, of the historicism that, as noted above in chapter 1, he found almost persuasive. European history is seen in the movement of political form, and that movement begins and continues with the action in history of individual, rational men who, in the city, learn from poets that their political moment has come from a pre-political world. These individual

---

44 *Metamorphoses*, 30–31.

45 Eric Voegelin, *Order and History* (Baton Rouge: University of Louisiana Press, 1957), 2:72, quoted in Manent, *Metamorphoses*, 32.

46 Manent, *Metamorphoses*, 32.

men come together in politics not as a result of historical forces but by their own nature and their own choices as humans.

Manent claims that in the poetic, pre-political world, all humans oriented themselves according to a tripartite division among animals, humans, and gods. "This prephilosophical regime—I am tempted to say this 'natural' regime—of the human mind is characterized by a twofold undertaking that appears to us necessarily contradictory."[47] The first aspect of the undertaking is that in pre-philosophical thinking, humans know themselves only by knowing they are not animals and are not gods; humans are known to themselves by knowing what they are not. Simultaneously, there is a dynamism to this tripartite regime whereby through metamorphoses, animals, humans, and gods constantly transform themselves into another part of the triad: gods with heads of animals, men with bodies of animals, etc. "The three great elements of the world exist only in becoming what they are not, or joining themselves to what they are not."[48] The breakthrough to rationality or the philosophical perspective that replaced this regime was a revolution that "consisted in saying that a thing—animal, human, god—is its being, or its essence, or its definition."[49] Beings are bounded by other natures, and the unfolding understanding of those natures will lead to the disappearance of the pre-philosophical, mythological world as we come to know not just what we are not, but what we are.

That disappearance paves the way for the rise of the city form from its poetic history, and Homer plays a decisive role. Unlike other pre-philosophical poets, he does not really take animals into account; his poetry is thus unconcerned with the metamorphoses that marked the non-Homeric mythologies. Moreover, the gods and men are both propelled by the same motives, so the defining distinction between them is that of human mortality contrasted to divine immortality. "[Homer's] *Iliad* is throughout, so to speak, a confrontation with mortality as there was never before, and will hardly be after."[50] The human feature of mortality equalizes all men, and this feature is the characterizing disjunction between men and gods by which men recognize themselves. The philosophical revolution will change the defining feature of humans from their death to their rational

47 *Metamorphoses*, 33.
48 *Metamorphoses*, 33.
49 *Metamorphoses*, 33.
50 *Metamorphoses*, 34.

capacity, with Aristotle's definition of man as the "rational animal." This rational capacity "tends to fill the gap between humans and gods since it naturally looks to what does not change, what is eternal—'natures,' 'essences,' 'ideas'—and as such is 'divine.'"[51] Thus, if Manent is correct that man becomes rational as he becomes political, becoming political is for man a move toward the divine. But if man's reason and philosophy close the gap between man and god, they also begin with man as animal, reviving that element of the tripartite pre-philosophical regime while, by the specificity of the definition of man as mortal animal and quasi-immortal or god-like reasoner, precluding the metamorphoses that prevailed in the pre-philosophical regime. The philosophical approach places man in nature. Manent notes, almost as an aside, that the "philosophers who place death at the center of their approach to the human phenomenon always end up privileging poetry and metaphors over philosophy and definitions."[52] Manent seems to give a clue here that the philosophers whose work is most definitively concerned with, and shaped by, their living in the city form (Athens)—Socrates, Plato, Aristotle—are aware of death. But they are principally concerned with the transcendent truths, forms, or universals that exist within a nature that, while filled with motion, does not allow for metamorphoses among beings of different essences. Political forms can and do undergo metamorphoses and change, which motion is the driver of European development in Manent's view. The constant throughout that motion is nature, including human nature with man as a political animal, which is the principle of that development as seen in political form. That principle emerged, with the city, from the age of epic poetry.

Manent continues his exploration of the poetic sources of the city form by turning to the *Iliad*, in particular and Simon Weil's interpretation of it. The question here is why the Greeks proved to be the first exemplars of the polis. Weil asserts, and Manent agrees within limits, that "the *Iliad* is 'the poem of force,' [which] can be our starting point."[53] Weil sees in the *Iliad* a certain equity between the Greeks and the Trojans, who are all gripped by a bitterness "that proceeds from tenderness and that spreads over the whole human race, impartial as sunlight. . . . Justice and love, which have hardly any place in this study of extreme and of unjust acts of violence, nevertheless bathe the work in their light without ever becoming

51 *Metamorphoses*, 35.

52 *Metamorphoses*, 35.

53 *Metamorphoses*, 35.

noticeable themselves, except as a kind of accent."[54] Weil, without raising this explicitly (nor does Manent), hits upon two key features of the Aristotelian and classical understanding of the political community, founded on a common friendship or love with the aim of justice for the citizens. In the pre-philosophical world, these notions remain undefined in political terms, still only in the background; man as rational philosopher and political actor will have to bring them to the foreground, define them, and recognize them as transcendental ideas that will be beyond metamorphoses in nature. Manent agrees with Weil that the Greeks and Trojans are presented as essentially the same, though the reader usually finds himself in sympathy with the "more likeable" Trojans "if only because of the presence of attractive or touching female figures—Helen (Trojan despite herself), Andromache, Hecuba."[55] Despite this likability in the midst of the general condition of bitterness where love and justice are in the shadows, Homer presents Greek civilization as superior. First, the Greeks are capable of silence. "[A]lthough this capacity for silence is the means of maintaining military discipline, it is not its result or effect. The silence of the Achaeans, in military actions as in councils, is not imposed upon them, but is a demeanor that is freely adopted as both the most useful and the most noble."[56] Silence permits the deliberation, both individual and collective, that can provide a basis for rational action; the Greek awareness of this positions them to become political. Further, the Greeks have a "capacity for superior collective action [that] resides in the felicitous relationship between individual interactions and common action. This harmony rests on the role of *aïdôs*, the sentiment of shame or honor before one's companions. . . . The common energy is a result of the affects that flow from companion to companion."[57] This sense of shame and honor reflects a superior relationship of the individual to the collective, whereby the Greeks are more effective singly and collectively. For example, in retreat during battle, they choose to protect one another, and they are also more effective in individual action when they are no longer protected by the group but on their own: Manent cites the contrast between the prudence of the Achaean Diomedes and imprudence of the Trojan Dolon. He claims that a "chain of weaknesses, running the familial

54 *Metamorphoses*, 37.
55 *Metamorphoses*, 38.
56 *Metamorphoses*, 38.
57 *Metamorphoses*, 39.

and sexual gamut, links the destiny of Troy to an erotic adventure [that of Paris's pursuit and possession of Helen] without illusion and without nobility. One could say that the human chain is here the prisoner of its weakest link."[58] Paris the individual cannot give up Helen for the sake of the Trojan whole. By contrast, Achilles relinquishes Briseis, "his legitimate captive whom he loves and by whom he is loved in return. . . . To be sure, Agamemnon's demand arouses Achilles's terrible wrath. . . . But if Achilles does not accept the injustice done to him and is prepared to ruin his companions to avenge it, he accepts being parted from Briseis because it is the order of his legitimate leader."[59] In the *Iliad*, one can find evidence of Trojans' accepting legitimate orders as well, which may call into question the strength of Manent's interpretation. But Manent identifies the Greek trait of respect for a legitimate authority that can grow into law beyond the tribe or family as the basis for a city; this authority is necessary but not sufficient for a political community. He draws from this contrast his politically relevant point:

> Troy stands for the familial and sexual dependence from which the Achaeans are freed. Troy, with all its endearing humanity, means the slope toward passivity and the power of bodily proximity while the camp of the Achaeans, with all its repugnant brutality, represents the tense movement toward activity and the power of spiritual distance. . . . [T]he camp of the Achaeans is not a city as such. . . . [I]t has in it nothing of a city in the classical and political meaning of the term, governed as it is by a king and innumerable princes, his sons. The Achaeans could appear to be but an expeditionary corps. In reality they are more and something other, just as their camp is more and something other than a camp or military base. . . . These men who have settled along the coast of the "wine dark sea" for nine years now seem to have attained self-sufficiency. They are not an army properly speaking, but a complete warrior society. . . . [O]ne can recognize in it a heroic or aristocratic republic, this republic of quarrelsome persuasion that is the invention of Greece and whose virtues democracy will spread and develop. In short, the camp of the Achaeans, the city "in speech" whose founder is Homer, was the common mother of the "real" Greek cities.[60]

---

58 *Metamorphoses*, 41.
59 *Metamorphoses*, 41.
60 *Metamorphoses*, 41–42.

Manent does not mention Aristotle here, perhaps assuming his reader will know that self-sufficiency is the Aristotelian quality of a city. But this city lacks the other natural relationships that form the city—family, household, village. Its excellences are thus the excellences of the city as a whole without the excellences of the subordinate communities of the city, resting on the individual virtues of the Greek soldiers and their capacity for silence during their deliberations and their action. This perhaps suggests another Aristotelian note as well in Manent's reading of Homer: that the excellences of the city are available prior to the other relationships or communities, that the city does in fact "take priority" over the other relationships and thus will, when the city eventually emerges, embody the final virtues to which the subordinate communities will point. Homer can thus be seen to forecast the first political form in the pre-philosophical poetic moment.

The warrior nature of Achilles reveals for Manent more about the change from pre-philosophical to political and philosophical life, to a more fully human condition. The life of the Homeric pre-city in the Greek camp

> is limited to war, and, one can add, to the sort of diplomacy that war implies (truces, embassies, etc.); it is limited to external action. These warriors are away from home and devote themselves exclusively to external action, to an aspect of politics, one is tempted to say, and perhaps not the most interesting aspect. After all, it will be of little interest to the philosophers. Plato and Aristotle have little to say about war and foreign policy; they tend to recommend that the city's external relations be kept to a minimum. But in barbarian times politics and war are one and the same; the progress of civilization is measured by the arts of peace and the development of internal politics.[61]

Though Manent does not mention it expressly here, he surely has in mind, among other things, Aristotle's critique of Sparta's inability to "live well" because its military ethos did not permit its proper use of leisure; Sparta fails to progress as a city as far beyond barbarism as did Athens. War as primary or absorbing action, to the exclusion of internal concerns, precedes the rise of the city form, and "[e]xternal war returns to absorb all the energies [of a city] only at the decline of civilization, in the case of Greece at the time of the Peloponnesian War of which Thucydides writes."[62] Homer,

61 *Metamorphoses*, 42–43.
62 *Metamorphoses*, 43.

the poet, provides the sources of the city, in the city-before-the-city of the Greek camp; Thucydides, the historian (though certainly a philosophically important historian), describes its decline into something that is "if not the city after the city, at least the city on the way to destroying itself."[63] The philosophers, Plato and Aristotle, describe the city in its prime and as it should be, the city that exists for the sake of living well and nobly in the condition of peace (though they, too, write at the time of the city's decline).

That city that can pursue the arts of peace emerges, again, from war, which "is the condition and the consequence of the self-discovery of 'mortals.' That is why the *Iliad*, while it speaks of nothing but war, nonetheless says everything about human life, or at least considers it in its entirety. Condition and consequence: this means that war produces the discovery of the self as mortal."[64] The critical step in the move from pre-philosophical to rational man is the discovery and awareness of mortality, which takes place in war.[65] "In war, death appears as the greatest possibility of human life since war holds for every man both the greatest possible action—inflicting death on the enemy—and the greatest possible passion—suffering death. And the true life, which is here the noble life, the heroic life, consists in constantly standing on the edge of this twofold possibility."[66] The best life in the age of the epic, the pre-city, is that of the warrior hero. Again, Manent does not make explicit the contrast between Homer and Aristotle, but in the *Nicomachean Ethics* and the *Politics*, the latter gives the best life in the city proper as the life of contemplation of the highest, most divine things; since such a life is too divine for men, the best available life is usually one of virtuous action in the political community. But before man can develop a city for the Aristotelian good life, he must discover his own condition of mortality. This discovery is illustrated by Homer especially in Achilles. Achilles does not permit Hector's corpse to be returned to Troy because his passionate hatred of the Trojans abates;

---

63 *Metamorphoses*, 43.

64 *Metamorphoses*, 43.

65 Manent's claim here seems to echo Socrates in Plato's *Republic* 2.369a3–2.374a1. When his friends reject the first, "healthy" city in speech that Socrates constructs in his search for justice, calling it a "city for pigs" that lacks what men want and should have, Socrates begins his remedy for the new, "fevered" city with the establishment of the guardian class, the warriors of the city, because this second city will need to expand to accommodate his companions' demands for more apparent, material goods. That expansion will necessarily produce war with the other cities that the fevered city will encounter in its growth. War is thus the first consequence and concern of the city that Socrates will endeavor to return to justice.

66 Manent, *Metamorphoses*, 43.

rather, he changes into a man with the ability to control his passions and his wrath "by his reason, by which is meant the more complete awareness he has gained of his mortality, and in general the fact that men are mortal."[67] In and through war, Achilles undergoes a metamorphosis into a rational, or at least more rational, human, and in this way closes the gap between man and the gods described above; but he must first be fully what he is by nature, a man. Homer (wittingly or unwittingly) paints Achilles as a figure who can, when looked back upon from the Greek city, exemplify man en route to politics. This demands a recognition of something in the nature of man that transcends family and tribal boundaries: "Being fully ready to die (as Achilles is just after he has killed Hector) does not suffice for one to recognize that one is mortal. It is not really different from being ready to kill. One still remains a monstrous hero."[68] Such a hero is little more than an animal, in the tripartite pre-philosophical understanding of the world.

> It is only when one recognizes that that honor is due to all corpses, including those of the enemies, that one is at last a man. Achilles, the son of a goddess and a mortal, was born a hero. He lived as a hero. At the end of the *Iliad*, as his death nears, he has completed his education, his education in humanity. He has become a man; he is at last a mortal.[69]

Man is first the mortal, then the political and rational, animal.

In what is presented almost as an aside, Manent then proceeds to contrast two figures, Socrates and Jesus of Nazareth, with Achilles.

> Socrates himself, in the *Apology*, compares himself to Achilles, to one who thought little of death when it came to doing an honorable deed (28b–d). And in the *Phaedo* the death of Socrates appears as a death without trouble or pain, and that leaves behind no corpse, so to speak. His last words are not about the care due to his remains, but about the cock he owes to Asclepius. The hero of philosophy, the new Achilles, is only a soul who is indifferent to his mortal body, a soul that does not cease to

---

67 *Metamorphoses*, 44.
68 *Metamorphoses*, 46.
69 *Metamorphoses*, 46.

reason and to speak until the moment of death. . . . His body
dissolves in words.[70]

This image of Socrates's death "is a representation of death that has
certainly and profoundly marked the European spirit, more even than the
image of Hector dragged by Achilles beneath the walls of Troy."[71] But more
profound yet is the image of the crucifixion of Christ, which Manent finds
"impossible not to point out" while admitting that it is not his subject:

> Jesus is both Patroclus [Achilles's Achaean comrade] and Hector.
> More precisely, in the Christian representation, Jesus is for each
> person what Hector and Patroclus are for Achilles: the enemy
> he has pierced with blows *and* the friend, the brother, who was
> pierced with blows for him. This is where I would see the para-
> doxical proximity between Homer and the Gospels, as much
> or more than in the impartial and pure appreciation of human
> misery where Simone Weil sees it.[72]

Manent leaves us to form our own conclusions from his aside, but the
implications seem as unavoidable as his comment: the figures of Socrates
and Christ point beyond the city that is achievable by mortal, political
man, beyond the domain of human action by the political animal. These
two figures represent, or are, the highest, and divine, exemplars of the
philosophical and religious vertices of Manent's triangle. Achilles shows
us what is necessary to be human, to be rational: the recognition of our
mortality and its necessary implications in recognizing what is proper to
all men by nature, in politics, the domain of human action in Manent's
triangle. Socrates and Christ, occupying the other two vertices, point
beyond, to the divine understanding of "what is."

In Homer, Manent finds the earliest pre-political traces of the
historical events that comprise one of his paths of inquiry (the other
being political thought). Poetry provides, if not political history in the
strict sense, a prelude to such history that can provide insights into the
political "what is" in the absence of a full account of political events (and,
perhaps, insights into historical actors that strict history might miss). In
his study of the city, Manent proceeds from the poetry that describes the

---

70 *Metamorphoses*, 46–47.

71 *Metamorphoses*, 47. This is one of Manent's first uses of "mark" throughout his work
to denote the effects of earlier cultural phenomena on European nations. It will become
his characterization of the political form he prefers, the "nation marked by Christianity."

72 *Metamorphoses*, 47.

Greek camp of Achilles as the setting for silent deliberation and successful human action, to the historical account of Athens, which he will interpret through the lens of Aristotelian political philosophy. The Greek camp of Homer is "the original city, the city before the city, or the heroic republic, which I call a 'republic' by anticipation, since the group of heroes has no idea of 'the public thing.'"[73] The Greek camp is a pre-political association without a *res publica*, yet "it is from that group that it [the *res publica*] is born," and thus the city form proper.[74] This development occurs in a kind of democratization of the warrior virtues of the heroes in the Greek camp. The transformation of camp into city is based, Manent asserts, on the human meaning of warfare itself, which "resides very simply in what takes place in the soul of the one who wages war. . . . [I]n varying degrees and modes, it is what takes place in the soul of Achilles," the recognition of the mortality of oneself and of all men, which is the crucial step to becoming human (and thus political and rational).[75]

> [W]ar holds for each man both the greatest possible human action (the "greatest" in the sense of "producing the greatest effects"), inflicting death, and the greatest possible passion, suffering death. The true life then can only be the noble life, the heroic life that consists in constantly standing on the cutting edge of this twofold possibility. This greatest of possibilities cannot but have the greatest power over the soul. If death— death received and given—is the most extreme possibility of life, then true life, the life that is most fully alive, is the life under the spell of death, the life of the warrior.[76]

The emergence of the Greek city requires the extension of this possibility of the greatest, most human life beyond an aristocratic few to the many, a transformation of many individual souls who will form the citizenry. Only in this way, one might derive from Manent's claims, can the city become capable of supporting man as he truly is, as the rational, deliberative, political animal.

The rise of the city depends on the transformation in some measure of the souls of the many, or at least many of the many, to a condition that resembles the souls of the virtuous, heroic few. Some sort of convergence

73 *Metamorphoses*, 51.
74 *Metamorphoses*, 51–52.
75 *Metamorphoses*, 49.
76 *Metamorphoses*, 49.

must take place between those who are superhuman and those who are subhuman, in order for human politics to come on the scene. There remains through and after this transformation a

> quarrel of people and heroes [that] is coextensive with our history, even if they are at times hard to recognize beneath their metamorphoses. Their polarity remains active even in the low tides of history seemingly peopled only with satisfied men. . . . One could say that the matrix or the first form of European life is the "heroic republic" constituted by a small number of "noble" or "good" or "excellent" people, and a great number of "nameless" or "bad" or "good for nothing" people—of a small number of the "more than human" and a great number of the "less than human" or "less than nothing." It is hard to speak here of a city; in Plato's terms, one can say there are here two cities forever at war with one another. At times, even, the "few" swear unending hatred for the masses. The heroic republic rests on war of a particular kind.[77]

From this heroic republic of Achilles and his heroes who fight the lesser Trojans, the city comes about when the many of Athens adopt the virtues of their heroes. Manent's language to describe the pre-political, heroic republic describes some men who are less than human, others who are more than human. But Aristotle describes the city as for "man" by nature, not for two groups who are above human and not political by nature— gods—or less than human and not political by nature—beasts. The war of the heroes and the many must somehow be brought into a political form that will include what was missing from the heroic republic, the common thing, in order to be rational and political. Referring again to the ancient-modern difference, Manent claims that this rise of the political form of the city takes place in a peculiarly ancient way, without an instituted state: "the virtues proper to the Greek city derive from the fact that the city achieved the immediate and direct participation of the many in the aristocratic 'values' of the few without the precondition or mediation of the State. Warfare between heroes and people gives way to people's participation in political life, not without conflict, but without any need to have prior recourse to the peacemaking of the State."[78] This role of the State will be examined more closely later. But the essential conflict between

---

77 *Metamorphoses*, 51.
78 *Metamorphoses*, 52.

the great and noble, and those who are not, continues from its basis in the first city throughout European political development; Marx will invert the virtue of the numbers of many-great-proletariat and few-capitalist exploiters, but the underlying "matrix" does not disappear after Athens or even in times of an apparently distinctionless self-satisfaction, when there is ostensibly little to animate the great-few versus bad-many conflict.

In the case of the first form of the city, how does this conflict resolve into politics? Manent will return to Aristotle to better understand how the city developed from this enduring conflict:

> Aristotle shows us the transformation of the war between two groups that have nothing in common but their mutual hatred into the conflicting confrontation of their respective claims to govern *the* city—the same city they now share. These claims are of course incompatible and in this sense the condition of war persists, but the parties work to find a method for adjudicating these incompatible claims, for evaluating them according to a common standard, which is precisely that of the *common good*. The process of adjudication and evaluation is what Aristotle calls political justice or "political right." War gives way to political justice, [and] justice is something that replaces war.[79]

This describes the outcome of the transition from camp to city, but it does not explain how that outcome is achieved. This replacement of war by justice is not a Hobbesian institution of a Leviathan over an undifferentiated mass of men in their war of all against all. It is the emergence of a political association of diverse elements, some virtuous and some not, through a natural process among men who have all or for the most part accepted their own mortality and the mortality of others and have thereby become political and rational; in forming the city oriented toward a common good despite their conflicts, they are doing what rational animals do, by nature. To see how this happened in the Greek city, Manent pursues his review of political events, the same events that were observed and catalogued by Aristotle, who would add his own philosophical explication.

Manent treats Sparta and Athens as a polarity. "Each has eminent claims to the glory of being the Greek city par excellence. Sparta was that city to the extent that it was the most typical, the most purely warlike city. It was continuously at war not only externally, against the other Greek cities, but also . . . internally, in the hidden war against subjected but rebellious

79 *Metamorphoses*, 52.

populations."[80] Sparta defeated its rival for preeminence in the Peloponnesian War. Athens, at the other pole, was—while still militarily very
active—more political than other cities, a trait that gave it greater power.

> Athens . . . was, of all the Greek cities, the one where internal
> war was the least bitter—the most visible perhaps, but the least
> bitter—because it was the one where the people took the great-
> est part in the life of the city.[81] Its greater internal pacification
> and democratization gave Athens forces for external expansion
> that were unknown elsewhere. Democratization and imperial
> expansion proceeded in Athens from the same movement, with
> tributes of the conquered cities making it possible to pay poor
> citizens to engage in their tasks as citizens in political, judicial,
> or military offices. Athens was the least warlike, in any case the
> least "military," and nonetheless the most powerful of the Greek
> cities for the same reason, because it was the most political. It
> brought the politicization of the polis to its highest degree of
> actualization.[82]

The "movement" Manent sees as the source of Athenian power is the
motion of politicization, which is the first instance of the motion of political
form as it becomes visible in the establishment and subsequent life of the
original political form, the city. The results differ from place to place and
instance to instance: Sparta and Athens politicize but to different degrees,
in different modes, with different results. But the essential point Manent
is bringing out is that of the city as the first result of the motion of man
as political animal, the motion that will explain European development.

Warfare is central to this first political motion. With greater degrees
of politicization, the warlike nature of the city diminishes: "As we pass
from Sparta to Athens, the warrior trait of the few fades. They tend to
become 'the rich.'"[83] But "a great part of their wealth bore no resemblance
to what we understand by that term. They indeed had lands but their titles
consisted of ancestral tombs, of religious shares."[84] The initial claims of

---

80 *Metamorphoses*, 52.

81 Manent's supporting citation (*Metamorphoses*, 331n24) for this point is from Aristotle's
The Constitution of Athens 22.4: "With the customary forbearance of the democracy, the
people had allowed the friends of the tyrants to continue to live in Athens." Trans. J. M.
Moore (Berkeley: University of California Press, 1986), 165.

82 *Metamorphoses*, 52–53.

83 *Metamorphoses*, 53.

84 *Metamorphoses*, 53.

the many were to participate in religious rites of burial and marriage. In pre-political, heroic ages, there is no politicization, "war does not give way to peace, war does not cease to reign, and inequality also reigns."[85] This inequality produces three kinds of warfare: warriors fighting other groups of warriors; warriors fighting those who depend on them, who might be thought of as a prototype of the many; and "latent" internal warfare among the warriors themselves when questions of honor arise. The heroic order is rife with conflict and utterly warlike. Manent begins with this war-laden order and makes a sweeping claim: "It could be said that our political history consists for the most part of the successive, though imperfect, pacification of the three kinds of war."[86] All political development is rooted in war, a pre-political fact, and is the motion of the process of politicization as pacification, first as a leveling among the warriors by a sovereign who distributes honors and adjudicates disputes, then through the metamorphosis of class warfare (presumably through wider participation first in religious rites, then in material goods), and finally through the pacification from within of democratic nation-states whereby "war—more and more rare but more and more violent—is relegated to the border that separates each nation from foreign ones."[87] Manent thus abruptly (and with little supporting argumentation) puts warfare in a central position in political development and the movement of political form not just in the Greek city but throughout European political history.

Manent uses this centrality to sketch "two parallel series" of polarities that help delineate the form of the city. These polarities are war and peace; external and internal; unknown and known; nature and law; and world and city. Manent does not attempt "to fully justify the parallelism,"[88] and this is a rare moment of diagrammatic schematism on his part. It serves to illustrate and summarize the distinction between the conditions of the city form in the latter nodes of the polarities (peace, internal concerns, attention to and preference for the known, law, and city itself), and in the opposite polarities not only the heroic order or camp but other non-city forms such as empire. In lieu of a formal argument or historical account to develop the polarities, Manent proposes a thought experiment, in which the pacification that has marked European history (in recent decades, at

85 *Metamorphoses*, 54.
86 *Metamorphoses*, 54.
87 *Metamorphoses*, 54.
88 *Metamorphoses*, 55.

least) "was to spread from Europe to the rest of the world and only peace without war would remain. Then the external and the unknown, which would no longer pose a threat, would join with the internal and the known. All people are *tourists* for one another. To regulate their lives, they have only to take into account the law, the internal law."[89] Manent does not make his conclusion explicit, but in such an experiment all of the distinctions or polarities would disappear, including the distinction between law and nature, as the internal law would seem to be merely a law we know by nature. "While there would be only peace and the interior sense of self in the world state, in the heroic age there tended to be only war and external affects, especially the 'glory' attached to 'victory.'" Again, Manent seems opaque as to the conclusion he wants us to draw, but one result of the experiment is that we see the city as a first form and one that contrasts both with the heroic pre-political camp and a fully modern state. But at this point we can note that both the pre-political camp with its warlike essence and the world state of total peace would seem to be without the law that controls or perfects nature and thus without politics and philosophy.[90] Manent concludes his experiment with a "very important remark.... It can be seen that philosophy, in revealing the distance between law and nature, the city and the world, preserves or restores in the element of peace what war brought to light but without understanding it."[91] To tighten points that Manent leaves loose, during the course of the events of politicization and pacification, philosophy preserves the reason found—albeit not fully or clearly grasped—by heroic warriors as they come to understand their own mortality and that of all men, which the poetic sources of the city begin to reveal and open. The city is the first political form and, if politics is reasoned human action par excellence as discussed earlier, the city is the first form of what is distinctly human: reason itself.

Manent's account of the transition from poetic camp to political city leaves many open questions, and it is more "asserted than argued" in the terms of contemporary political science. He considers no "alternative theories" to the notion of the city rooted in the pre-political camp of Homer's poetry: the reader is left to gauge the success of his account without metrics or data. But his determination as a political philosopher not merely to

---

89 *Metamorphoses*, 55.

90 There is a hint here that as the pre-political camp is found in mythology, so too the universal modern state, or rather its ideal, is a mythological entity that can exist only in the eschaton of post-reason, post-philosophical man.

91 *Metamorphoses*, 56.

return to an ancient view of politics and man, but to understand from all available sources the emergence of the first and most important political form—the great metamorphosis into the city, from which all other political metamorphoses would flow—is distinctive.

THE CIVIC OPERATION AND THE COMMON THING

Manent's examination of the city form continues from its poetic sources to the emergence of its central characteristics. Here, Manent is concerned to alert his reader to the modern lens of political thought, at least in an introductory way, in order to clarify the profound difference of the ancient city with its associated philosophy and understanding of "what is." The city is thus illuminated by a contrast with what moderns see around them and how they see it. We will consider here what is essential to understand the city. Manent returns from poetry to his inquiry into political thought in order expand his inquiry into the nature of the city.

The city and the modern state share the characteristic of producing peace and thereby changing the condition of their citizens from warlike to peaceful; both dwell on the peace side of the war and peace polarity. But neither changes the underlying political nature of man, and the two forms do not yield peace to the same degree or in the same way.

> It has been said that the modern State, with its monopoly on legitimate violence, overcame the natural state of war thanks to a "homeopathic" use of violence. But the ancient city did not deal so directly with the condition of war that preceded it. It largely overcame it, it is true—otherwise there would be no city—but by transforming it in a way that was both more subtle or profound and less complete. Our view of these things is necessarily conditioned both by the univocal character of modern political philosophy that makes us pass from a state *defined* by war to a state *defined* by peace, and by the corresponding effectiveness—that corresponds to this univocal character—of the modern State that in effect brings an unprecedented peace. We are speaking of a complete transformation here, since it makes us pass from one pole to another or from one opposite to another.[92]

---

92 *Metamorphoses*, 63.

The peace that obtains in the ancient city did not represent the extraordinary enforcement of a new condition by a political agent, a sovereign, beyond the people themselves. Yet it was the peace of the city, not the State, that rested on a true change in human nature, the transformation of man into rational and political animal:

> At the same time, this complete transformation of the state of humans does not constitute, or does not imply, a profound transformation of their nature since it is essentially the same human being who lives in the two states, namely the individual who craves security. . . . Unlike the modern State, the ancient city presupposes and produces . . . a transformation of human nature that is both more profound and less complete: less complete, for war persists or is felt more in the ancient city than in the modern State; more profound, for the transformation is not accomplished by a State that remains in some way outside individuals, but directly concerns the individuals themselves whose nature is transformed since they become participants in a *common thing*.[93]

The ancient city, Manent tells us, involved its people in the pursuit of a common endeavor that is the operational definition of politics properly understood. "The ancient political condition is oriented by the question of who participates in the common thing, which is inseparable from the more radical question: what is the common thing?"[94] In the city, politics is oriented not by the development of "external instruments" that control the citizenry but with "the elaboration of a more and more refined internal tension." Where the modern politician is an expert on political mechanisms, "the ancient politician was an inseparably political and moral educator who strove to arouse in the soul of the citizens 'the most noble and most just' moral dispositions."[95] Politics was, as Aristotle claims in the *Nicomachean Ethics*, the science whose end "must be the human good,"[96] and which, to understand that good, "must study . . . human virtue; for the good we were seeking was human good and the happiness human happiness. By human virtue we mean not that of the body but that of the soul; and happiness also we call an activity of soul. But if this

---

93 *Metamorphoses*, 63–64.
94 *Metamorphoses*, 64.
95 *Metamorphoses*, 64.
96 Aristotle, *Nicomachean Ethics* 1.2.1094b6.

is so, clearly the student of politics must know somehow the facts about the soul."[97] Ancient politics was concerned with the human good, the telos of happiness, and thus with the virtue of soul necessary for that good both in individual citizens and in the city as a whole. Only with that understanding of the science and aim of politics could the city realize its own good, its common thing. This effort to achieve a common thing is the civic operation, the political and rational action that Manent tells us is seen in its most concentrated instance in the city.

If the common thing in the city is, ultimately, human happiness in whatever degree it is achievable, the other question for ancient political science is who participates in this civic operation of the common thing. Manent argues,

> The heart or soul of ancient political philosophy resides in the analysis of political regimes. These regimes are particularly delineated in Plato and Aristotle, but we have already met with some elements of analysis in Homer. In the classification, number plays a decisive role: according to whether one or a few or the many govern, the regime of the polis, that is, the form of common life, essentially changes. Human life changes profoundly depending on whether one lives in a monarchy, an oligarchy, or a democracy. This threefold division finds numerous refinements in Aristotle as in Plato, but they do not affect the central character of the question of number for Greek political philosophy.[98]

The sixfold scheme of regimes—three good and three deviant—is introduced by Plato in the *Statesman*[99] and forms the basis for Aristotle's *Politics*. Manent chooses here one good and two deviant regime types to illustrate the point of quantity. Both Plato and Aristotle share the one-few-many framework. Manent argues that such a framework is natural, because one, or few, or many represent "real, effective, active numbers.... [T]here is no need to count them. How many are several? One does not know exactly; one does not need to know: the few are the few, and that is in fact a qualitative determination."[100] The same holds for the many. Whereas the modern form is distinguished not by "real" numbers but by

---

97 *Nicomachean Ethics* 1.13.1102a13–19.

98 Manent, *Metamorphoses*, 64–65.

99 Plato, *Statesman* 290d1–292a3.

100 Manent, *Metamorphoses*, 66–67.

a *relative* majority-minority whose counting determines its legitimacy, the city form rests upon quantities that are themselves qualitative: "In the classical tripartite division, there are three real, qualitative numbers that do not need to be counted in order to be defined in themselves and in relation to one another. In this sense it is a natural tripartition that belongs necessarily to human things."[101] By contrast, the modern state answers the question of who should rule by the act of counting votes, which would seem—Manent is not explicit—to rest the civic operation and the common thing on a human act of a contingent measuring, rather than a quantity that can be described by definition and found in nature. Manent does not elaborate further on the natural necessity of these quantities; rather he argues that they are found in all places and all times, even in the modern state though not in a politically natural way. "After all, the few and the many, although they have no place in the constitutional mechanism, play a considerable part in the social and political life of modern peoples."[102] His example is the outcry in France against the "two hundred families" who supposedly influenced politics disproportionately outside of the constitutional majority's control; an example from recent American experience is the denunciation of "the one percent" by progressive politicians, or the rally against Wall Street in the Occupy Wall Street movement. In these examples, no counting takes place (the two hundred or one percent are notional figures), but the appeal is to call attention to the power of "the few," an "active" quantity with a qualitative characteristic rather than a measurement. Likewise, the original quantity of "the one" appears in the executive function of modern states. Thus, like the human nature that remains the same from the city through all forms to the modern state, the threefold quantitative description of regimes in ancient political thought retains its natural explanatory force today. The city's three possible regime quantities are at work beneath all political forms, though perhaps in conflict with the constitution of the modern state.

The origins of the three quantities of the city's regimes are found, again, in pre-political life. Manent relies here on the political philosophy of Vico in the way he relied on Homer to elucidate the poetic sources of the city. The "one" is apparent in the

> the first fathers of families that Homer and following him Plato and Aristotle describe under the figure of the Cyclopes. . . .

101 *Metamorphoses*, 67.
102 *Metamorphoses*, 67.

> In the life of the Cyclopes, one, the father, encompasses and
> determines every plurality: since no one concerns himself with
> another's affairs, each cave constitutes, so to speak, a unit of
> justice.... What is ... confirmed in all sorts of ways in the whole
> breadth of the historical field is the pervasiveness of this type
> of human association, dedicated to intense unity ... under the
> pressure and attraction of paternal power.[103]

The pre-political "one," predecessor of the king or tyrant, in abundantly
attested to. Vico also suggests that the early type of the "many" can be
found in the *famoli*, "the fugitives, the bandits, the wanderers, all those
beings with no faith or law, with no hearth or home, without marriage or
burial rites"—recalling that the first claim of the many in the city was not
to the material goods of the rich but to such rites—"who found asylum
in the cities."[104] The phenomenon of such persons "is as it were coeval
with human history. It does not necessarily concern 'large numbers' in
the quantitative sense, but it possesses the qualitative characters of indetermination—how many are they? —of opaqueness, alienness, recalci-
trance, and threat of the 'large number.'"[105] Whether this constitutes a
"real, active number" as the many would be in the city, Manent does not
directly address, but there is at least a possible antecedent of the many in
the pre-political world. The few, of course, are the heroic warrior groups
who have been discussed already. Thus, Manent shows that the tripartite basis of regime analysis of the city, illuminated in classical political
philosophy, existed before the arrival of politics and extends through
all political history. This endurance strengthens the conclusion that it
is somehow natural to politics and must be accounted for in human and
political nature.

The Cyclopes, like the Greek heroes, lack a notion of a common
thing. They have a highly developed awareness of the particular, what
is theirs, what is proper to each self-sufficient family association. This
understanding of the particular, according to Vico, will become the basis
for a common thing. The particular private interests of the great heroes
or paternal kings at some point become threatened by the demands of
the many, the *famoli*, who had come to congregate around the great for
survival but at the cost of enormous oppression, which became unbearable

---

103 *Metamorphoses*, 68.
104 *Metamorphoses*, 69.
105 *Metamorphoses*, 69.

and provoked revolt. This mutiny is "the catalyst of political crystalliza-tion, into a city of the one, the few, and the many."[106] The great few now have a shared, non-particular interest in preserving their proper goods and perquisites against the many. The first common or public thing is common to the few, the aristocratic kings of families, and their unity under a leader is "but the instrument and . . . annex of familial monarchy."[107] How do these great family monarchs proceed from this tentative understanding of a common thing to the more robust common thing of the city? One possible explanation, according to Manent and Vico, is that the pride of the great heroes and Cyclopes actually intensifies within this new alliance and can then be turned to a more intense notion of the common good. But this explanation does not follow easily from the facts, from the great particularity of the interests of the few. As Manent points out, Vico relies on a providential force to explain the transition of soul from Cyclopes to citizen. In keeping with his determination to examine politics as a human activity with little or no reference to the religious vertex of his triangle, Manent appreciates Vico's description and sees its value, but he wants more than a deus ex machina to explain the emergence of the city.

To develop Vico's account into a more satisfactory explanation, Manent turns to two modern philosophers with contrasting views of the ancient world: Montesquieu and Rousseau. He finds in their views on ancient thought important clues to the nature of modern thinking. He recounts Montesquieu's explanation of the emergence of politics and then looks to Rousseau, whose views on the possibilities or lack thereof for a natural politics were discussed earlier. For purposes of understanding Manent's form of the city, the critical insight of Rousseau (among many errors) is that the rich few have a specific vulnerability: They have such extended particular interests that they are easily attacked. "They are more exposed because they are more extended. The more extended being of the rich is thus decisive for the birth of political reason. Such is the mystery of the city in full light: those who are manifestly the strongest are at the same time and for that very reason—it is the reverse side of their strength—the weakest."[108] The rich therefore come to reason from their weakness and their desire to protect their interests. Their reason permits or requires them to see beyond their particular interests in order to defend those very

---

106 *Metamorphoses*, 71.
107 *Metamorphoses*, 72.
108 *Metamorphoses*, 84.

interests, and in that extension of reason their souls become political. Manent draws the relevant conclusion from Rousseau: he "rediscovers the necessity and eminent dignity of common reason. Each one of us lacks strength as well as reason. Each needs to be strengthened and justified by public force and common reason."[109] Rousseau is helpful in explaining the emergence of the city because, in this case, he rediscovers the Aristotelian principle of man as rational animal and, by virtue of his lack of self-suffi-ciency, political animal. But this is not a Hobbesian state of nature among equals; it is driven by the disproportionate wealth of the few. That few "ceaselessly increase their goods, the 'surface' of their domination and of their weakness in the same proportion."[110] They do this not as a class bound together as one, but as individuals whose rationality appears in them as individuals.

The city's emergence must then include the many. The poor are persuaded in an act of self-reflection to accept a political arrangement in the city.

> The kind of irresistible pull of half-socialized people, or, more precisely, of people bound in a knot of domination and servitude is clarified and resolved in the great act of reflection that Rous-seau depicts in such solemn terms. Reflexive reason emerges at the same time that nascent society takes shape by closing on itself and becoming a properly political association. For Rous-seau, too, people become rational at the same time they become political. This twofold and unique transformation takes place once people who are still rude yet already dependent turn toward and bring their forces to those few who, as a consequence of the extension of their being, are led to imagine a still greater exten-sion, one that envelops not only themselves and others, the rich and the poor, the few and the many, in short an extension that for the first time envelops and defines a whole, that is, a city.[111]

Thus, Manent finds in Rousseau an explanation of the leap to politics in reason that Vico describes, but with Rousseau's help, Manent can develop the emergence of the city within the human domain and without need of providential intervention. This leap occurs initially on the part of rich

---

109 *Metamorphoses*, 85.

110 *Metamorphoses*, 85. This ceaseless desire for more becomes important again later when considering the thought of St. Augustine.

111 *Metamorphoses*, 86.

individuals, not a wealthy class as a whole. But Manent finds that he must correct Rousseau as well as Vico.

> The objection I am raising to Rousseau could be summarized in the following way. Let us allow that the rich person, who is the owner, becomes a citizen *in order to* be assured of his ownership. But once he is a citizen he is no longer simply an owner. Citizenship cannot be only a means; it is a new determination of being. Let us also allow that once he is a citizen, the rich man still thinks only of himself [Rousseau's claim], of his property, his goods, but he must nevertheless take into account this new extension of his being that civic life implies. Perhaps against his inclination his soul is open to a possibility that it cannot again close at will.[112]

The citizenship that is the "new determination of being" brings the second birth of each citizen that Manent earlier described as the tragic nature of the city. Here we return to Manent's point that Rousseau, in believing that the rich could never overcome their own selfish concerns to consider a common thing or common good, misses the distinction between imagination and will. "The most extended imagination has its center in the body itself, in the sentiment of self."[113] Imagination is limited by and to the interest of the self. Reason, on the other hand, "involves a decentering movement toward a point that exists only through it, the point of justice or the common good."[114] Rousseau correctly identifies the key elements of the pre-political social association as the haves and the have-nots, or the dominating and the dominated. "But the deployment of these two possibilities in the framework of the city modifies their nature and meaning."[115] The few haves want not just to enjoy their goods but to rule; the many have-nots want a share of the rule. The disparity between the two quantities, to use Manent's own typology as aided by Rousseau, between the few and the many, becomes not just the social arrangement that is the pre-political "principle and goal of all human movements."[116] With the onset of reason, the dispute over who should rule "in the civic state of the city [is] also the starting point of a vast and very complex, an unprecedented

112 *Metamorphoses*, 89.
113 *Metamorphoses*, 90.
114 *Metamorphoses*, 90.
115 *Metamorphoses*, 91.
116 *Metamorphoses*, 91.

category of human movements, those that are proper to the citizen. And the city, or the public thing or the common good, is the object and goal of these movements."[117] Thus the first political form, the city, is identical with the common thing or common good, and with reason. The movement of the citizens toward some interpretation of the common good is the activity of reasoned politics.

To round out his account of the city, Manent again turns to Aristotle, first recapitulating and clarifying his own earlier conclusions on the two quantities of the few and the many:

> The rich person wants more than to guard or increase his property. The poor person wants more than to seize the property of the rich or have it distributed. The rich wants to set the tone for the city, to be recognized as one of its *first* citizens. The poor wants to have a share in the city, to participate in it, to give his opinion with as much right as the rich, in short to be recognized in his *dignity* as a citizen. The movement of politicization, by which the one and the other become citizens, transforms the nearly animal confrontation between those who have and those who have not—it is "animal" because the sentiment of the body plays such a large role in it—into a contest over "honors" and "dignity." The city engenders itself in this movement where cupidity develops into pride. The city takes its form from the development of the human form. In the city, one constitutes oneself by deploying and moving through one's being from the body to the soul.[118]

There is much to consider in this dense and elegant passage that Manent leaves to the reader. Both the few and the many, in politicization, somehow come to the reason of politics that is the seeing beyond the self-centered imagination to a common good. This occurs not as a result of some transformation of man from self-interested to altruistic being, but by the transformation of the kind of self-interest from merely private property, what is proper to each king or family, to something that is public and must be publicly acknowledged, a status of "first" or "possessing dignity." That acknowledgement can only be granted by a whole association; the many must grant the status of first to its few claimants, who must in turn accept the dignity of the many. Moreover, the status derives not from being part

---

117 *Metamorphoses*, 91.
118 *Metamorphoses*, 94.

of a class but from the qualities of the individual and what is, beyond wealth or poverty, proper to the individual, the "firstness" of the few and the citizenship of the many. Further, Manent here describes the city as engendering itself as a result of this dynamic movement among its citizens, who themselves are deploying and moving through their being from body to soul. Both the city and the citizen are in motion, and both are acting in some sense of bringing on their own change from pre-political to political. Man is, as discussed in chapter 1, Manent's principle of political movement and development. The city must realize itself as the common good, and man must realize himself as body and soul, political and rational animal. The sources for these movements and actions are there in the pre-political world, in the nature of man. Politicization is the playing out of these sources according to nature as men make choices about their property, the honors they seek and will grant, their selves, and their common thing.

It is then short work to arrive at the Aristotelian characteristics of the city. "Then as the city emerges, as the polis becomes, if I dare say, more political, what makes one worthy of governing is more and more a properly political quality that Aristotle calls precisely *political virtue*."[119] The hallmark of the virtuous ruler or regime is commitment to the now-discovered common good of the city over the particular interests of the ruler. "[T]he city, since it exists, must have a life of its own. 'Political life'—the life of the polis—must have a content of its own. What is this content? We know Aristotle's answers: sharing in happiness, life according to deliberate choice, or life for the sake of noble actions."[120] There is little to be added that Aristotle did not already explain in the *Nicomachean Ethics* and the *Politics*, aside from modern ruminations about these characteristics and the problems of those ruminations.

Manent's account of the emergence of the common good as the political form of the city is elegant and draws on an impressive array of Western sources, ancient and modern, but it leaves gaps that we might make a very preliminary attempt to fill. First, Manent gives us the account of the Achaeans'—and, in particular, Achilles's—recognition of their own mortality and, with equal importance, the mortality of others, as the key condition for the advancement to political rationality. Yet he also offers the needs of the rich few to defend their interests as the "driver" for the

---

119 *Metamorphoses*, 95. Aristotle speaks of political virtue throughout the *Politics*, e.g., 3.4.1276b16–1277b32.

120 Manent, *Metamorphoses*, 96. See Aristotle, *Politics* 3.9.1280b–1281a9.

extension beyond self-centered imagination to a reason that can perceive a common thing. He does not seem to connect these two accounts. We might draw that connection in this way: death in the pre-political mind is particular to oneself and to one's closest comrades, and one hopes for the honors that accompany a heroic death for oneself. The dawning awareness that death is universal and so must its honors be, is a comparable move beyond imagination to the awareness that a good beyond one's particular goods may be possible. Both suggest that reason comes in the awareness of a less particular, more public or general good. The honors that the pre-political hero seeks, while in some ways measured by possessions, are also suggestive of the power of the pride that leaves both the few and the many demanding their respective status in the city. Reason, mingled with pride, is associated in both cases with the enlargement of awareness beyond the possibilities of the particular.

Manent also leaves open the question of how the many come to political reason. This is an important lacuna, as the city in full demands the reason of all in the kind of reflection first anticipated in the silence and council of the pre-political Greek camp. Manent allows that the few can employ political speech to persuade the many of a good beyond the particular interests of the few that nevertheless serves to protect the interests of those few.[121] Yet to recognize such a larger or public interest, at least in a meaningfully political or city-like way, the many or poor must have the reason-beyond-imagination to recognize that basic common thing; in order to be Aristotelian citizens, they must be more than the gullible automatons manipulated by the few that Rousseau imagined and Manent rejects. As men, they have reason by nature, and while they have as appetites the usual wants of more goods, they too must see, like the few, the possibility that will transform their interests from a share in the wealth of the few to the honor of being recognized for their dignity—a share of the city's life. One explanation is that they see and imitate the reason of the few; the few act as the "vanguard" that activates the broader reason in the many. Another is that the poor, though they lack the wealth of the many, nevertheless have some minimal particular goods that are worth preserving, from other poor people or from the predations of the few. Their motive would be the same as the rich but on a smaller scale, and their claims to the dignity of citizens would stem from their own protectiveness of their small but real interests. A final possibility is that the poor, to an

---

121 Manent, *Metamorphoses*, 89.

even greater degree than the rich, know the inevitable truth of death from which they are less able than the rich to protect themselves and their friends and family. This leads them to understand, perhaps even more quickly than the few, the common fact of death, the common respect due to other men, and thus the common good of living and living well in a city.

Manent's entire account of the emergence of the city provides the substrate for the city form as described by Aristotle, but also for the subsequent political development of the West. Pre-political poetry and modern political thought (when corrected as Manent does for Rousseau, or when brought back into accord with nature) help explain this first and foremost form of the city as the common good. Those are only supplemental to the essential science of Aristotle, but they clarify that science and provide the basis for Manent to extend Aristotelian political philosophy beyond the era of Greek city states through the history of the development of European political forms. This city, the most definable and most clearly observable form of all that Manent examines, is illuminated in motion, in the metamorphosis from pre-political conditions to the incompletely pacified but completely politicized human association, and in the motion of the city itself and its citizens. This form and the action it permits show most clearly what it is to be rational, political, and fully human, to participate in its "vast and very complex, . . . unprecedented category of human movements . . . proper to the citizen." The remaining forms will be further metamorphoses from the city and will be viewed always in comparison and contrast to the first form.

EMPIRE AS A FORM BEYOND THE CITY

From city comes empire. "The two great political forms, the two mother forms of the ancient world, are the city and the empire. They are the mother forms, but they are also the polar forms: the city is the narrow framework of a restless life in liberty, the empire is the immense domain of a peaceful life under a master."[122] The empire is seen as a phenomenon in comparison with the city. We can return here to Manent's matrix of polarity, in which the city, by contrast with the pre-political condition, represents peace, internal focus, the limits of a known place, and rule of law. The empire, like the city, exists for peace, but it achieves that peace by domination and at the expense of liberty. It turns its attention to the

---

122 *Metamorphoses*, 105.

external and the unknown beyond its confines, and it attempts to bring them into its realm and thus make them in some sense internal and known under its own law.

Manent establishes an axiom of political form: "It is moreover a sort of general rule, a law of the physics of political forms, that they do not directly transform themselves one into the other."[123] Manent stipulates that Athens, despite its power and adventures outside its city limits, always remained a city in form:

> In spite of its tormented history, in spite of the great transformations produced by regime changes, by the modification of domestic and foreign circumstances, Athens, as a living entity and as a lasting "whole" that keeps the name of Athens, never ceased being a city. . . . At the head of a maritime empire, the city of Athens did not transform itself into an Athenian empire. Its action was imperial . . . but its form remained "civic" or "political."[124]

But there is one exception to this axiom, and of the different kinds of empires that Manent has noted, the exception is the empire that is of principal interest to him: Rome, whose republican phase was a city form that then became a polar opposite form of empire.

> The Greek historical experience, like the European experience, establishes that the political forms are true forms; that is, if they each indeed have their genesis, they are not moments or aspects of a process; they exist by themselves and from one to the other there is not continuity but rupture. Now, there is one exception to this rule or law, a unique example of a political form transforming itself directly into another political form, of a city transforming itself directly into an empire. At Rome, or starting from Rome and under the name of Rome, a properly unique political phenomenon developed, a phenomenon contrary to the ontology of politics—I dare say—namely, the effective and

123 *Metamorphoses*, 105.

124 *Metamorphoses*, 113. Athens's transition to empire did not happen as a change of political form but as a process of being subsumed into another empire: "After the Greek cities had been exhausted in the Peloponnesian War, there came the hegemony of Philip of Macedon, followed by the empire of his son, Alexander the Great, that covered the east all the way to the Indus. Thus the Greek world passed from city to empire." Manent, *A World Beyond Politics?*, 48.

direct continuity and communication between the two mother
and opposed forms, the city and the empire.[125]

Rome instantiates two forms and, as already noted, the empire will retain
the principle of the city. It is significant that the political entity that will be
the basis for European politics is a one-of-a-kind "freak of nature"—again,
Manent considers both city and empire to be natural forms—whose history
defies Manent's own axiom.

Rome enjoys a historical prestige as a model for rule that Athens
lacks; Manent cites the *Federalist Papers* as an example of regard for Rome
and of disapprobation of the governance of Athens. He distinguishes the
two by the presence in Athens of leaders who appealed to the many in a
movement of democratization that was absent in the Roman republic.

> What gives the Athenian political development its specificity,
> its direction, and its wellspring is that it consisted in the grow-
> ing power of the people thanks to a succession of eminent men
> who sided with them in order to guide them. If we now turn to
> the history of Rome, we are obliged to observe that it has noth-
> ing of the sort. The *elements* of its history greatly resemble, as
> I have said, those of Athens. In both cases one finds the many
> and the few, their dissensions, and those eminent men of whom
> some are leaders of the party of the people, others of the party
> of the nobles. One can in addition say that at Rome also, the
> claims of the people, of the plebeians, provided the energy of
> the collective movement. But one could not describe the axis of
> Roman history as formed by a succession of patrician leaders of
> the plebeians.[126]

Manent extends here his path of the study of political history of two actual
forms, so that Rome is seen in relief against Athens historically as well as
formally. In Athens, democratization proceeded through an increasing
power of the many "*guided* by a brilliant succession of leaders of the people
of generally aristocratic origin, [while] in Rome, it was *controlled*—that is,
at once used and checked—by an aristocratic body that resembled nothing
in Athens, namely the senate."[127] The divergence of the two continues in that
Athens, following its decline after losing the Peloponnesian War to Sparta
and coming under the dominance of the Macedonian empire, remained

---

125 Manent, *Metamorphoses*, 105–6.

126 *Metamorphoses*, 112.

127 *Metamorphoses*, 112.

a city, if a rump version of its earlier self. Rome, "though bruised within by the bloodiest strife, instead of foundering over itself engaged in a new career, or rather pursued its expansion, but under an altogether new form, the imperial form."[128] Even as it headed a kind of maritime empire, Athens remained a city with its limits, internal focus and energy, and other civic attributes.

Manent notes that the inattention of Aristotle ("who knew every-thing and whom nothing escaped") to the form of empire is "very puzzling. What we can say is that this silence suggests at least a certain perplexity on his part, perhaps a decided hostility, regarding a political form that extended the territory of the body politic indefinitely and that also multiplied indefinitely the number of citizens, although the term is not appropriate since they must henceforth follow a combination of Greek and barbarian customs under the power of a tyrannical king."[129] Indeed, Manent suggests that Aristotle might not even consider empire to be a political form because its extension dilutes civic action to such a degree that its activity might not even constitute politics. If Manent is correct that city and empire are polar forms, Aristotle's skepticism might be justified, and one can ask why Manent considers the empire a natural form. Manent would certainly concede that empire is natural in a weaker way than the city. But Manent apparently finds sufficient presence of the three natures of the city—birth (and a second birth for its citizens beyond their families), finality or an end, and movement of political life—to justify its description as a natural form.

Rome-the-empire emerges from the corruption of Rome-the-re-public as city. "The self-destruction of the republican city was in a certain sense the cause of the empire coming into existence. In the case of Rome extreme corruption did not signify death or the end, but the introduction to an unprecedented metamorphosis. Whereas Athens had consumed itself, so to speak, Rome renewed itself entirely."[130] Manent has already stipulated that Rome was thus a contradiction to his axiom that political forms do not directly transform from one to another, and thus an exception to political ontology; here, he adds that Rome is even more—a contradic-tion to ontology *tout court*. "In Rome death was not deadly."[131] Again, Rome-the-city has the natural feature of birth but lacks the natural characteristic

---

128 *Metamorphoses*, 113.
129 *Metamorphoses*, 113–14.
130 *Metamorphoses*, 114.
131 *Metamorphoses*, 114.

of death; it transcends its being as a city to transfigure itself as empire, seeking to bring as much of the world as can be known under its laws.

The transformation of Rome into empire "comes together or is summed up in the figure of Julius Caesar—who became more, and something other, than a Roman citizen . . . without however seizing the royal crown."[132] He founded both the empire and "an unprecedented political phenomenon, 'Caesarism,' . . . a monarchy that *follows* a republic no longer able to govern itself."[133] Manent argues that monarchy usually precedes a republic in the regime cycle, and thus in Rome we find that a "new historical sequence is added, one that was absent from the Greek experience." Again, Rome-the-empire is seen in contrast to Athens-the-city as Manent traces the course of political events. In evaluating these events, Manent strikes a phenomenological note that reminds us that his examination of events aims to discern a science of politics, a political philosophy: "[O]ur hypothesis is that 'Rome' designates unprecedented political phenomena. It is in order to make this unprecedented character appear that we have set the stage with the Greek civic experience, a complete experience or complete cycle of experiences."[134] Athens had lacked monarchical "experiences of the government of one alone that, good or bad, had remained foreign to the Greek city."[135] Manent wonders whether the Caesarism is really new, something beyond the range of Greek political science, or whether it is accounted for in Aristotle. "One [might] maintain that on the admittedly limited basis of the experience of the city, Greek political science elaborated an explanation of the political phenomenon that is so complete that it could be said to be exhaustive. . . . If the city is the original form of politics, it [would] contain in some way the whole of politics."[136] Is Greek political thought so complete that it can enfold Caesarism under its science, so that in fact there is really nothing new in the transformation of Rome from city to empire?

Manent's early influence, Leo Strauss, believed that Greek thought is indeed that complete and can account for Caesarism, the regime of the corrupted city-turned-empire. Strauss, in contesting Voegelin's claim that Caesarism is not a form of tyranny because it represents a

132 *Metamorphoses*, 114.
133 *Metamorphoses*, 114.
134 *Metamorphoses*, 115.
135 *Metamorphoses*, 114–15.
136 *Metamorphoses*, 115.

post-constitutional government that emerges only after a return to a consti-tutional regime is impossible, responds: "There is no reason to quarrel with the view that genuine Caesarism is not tyranny, but this does not justify the conclusion that Caesarism is incomprehensible on the basis of classical political philosophy: Caesarism is still a subdivision of absolute monarchy as the classics understood it."[137] This is because Caesarism's difference with tyranny consists in the fact that with no prospect of return to something like an aristocratic or mixed regime that seeks the common good, the Caesar provides the best available regime and is thus good in one of two possible senses. Either the Caesar is just and seeks the common good rather than his own interest, in which case he is like Aristotle's king; or he is unjust and rules over a corrupt and unjust people, that is, he is suitable for that people in the way that deserved punishment is just. Such a Caesar is "under certain conditions . . . necessary hence legitimate."[138] Aristotle's regime analysis can account for Caesarism without elaborating a new political form of empire; the science of the city is sufficient.

Breaking significantly with Strauss's thought, Manent disagrees with this analysis. To state the conclusion first, Manent argues that abso-lute monarchy as a regime does not really exist in Greek history and is a regime incapable of actually existing. He returns to Aristotle, who claims that most cities, based on the opposition of the few and the many, are "mixtures or composites of oligarchy and democracy,"[139] deviant regimes that are the most common in the Greek world (which, again, is the whole political world if Greek science is itself complete). Kingship defined simply as rule by one is relatively rare. Aristotle identifies five kinds of kingship, two of which are in practice tyrannies. Of the remaining three, Laconian kingship is not truly a kingship but a perpetual generalship that is not properly a regime but a "legislative provision" for a post than can exist in any regime.[140] The two remaining kinds of king are the king-ship of heroic times and the absolute king. Manent recounts Aristotle's answer to two questions, what to do with the individual whose virtue clearly exceeds that of all other citizens, and whether rule by law or rule by men is better. Manent notes that Aristotle's answer to the first question

---

137 *Metamorphoses*, 116. Manent indicates that Voegelin's claim appears in a review of Strauss's work on *Hiero*. Strauss refers to and contests Voegelin's claim in Strauss's book *On Tyranny*, (Ithaca, NY: Cornell University Press, 1968), 190.

138 Manent, *Metamorphoses*, 118.

139 *Metamorphoses*, 119. See Aristotle, *Politics* 4.11.1296a23–24.

140 *Metamorphoses*, 120. See Aristotle, *Politics* 3.14.1284b35–1285b33.

"seems unequivocal: absolute power should be given to such a superior person—or lineage."[141] Manent notes that this argument will be deployed throughout the later history of European monarchs, implying that Aristotle's science will remain foundational to European political development. In answer to the second question, Aristotle explains that "laws can only enunciate general rules and are unable to prescribe anything concerning particular situations. . . . [But] those who govern must have at their disposal this universal rule. One cannot do without laws."[142] Thus, if there is one exceedingly virtuous person, he should rule with the law. But his rule of one quickly becomes the rule of a few, including those magistrates who are needed to interpret the law in particular cases, who may be of lesser virtue than the king but can and must participate in the administration of justice and the consideration of the common good. This is advantageous because "a numerous mass judges many things better than one person, whoever that may be."[143] Thus, while the notion of rule by the best one person seems appealing, in practice it inevitably extends into rule by the few and by the many. This argument for a democratic tendency is not based on the equation of the politically just and the will of the majority. Rather, it "is an essentially or intrinsically political argument, . . . not only an argument whose object is the political thing"—the common thing or good—"but one whose tenor and so to speak whose life imitates our political condition."[144] Manent is claiming that this democratizing tendency is in some important sense natural, not because of the moral superiority of the majority or the many but simply as a practical matter of how best to decide the common good. In effect, the power of a supposedly absolute king is "diffracted" among the many, who can together produce a vision of the common thing better than the one, and the few who are the friends and close assistants of the king. Our "political condition" renders absolute kingship impossible as a realistic alternative: the "notion of absolute kingship . . . has in the end no substance of its own in the Greek political experience explored by Aristotle."[145]

The remaining sort of Aristotelian king, the king of heroic times who ruled "over willing subjects, hereditary, and in accordance with law . . .

---

141 *Metamorphoses*, 121. See Aristotle, *Politics* 3.17.1288a15–30.

142 *Metamorphoses*, 121. See Aristotle, *Politics* 3.15.1286a9–26.

143 *Metamorphoses*, 122. See Aristotle, *Politics* 3.15.1286a30–31.

144 *Metamorphoses*, 122.

145 *Metamorphoses*, 123.

was the only effective kingship in the Greek world."[146] And this, according to Manent, is a very weak and short-lived regime that came only at the beginning of the city form and quickly ceased to exist. During this transition period from pre-political to political life (Manent does not identify such a period, but that seems the obvious characterization), cities are small "with a paucity of excellent persons [and] the least physical or moral quality . . . was enough to make one worthy of kingship."[147] As soon as men equal to or nearly equal to the king in whatever qualities he might have been eminent appear, the kingly office becomes untenable.

The impossibility for kingship to endure as a political regime, at least in cities, also explains the regime cycle. With one short sentence, Manent both explains the origin of this cycle and points ahead to St. Augustine: "The progress of the love of gain led to oligarchies."[148] Man's desire for more and for dominance produced the corruption of the city from aristocracy to oligarchy. Then, it is a short step to democracy as deviant and ruling regime: "Aristotle suggests that because of its sordid love of gain, the ruling group shrank and so made the latter stronger. With the latter revolt, democracies arose."[149] Thus the conflict between the few and the many produces the city and leads as well to its corruption. This is Aristotle's "natural history of the city . . . [in which] democracy—wholesome or corrupt—is the final regime of the city, the end of its 'natural history,' or the natural end of its history. . . . With this final regime, the city has become all that it can be. . . . A 'Caesarian' future is not envisaged."[150] A tyrant may arise, but not an imperial Caesar. Strauss is wrong on two counts: the inclusion of Caesar under the regime type of absolute king cannot hold, because the logical interpretation of Aristotle's own thinking is that such a regime cannot really exist or exceeds the Greek experience. And he is wrong that the necessity of a Caesar as a form of deserved punishment for a people accords with Aristotle's notion of a good regime. Aristotle's "good regime" is one that seeks the common good, and necessity in his regime analysis involves democratization and corruption stemming from desire for gain, by the few and by the many; there is no place in his analysis for a

---

146 *Metamorphoses*, 123–24.

147 *Metamorphoses*, 124.

148 *Metamorphoses*, 124.

149 *Metamorphoses*, 124. See Aristotle, *Politics* 3.15.1286b12–20.

150 *Metamorphoses*, 125–26. Manent relies here not on any text from Aristotle but on the absence of any reference to such a Caesar.

regime that does good in some unintentional sense by inflicting punishment through the self-seeking gain of the ruler.[151]

Caesarism thus exists outside the Greek understanding of regime. It calls for a broader category than regime in order to accommodate Caesar, an absolute king who not only existed but existed beyond the corruption of the city, which concludes the Aristotelian regime cycle of the city. The unprecedented case of Caesar and Rome can only be understood by introducing the notion of political form, which enlarges the boundaries of Aristotelian political science beyond the city, and within which regimes that instantiate all political forms can be understood more fully as good or bad. Manent's inquiry into political form thus expands Aristotle's science without contradicting it. Aristotle's principles remain valid as expressing the reality of the political "what is" of the rational animal. With political form thus made visible as a phenomenon observable in the contrast between Athens and Rome (and that, after being made visible, can be applied to understand both), Manent has a powerful concept with which to proceed with his examination of European political development. Rome, with its unique transformation from city to empire, gave him that concept, and the science of Rome with its exceptional formal transformation is the basis for Manent's study of both political philosophy and of European political events, two vertices of his religion-philosophy-politics triangle.

ROME'S CONTRIBUTION
TO EUROPEAN DEVELOPMENT

We have already seen the general characteristics of empire as Manent describes it, as well as the place in Aristotle's science, or lack of such a place, of the Roman empire in its Caesarian phase—a problem that demands Manent's introduction of the category of political form. The empire form becomes visible as a form in contrast with the city, from whose corrupted example of the Roman republic the empire emerged. The remaining question for empire is how it contributes to the overall development of political form in Europe.

Cicero is, after Aristotle, the second major classical source who informs Manent's inquiry. Cicero was forced by events to turn from active

---

151 Manent seems to point here again to St. Augustine, who in the *City of God* will see providential good in all governance, good or evil. One could say that Manent is arguing here that Strauss agrees more with Augustine than with Aristotle on this point.

politics to philosophy. He does so as the city-republic is transforming to empire, thus he is an obvious candidate to provide insight into Manent's question regarding the uniqueness of Rome as city-turned-empire. The "death and deification of Caesar as the founding cause of the Roman Empire,"[152] the cause of the unique and even unnatural transformation, is the event that prompts Cicero's turn from one of Manent's vertices, politics, to another, philosophy. Manent's concern here is not empire in its various kinds, but the particular case of Rome. The deification of Caesar must be understood in formal terms:

> This extraordinary elevation of a citizen above those who were his equals presupposes a considerable modification of the form of the city. For such an elevation to be possible, its base—which is the city itself—must first have been considerably extended to be able to sustain this elevation. The surface area of the base, dare I say, must be proportional to the height of the new prince. The narrow city, "where all that is odious becomes even more odious," had to undergo such an extension and deformation, such a distension, that the laws of hate and love, the chemistry of the passions, were profoundly modified. The consequences of this distension of the city can best be seen in the period immediately preceding the institutionalization of empire, in the "Caesarian" period. The political and moral order becomes blurred or, better, indeterminate.[153]

It is in this blurry moment that Cicero writes *De officiis*. Manent finds here a diminution of the clarity of Aristotle's understanding of the natural relationships of family, household, village, and city. "[T]he differences and articulations among the diverse human associations that were brought out so clearly in Aristotle's description dim, weaken, or fade in Cicero's exposition. The landscape becomes flat and at the same time confused."[154] These differences among natural relationships become lost in the

---

152 Manent, *Metamorphoses*, 132. Again, this would seem to be a case of the resolution of the theologico-political question by the convergence of human ruler and divine presence in one person, but Manent does not explore this further.

153 *Metamorphoses*, 132. Regarding the height of the "new prince," Manent cites here Shakespeare's *Julius Caesar*, act 1, sc. 2: "He doth bestride the narrow world like a Colossus, and we petty men walk under his huge legs" (*Metamorphoses*, 336n76). Manent returns to this play elsewhere, as in an essay on its contemporary relevance to European decay, "The Tragedy of the Republic," *First Things* (May 2017), accessed April 19, 2017, https://www.firstthings.com/article/2017/05/the-tragedy-of-the-republic.

154 Manent, *Metamorphoses*, 134.

transformation to empire, and Cicero introduces a notion of the "'fellow-ship of the whole human race' [that is] unknown to classical Greek philosophy."[155] The human nature based on common logos as the Greeks understood it becomes a bond among all persons outside of a particular political association; Manent attributes the origins of this notion to Stoicism. With Cicero's leap from particular to universal, we can no longer be sure that reason and politics arise together, as they arise in a common humanity or brotherhood (or, elsewhere, "commonwealth") of man. Manent here objects to Cicero's move in a way that foreshadows his objections to the modern state: "It is impossible to consider humanity as such a political form. . . . [If we try to do so] human action . . . is no longer located in a concretely determined *political* order but in an order that will later be called civilization or what Cicero himself begins then to call the 'universal society of the human race.'"[156] In such a circumstance, reason serves only a general morality that is "detached from political forms and regimes and thus applicable in all political regimes and forms, in all political conditions, for the citizen of the smallest city as well as the emperor of Rome."[157]

With such an innovation, Cicero raises the importance of *jus gentium*, the law applicable to all peoples, or what he also calls natural law. Such a law has no boundaries and thus obliterates the limits of the city and the distinction between the internal and the external on Manent's polar scheme. The beginning of the polarity between city and empire is evident. Manent attributes then a "flexibility, plasticity, malleability of the Roman substance that forms a vivid contrast with the firmness and compactness of the Greek civic substance, especially the Athenian."[158] The Roman plasticity derives from the account of the founding of Rome, again seen in contrast to that of Athens. Athens had, in its own self-understanding, always been there from the pre-political era forward; the Greek camp in Homer had come from a place that was pre-political Greece. Rome, on the other hand, is founded by those who come from elsewhere, such as Aeneas and Ascanius. At the same time, "Rome comes from nowhere. . . . [T]he accounts, legendary or historical, of the origins of Rome emphasize that it was born from nothing: those who will make up Rome are

155 *Metamorphoses*, 134.
156 *Metamorphoses*, 135.
157 *Metamorphoses*, 135.
158 *Metamorphoses*, 136.

nobodies, ... outcasts, ... cityless."[159] As a result, Rome "understood itself
as a process of association or consociation whose starting point could
be known rationally,"[160] as opposed to the indefinite and prerational
beginning of Athens. In Cicero, Manent understands that "Rome is not so
much a city to be compared to Athens or Sparta as a dynamic process of
human consociation, a process that unceasingly pushes and in the end
abolishes the limits of the city form."[161] This is a critical point for European
development. Rome-as-empire introduces, in polar opposite to the city
form, the limitless that will always compete with the attraction of the city's
limits. The sources of modernity's characteristic of constant and endless
searching is found first in the empire whose own characteristics are elaborated in Cicero. European political development will then proceed as a
contest, a motion, between these two forms.

Cicero also provides the philosophical basis for another innovation
in the politics of the Roman empire. He "substitutes for the [Aristotelian]
citizen who is both one and double—sometimes commanding, sometimes
commanded—the duality of the magistrate and the private person. The
magistrate is elevated at the same time the private individual is abased, or,
more precisely, the citizen is reduced to the condition of private individual."[162] In the city form of Athens or the Roman republic, the magistrate was
simply a governing function. In the empire that is no longer surveyable
within political limits, the citizens must be represented by the magistrate.
Manent claims that in these circumstances of the "extended or distended
city [i.e., the incipient empire] the part and the whole have lost their
mutual actuality and need the mediation of a third term."[163] The citizen
and the political association are no longer real to each other, perhaps
suggesting a further blurring of the natural relationships identified by
Aristotle that characterizes the empire. The third term is the *persona civitatis*, a relatively abstract and non-concrete "moral person." The magistrate carries the abstract person, this third term, on his shoulders. The
private citizen is then relieved of the need to carry the political burdens
of ruling and being ruled; his role is to live in equality with other private
citizens. Manent sees here a "sketch of the modern State" that assigns

159 *Metamorphoses*, 137.

160 *Metamorphoses*, 137.

161 *Metamorphoses*, 137.

162 *Metamorphoses*, 138.

163 *Metamorphoses*, 138.

to and guarantees each person his rights.[164] In Rome we find the beginning of the end of the authentic diversity of human action that Manent
considers central to a good politics; the citizens are, whatever their chores
and manners, essentially the same, the recipients of the rights provided
by the *persona civitatis*.

Finally, Cicero and the empire form inaugurated in Rome provide
a third element to the trajectory of European political development, one
that is apparent in his elevation of the importance of private property.
Such property is particular, indeed it is a right, to each citizen, and it is
distinct from the common good. With this emphasis, Cicero divides the
one human nature of Aristotelian science into two natures with separate
goods, one common and one individual. In Cicero's account, "[n]ature has
thus endowed us with two kinds of persona: a *persona communis* that is
our rational nature common to all human beings; and a *persona singulis
tributa,* a particular or singular persona that is out individual nature, our
individual character. . . . Cicero [strikingly] insists on this second persona."[165] The authority of the individual nature trumps that of the common
nature: we "must not do anything against our common or universal nature
but on the contrary preserve it, [but] we must on the other hand follow our
own proper nature."[166] Manent does not put it in these terms, but Cicero
places the particular nature of the individual in priority to the common
nature, removing Aristotle's priority of the city. Cicero's combination of
the universal humanity that is the ultimate distension of the city and the
split human nature of common and particular (with the latter in control)
in Rome has profound ramifications for all that has followed and for the
modern interpretation of "what is":

> The dissolution of the "ethical substance" of the republic
> liberates on the one hand human generality, a human nature
> abstractly said to be rational or reasonable, and on the other
> virtues and vices that appear as strictly individual characters.
> One can see that the most delicate questions of morality, and
> even the most difficult questions of ontology (such as the status
> of individuality) are linked to the question of political form. The
> human as pure moral agent and the human as pure particu-
> larity, pure individuality, two phenomena that appear to us [as

---

164 *Metamorphoses*, 138.
165 *Metamorphoses*, 139.
166 *Metamorphoses*, 139.

moderns] to be given, that is, as determined in themselves or by themselves, are shown to be in fact derivative phenomena, if we judge by the Roman experience. From what do they derive? They derive from the distension and finally from the decomposition of the first political form, the original republic.[167]

In Rome, in its transformation from city to empire, and in the contrast between city and empire, the key elements of European political development are found. Manent implicitly reinforces the deep intertwining of the human soul and the political association that pervaded Greek political thought, an intertwining that will be later be rejected with the individualism whose roots in Cicero grow into the modern rights-bearing man of the modern state. The first metamorphosis from the pre-political to the political condition in the city depended on and activated the original intertwining. The next metamorphosis from city to empire introduced the tensions between citizen and political community that would drive the later metamorphoses in European political form, in particular the rise of the nation.

167 *Metamorphoses*, 142.

Chapter Four

NATION AND CHURCH

THE POLITICAL FORM THAT MANENT WILL ULTIMATELY CONSIDER the best available for Europe is the nation that developed there after city and empire, the nation that is neither natural nor anti-natural, nor morally neutral: the nation form that, as we will see in this chapter, developed under the pressure of the Church and bore the Church's mark. The nation remains, even in our day, the form most likely to provide the possibility of a good life for Europeans, who remain political by nature even if their modern tendencies cause them to seek to flee that nature.[1] But Manent spends less time defining or describing this form and its closely related sometime-nemesis and sometime-formator, the Church, than any of the other forms he explores; he instead observes and examines the nation's emergence in historical events. Like the empire, the nation cannot be understood without reference to its predecessor forms, as it emerges from Europe's inability to find political satisfaction in either city or empire. The development of the nation is inextricably linked to the Church, which Manent also identifies as a political form, if an odd one. The nation is the "in-between form": it is in between the particular interests of the city and the universal aspirations of the empire, in between the Church and the civil authorities of Europe, and in between the classical or pagan understanding of what is and the modern understanding. This in-between form is Europe's answer to the theologico-political question.

Much of Manent's work on the nation appears in the context of his explication of the motion of political form in Europe toward the modern nation or state and the dangers of that state; the nation is visible in that

1 As will be discussed later, Manent contrasts the nation with the modern state that arose from the nation of Christian confession when it democratized and began to declare itself in a morally neutral way. Manent favors this nation form as an alternative to the modern state, the false universalism embodied in the "post-national European nation" and the European Union, and the moral void in contemporary European nations that permits and even abets the rise of Islam.

movement. The nation form becomes fully visible and open to description, then, from the perspective of its successor form, the modern state. Manent argues that the consequences of failing to understand the nation are catastrophic, yet achieving such understanding is a very trying part of his project: "If our nation suddenly disappeared and its bonds were dispersed, each of us immediately would become a stranger, a monster, to himself. . . . But how difficult it is to describe the nation and its effects!"[2] We turn now to Manent's effort to confront this difficulty. We will first examine Manent's description of the nation form as self-sufficient and, more tellingly, as a response to two indeterminacies, one political and one theological, that demanded a choice on the part of Europeans; these descriptions offer as general a depiction of the nation form as we will find, but it is not at all abstract. It is grounded in the concrete political choices that Europeans made over a long period of history. We will then see how the nation that responded to these indeterminacies comes to be visible as a phenomenon in historical events and is only fully visible as it is already being overcome by the modern nation or state. The nation form is the "look" of the political association that emerges in these events. We know it in limited measure by describing it, but we know it more completely by seeing it in its emergence and its eventual eclipse. The role of the Church in the emergence of the nation and the shaping of the European citizen will be shown in two respects, first in how the claims of the Church as a form, or a form above the nation form, rendered necessary some replacement form for the city and empire, then in how the Church's proposition of charity and its critique of pagan pride, demanding humility instead, left the national Christian citizen "seeing double" and set the stage for modern thinking.

THE NATION DESCRIBED AS SELF-SUFFICIENT

Aristotle describes the city as reaching "a level of full self-sufficiency."[3] Manent, focusing "attention on the national form for its own sake," also chooses self-sufficiency as a key aspect of "the fact or phenomenon of the nation."[4] Citing the work of Jean Baechler, Manent ascribes three forms of self-sufficiency to the nation form: economic, diplomatic and strategic, and affective. Economic self-sufficiency

---

2 Manent, *Democracy without Nations?*, 4.

3 Aristotle, *Politics* 1.2.1252b29.

4 Manent, *A World beyond Politics?*, 51.

> means to live on one's own resources, without needing to import goods or services or to engage in commerce or trade. . . . The idea of self-sufficiency [today] evokes a closed path of narrowness, when we would rather be open. Until fairly recently, however, a certain amount of self-sufficiency was the desire and the law of all political bodies, except of course those for whom commerce was the principal activity, like the cities of northern Germany long ago.[5]

Markets developed over the course of the era of the national political form, to the degree that the "market was at first and for a long time principally the *national* market."[6] With Great Britain as an exception, until World War II, most nations opted for a high degree of economic self-sufficiency; only after the development of the modern nation or state do nations open their markets broadly in an effort to counter the destructive effects of the nationalisms thought to have driven the violence of the two world wars.

Diplomatic and strategic self-sufficiency refers to "national independence and sovereignty. Each nation—and this is what defines it as a nation—determines its external actions in sovereign fashion: chooses its alliances, wages war, or makes peace."[7] Like economic self-sufficiency, this characteristic of the nation is diminished substantially in the twentieth century, especially as American involvement in Europe grows in and after World War I.

Affective self-sufficiency, Manent quotes Baechler, "means the possibility of concentrating on the polity every affective identification with a community and of focusing all negative feelings of hatred, spite, and fear on other polities."[8] Manent elaborates: "This 'affective identification' is something more than a 'national feeling.' It causes a nation to fuse into itself and subordinate all other identifications that a citizen might feel."[9] In the case of France, this fusion comes in two stages, first in the fourteenth and fifteenth centuries in opposition to the English, then more completely in the French Revolution. This affective self-sufficiency, like the nation form itself, only comes into its full realization as the nation form is in transition to the modern state. In this description of the nation, Manent

---

5 *A World beyond Politics?*, 51.

6 *A World beyond Politics?*, 52.

7 *A World beyond Politics?*, 52.

8 Jean Baechler, "Dépérissement de la nation," in *Contrepoints et commentaires* (Paris: Calmann-Lévy, 1996), 486–87, quoted in *A World beyond Politics?*, 53.

9 *A World beyond Politics?*, 53.

identifies clearly the self-sufficiencies of the nation only in hindsight; the features of the form become apparent only as the nation, which Manent argues was a condition for democracy, became democratic, representative, and industrial—modern. For a more complete and dynamic description of the nation, we must turn to its operation and its emergence.

THE NATION DESCRIBED AS OPERATIONAL RESPONSE TO TWO INDETERMINACIES

Manent's most complete and, at the same time, concise expression of his understanding of the nation comes in his book *Beyond Radical Secularism*. The nation is to be understood in its historical and operational dimensions, within the context of the movement of political form as the driving force of European development. This movement is the history and operation of two freedoms or indeterminacies, the freedom to obey God in conscience with a hope for union with him, and a simultaneous freedom for self-government according to human prudence.

> This was, then, the starting point and the principle of European history: *to govern oneself in a certain relation to the Christian proposition*. Now, . . . it was through the effort to align these two determinations that the Europeans left behind the [Roman] imperial matrix or renounced the project of restoring it. . . . There is one observation . . . that will help us to find our way between these two great intimidating entities [the Roman Empire and the Catholic Church]. The Roman Empire emerged from the *corruption* of the Roman Republic, and yet it is from the corruption of a *Republic* that it emerged. Under the Western empire, there was always the city as a living, even if almost smothered principle; beneath the *princeps* or *imperator*, there was the *populus romanus*.[10]

Manent alludes here to the "determinations" that responded to two indeterminacies: the indeterminacy of political form and the indeterminacy of the response to Christianity. Both indeterminacies are answered by human choices; they are not predetermined or necessary. He also refers to the freedom of self-governance in pagan Rome that extends as a political principle into the fundaments of the nation form. As in the case of

---

10 Manent, *Beyond Radical Secularism*, 64.

the cities of Athens or the Roman Republic, the nation assembles itself from different principles: "The nation-state was to modern Europe what the city-state was to ancient Greece. It produced the unity, and therefore the framework of meaning of life by producing, in Aristotle's phrase, 'the things held in common.' . . . [T]he city-state and the nation-state are the only two political forms that have been capable of realizing, at least in their democratic phases, the intimate union of *civilization* and *liberty*."[11] The nation resulted when the political freedom of the city encountered "the Christian proposition of a 'new life,' henceforth accessible to every person of good will, which consisted in participation in the very life of God in Three Persons."[12] Christianity demands the freedom to respond to this proposition in obedience to God, not man; it demands its own union of civilization and liberty.

> On the other hand, obedience to God's law is not all there is to Christian life. This God seeks a covenant with human beings; His grace seeks their freedom. Beneath the apparatus of the empire as well as that of the Church, there is a principle of freedom. Beneath the rivalry of the two giants brimming with authority, we find the divergent and complicit operation of two principles of freedom. This operation was incompatible with the unity, the extent, and the immobility of the empire, and so progressively abandoned it in order to work itself out in the ardent pursuit of new and ever-more intimate alliances between the government of men and divine Providence. In this collaboration, the theology of St. Thomas Aquinas was able to provide the principles, but not to show the way concretely to put them into practice.[13]

As we have seen, Manent believes that not just St. Thomas but all Christian medieval thinking was deficient in its capacity to provide a political philosophy adequate to its theological challenge to paganism. It could not define or describe a form that would suffice for the cooperation of the two principles of freedom. Thus, the two "divergent and complicit" principles were left to be reconciled in their compatible if often tense coexistence by bringing into place a new political form, the nation.

11 Manent, *Democracy without Nations?*, 30–31.
12 Manent, *Beyond Radical Secularism*, 63.
13 *Beyond Radical Secularism*, 64.

Europeans thus strove to bring this collaboration to fruition in a new political form, a political form ignored by the ancients. They undertook this unprecedented political and religious project through an unprecedented political form: to govern oneself through obedience to God's benevolent intention, to seek ceaselessly to combine the pride of the citizen, or more generally of the acting human being, and the humility of the Christian. In this sense, what distinguishes Europe is not the separation between religion and politics, but rather the pursuit of an ever more intimate union between them.[14]

We will examine the conflict between civic or pagan pride and humility further below. Manent's language in these passages can tend toward suggesting the possibility that principles or operations are the actors and agents of movement in political history. But this last citation pulls him back to his essential premise that man is the principle of all political history, that it is Europeans as persons, prideful or humble or some combination of both, who determined what the responses to the indeterminacies of political form and the Christian proposition would be. "Each form of common life in Europe was a way of resolving this double indeterminacy by in a way linking the concretization of a way of governing oneself with the concretization of a certain relation to the Christian proposition."[15]

Just as Manent describes the ancient city by its two acts of taking the young from their families for its own purposes and of declaring the world beyond the city to be hostile, the European nation is also known by its act or operation: the operation of its persons collectively bringing into political force the two freedoms of the Roman Empire—more precisely the freedom of the citizen of the Roman Republic that lingered in the imperial form, and the freedom of the Christian to respond God's offer of salvation. We know the nation by seeing in political events what it does in bringing these two principles into itself as a political form, and the science of the nation, more than a definition of the form or a description of its various regimes, must be the understanding of its operation or motion in resolving these two principles:

The object of Europe's ceaseless quest can be defined, in theological terms, as the common action of grace and of freedom and, in political terms, as the covenant between communion

---

14 *Beyond Radical Secularism*, 64–65.
15 *Beyond Radical Secularism*, 86.

and freedom. The Church cannot prevent the covenant that God entered into with the old Israel, a covenant of which Israel saw itself as the sole heir, from being diffracted in Europe among several rival peoples who are equally covenanted with God. Whereas the Church saw itself as the unique path to salvation, the various nations entered into their particular covenants with the Most High, first under a Christian king, and then, after the Reformation had abolished ecclesiastical mediation, rendering the nation in a way immediately Christian. . . .

[T]he European nation, which, beginning in the Reformation, tended to take on the attributes of the Church, remained throughout its history this kind of community of spiritual education that wove together self-government and a relation to the Christian proposition, a two-fold *intention* that opens up a plural and indefinite history, the history of European nations.[16]

The effects of the Reformation will be discussed in greater depth below. For now, we can see that, again, the history of political form is indefinite or undetermined, until it is given determination by freely acting people. The "in-between form" of the nation is a woven form whose essential materials are the freedoms of self-government and Christian response; it is the "covenant of communion and freedom." Manent's path of inquiry through political philosophy has little to say about this form. His path of following historical events allows him to identify the nation by its determination to enjoy the two freedoms in operation and, ultimately, will lead him to consider that operation, the nation, to be the best available political form for Europe, situated as it was between the ancient city and empire before, and the modern state after.

THE NATION SEEN IN ITS EMERGENCE

The lack of direct definition and explication of the nation form, and the nation's importance in Manent's prescriptive political commentary for Europe, demand that we examine the nation from the limited remarks Manent does offer about it and derive all that his discussion permits. He makes several claims, implicitly or explicitly, about the nation:

• Implicitly, Manent writes with the awareness that the nation was the dominant political form in European history before modernity, and its

---

16 *Beyond Radical Secularism*, 65–66.

detritus is still present; therefore, most people will have some intuitive understanding of what the nation is.

• Explicitly, he claims that the nation emerges from the tension between the city and the empire, the two natural political forms of the ancient world, neither of which could satisfy the political needs of post-Roman Europe. Further, the nation emerges under the pressure of the Catholic Church, which is itself a political form of sorts, though not a natural political form. In its historical dependence on the Church and in its difference from city and empire, the nation itself is not a natural form. It is the form that is Europe's answer to the theologico-political question, at least for a time.

• The nation emerges over the long course of what Manent will describe as the Ciceronian moment, which will be considered at greater length momentarily. This period was marked by political disorder and absence of clear form. That disorder is brought to an end not by the nation but by the moderns. The precise "phase" or timeframe of the nation is not pinpointed. It is evident first in the age of the Christian kings, then in the process of nationalization accelerated by the Protestant Reformation. It is still evident as the later modern political form based on representation comes into existence, and it is still available and influential, if in a weakened condition, today. The nation seems to come into its full realization only as it is already being overcome by the modern state.

• Christianity has little to say about politics, but its critique (especially by St. Augustine) of pagan thinking has profound political implications and effects, and that critique deserves extended attention as it relates both to political form and to the persons who live within the nation shaped by the Church.

• The nation or its elements are thus present in each of what Manent calls the three great waves of European history: it is present potentially in the ancient, pagan forms of empire and city, which were its sources; it is present in Christianity, which shaped it; and it remains present in modernity, which departed from it but still rests upon it. The waves correspond to different claims to the authority of mediation between man and God, or in the case of the modern state, the privatization or elimination of such mediation. But the nation form is not itself one of the great waves. It is an operation that draws from, responds to, and ultimately fades into these waves, a movement within the larger movement of European history that is visible in political form.

THE STILL-UNDERSTOOD REFERENCES TO THE NATION

Europeans know that they are French, Belgian, Italian, Slovenian. They know their own nationality, if only in a way quite distant from the intensity of the religious profession with which their nation began in a common response to the Christian proposition, though the references to that profession in architecture and art, historical memory, and even contemporary religious praxis still resonate within national boundaries. "Of course, the European nations developed their respective physiognomies, their 'general spirit,' on the basis of various different elements, both natural, such as climate and geography, and human, with all the variety of social, moral, and political circumstances, both internal and external."[17] A Croatian knows by nonreligious and religious references that she is a Croatian, not a Swede. "[T]he framework of our lives will retain a national character for the foreseeable future. Our nations are here to stay for a while longer."[18] Manent can thereby assume a common framework of reference for discussing the nation that he could not assume for the city or empire, even if in the modern state the principle of freedom inherent in Christianity and in the pagan city is submerged, forgotten, or otherwise inoperative.

Of all the references that remind Europeans of the nation form, language is perhaps the most important in politics, as it shapes political speech and records the political events that comprise the visible operation of the nation.

> We Europeans ought to be particularly sensitive to the political character of speech. European languages, we are told, are "national languages." That is true if one understands by "nation" a *political* body of a certain kind. Our languages in fact do not send us back principally to an ineffable lost origin or a series of incommunicable experiences, but to a rather intelligible political history, one to which our familiarity with the language gives access. Our languages do not express a sublime "cultural" essence that is fundamentally apolitical or metapolitical. Rather, they express the history of our respective political regimes.[19]

---

17 *Beyond Radical Secularism*, 66.

18 Manent, *Democracy without Nations?*, 90.

19 *Democracy without Nations?*, 30.

Language marks and differentiates the different examples or regimes of the nation form. The speech that records the particular political history of each nation is thus central to its realization of the operation or form of the nation. Yet, as with Homer for the emergence of the city form in Athens, it is national poets rather than political philosophers or statesmen whose speech plays the seminal formal role. Manent's examples are Jean Racine in seventeenth-century France and William Shakespeare in Elizabethan England.

> For each country, the poet embodies the political moment when the nation became self-conscious by attaining, as it were, its definitive form. He actualizes the potentialities of the language and at the same time "fixes," in a manner of speaking, its quantity and quality. French was the language of the court and was so firmly set in its abstract categories that it almost naturally became the language of a republic that set itself up as schoolmaster and lecturer. It is a language of the narrative discourse that prefers the sign to the thing, a language of the tiniest and most subtle inflections. English, by contrast, had been a "barbarous" language, but one that the greatest poet of Europe very soon brought to its highest degree of expressive "ruddiness." At the same time, English was endowed with enough simplicity and force to become the very language of utility. It also is a language of imitation in which one still hears the cry of the beast, as one can regularly verify in the House of Commons. Our European languages—I have only invoked two, those best known to me—are admirable distillations brought about by that great synthesizer of European life, the nation-state.[20]

Similar roles are played throughout Europe by poets from Poland to Germany to Ireland. This intimate relationship between poetry, with its sources in and effects on the imagination, and politics persists from the inception of the city (and of politics and philosophy), as seen earlier through the form of the nation. It ensures that each political association's record of political events will be distinctive to that association. But it is the form, in this case the nation, that "distils" the language by "synthesizing" that which must be brought together—in the case of Europe the principles of political and Christian freedom. Language, for Manent, both precedes

---

20 *Democracy without Nations?*, 30.

and follows political form, and then records the movement of that form; as in the city, logos and politics go together in the nation.

THE EMERGENCE OF THE NATION FROM CITY AND EMPIRE, AS THE CHURCH WATCHES

The change in prevailing political form from the ancient city and empire to the nation is not a radical or abrupt new beginning, but an emergence in which the past is both prologue to and part of the new period of the nation. "[T]he phases of the past, those we have left behind, never simply disappear. They have reached their limits, but they remain present and active."[21] The limits of the city and empire forms were reached as Christianity introduced new pressures on Europe. Manent writes,

> During the first centuries of the Christian dispensation and for quite a long time afterward, city and empire were the only available political forms. Cities naturally grew up, particularly, as I have recalled, in northern Italy and northern Europe. And the prestige of the Roman empire was such that a Holy Roman German empire evolved in western Europe. However, despite this imperial prestige, despite the magnificent flowering of so many cities from Florence through Venice to Cologne and Amsterdam, the most significant fact of our history is that Europe did not organize itself durably in the form of cities or an empire. Instead, it was forced to produce a radically new political form. The way to break the stand-off between city and empire, between Guelphs and Ghibellines, was to invent a political form unknown to the ancients. This . . . was the nation, the European nation, the political form that is so familiar to us. The ancient or natural conflict between city and empire, therefore, did not issue in the ancient or natural outcomes, whether the victory of one or a complex equilibrium between the two.[22]

Manent is tracing here the political events of Europe that occurred in the absence of a prevailing political philosophy, the period known as the "Ciceronian moment" that will be further discussed shortly. His understanding of the emergence of the nation is grounded in concrete developments that

---

21 Manent, *Seeing Things Politically*, 192.
22 Manent, *Democracy without Nations?*, 95.

were not natural in the Aristotelian sense (of the building of natural relationships) and also not "thought into existence" or preceded by a guiding philosophy of politics.

> We are struck, in considering European history after the fall of Rome, by the persistence of empire: the Germanic Holy Roman Empire, the French Empire, the German Empire, and contemporary Europe, which many speak of as the new empire. And yet it was not these empires that gave Europe its form. Similarly, there have been brilliant examples of the city in Europe, whether in Italy, in Flanders, or in the Rhineland. But European life has not been organized mainly in cities. In any case, this has not been the dominant political form. . . . Why were the two natural forms of human association gradually set aside? And why was a third form finally victorious, a form without equivalent in the ancient world, the nation? Even with all the prestige that was associated with the city on one hand and the empire on the other, European life was finally organized in a political form that was neither the city nor the empire.[23]

Manent insists on answering this question of "why the nation?" with a language that is not technical or specialized, but available and comprehensible to all citizens, and this is the language of political forms: "By identifying a process that rests on political forms, I propose a history that I can recount in [simple, natural] French: the city, the empire and the nation got their names from political life itself."[24] Unlike the city and the empire, the nation is not a natural form, as will be further discussed below; but like the city and the empire, ordinary citizens recognize what the nation is from their own political experience, even though the nation is more difficult to articulate in formal terms than its classical predecessors.

Why is the nation not a natural political form? Manent is strong on this claim: "These political bodies—the nations—have nothing natural about them, even though, and I say this on good authority, man is a political animal."[25] Yet he does not make the reasons for the claim obvious, so we must speculate. At the least, if city and empire are the two classical, natural forms that are in some sense opposed to one another, then the nation is not natural simply because it is not one of those forms. It lacks

---

23 Manent, *Seeing Things Politically*, 109–10.
24 *Seeing Things Politically*, 110.
25 Manent, *Democracy without Nations?*, 103.

the surveyable scale of the city and the boundless aspiration of the empire. Yet it suffices as a political association for man, who remains in his own nature a political animal. While the nation is not a natural form, it is also not anti-natural. It accommodates man's political nature without fulfilling it completely or seeking to destroy it or escape from it.

Perhaps more powerfully, we can return to Manent's account of the three natures of the city in *Metamorphoses of the City*: its tragic nature, which stems from the fact that it has a birth and offers a second birth to its citizens; its philosophic nature that "arouses and constrains the desire to accede to the world without borders, the pure world that is beyond the city"; and its natural political movement "of internal struggle and external war." These natures could be absent or very different in the nation. This absence or difference might be because the city's natures were displaced by the political form, the Church, whose pressure produced the nation, and which makes claims and propositions that exceed the natural, introducing a supernatural force that rendered the pagan forms incapable of enduring response.

As already noted, this nonnatural form of the nation responds to the inability of the natural forms to provide a political determinacy that could cope with the divisive Christian proposition as offered by the Church: "One could say that at least since the thirteenth century or the start of the fourteenth, since Dante's *Monarchy*, Europe has been in search of the unification of human life in order to overcome the division induced by Christianity. . . . This is the very theme of European history and in particular the well-spring of the modern State."[26] The profound division brought by the Church extends throughout the era of the nation and beyond it. Manent writes,

> The old dynamics [of city and empire] no longer ruled, no longer produced the accustomed order or disorder. Why? A third party— not a political one—had introduced itself, purporting to mediate the conflict or tension between city and empire. I allude to the Catholic Church, of course. The church is not strictly a political form, but it introduced such a deep reconsideration and recomposition of human association that it would be prudent to include it among the political forms, if only never to lose sight of the part it played in constituting the European political

26 Manent, *Metamorphoses*, 214.

landscape, especially through its role in giving birth to the political form proper—even exclusive—to Europe: the nation.[27]

The Church is an odd entity, a kind of form that carries a strength stronger than the earlier forms. It is, paradoxically, not political in itself yet wields vast political force:

> In some politically relevant sense, the church is stronger than either the city or the empire. It is stronger for spiritual reasons, which have political consequences. The church, as a purported perfect society—if you prefer, as an imagined perfect society— undermines the moral components and conditions of the city and the empire as human associations. Through the specific characteristics animating it—that is, through charity—the church goes deeper than the city and further than the empire. The mere notion of charity—love of the neighbor for the love of God—opens up perspectives and possibilities that are enough to reorder the way we look at the human association.[28]

Manent rarely speaks explicitly and directly of the political power of love in such unvarnished terms, usually preferring instead to focus on that love in the context of the critique of paganism to be discussed below. But here he makes clear that, although he does not use these terms, the Church "de-natures" the political form through its proposition of a love that transcends those forms. With its transcendent claim, it at least divides man's understanding of politics and its place in human action, and it ultimately demands its own understanding of the original three natures of the city or political association—birth, death or end, and movement—which must now be ordered to the larger supernatural principle revealed by Christ and proclaimed by the Church. The second birth of the citizen must become a second birth in Christ; the end of a man or a community as defined by the ancient philosophers is superseded, or enlarged, by their Christian end in God; and the motion that matters most is the motion that leads to that God. The Church calls to man in his human action, in politics, in a way that transgresses the barrier between faith and politics in Manent's philosophy-politics-faith triangle. Yet man is still the principle of politics, for it is man who must choose how to respond to the Christian proposition and who, even after accepting it, remains in the human domain and must

---

27 Manent, *Democracy without Nations?*, 95–96.

28 *Democracy without Nations?*, 96.

still act in that domain, where Christianity has little to offer in practical terms beyond its powerful, guiding principle of love of neighbor and God. Man must still respond to the indeterminacy of political form and to the desire for self-rule. But he now does so in the absence of the natural political forms of city and empire. He is now a political animal by nature who is also directed by a supernatural principle. As St. Augustine will explain, he now resides in two intermixed cities.

The Church, of course, "is not of this world. It is, or was, unable to make charity the animating principle of our political associations."[29] The Church "decisively and definitively changed the way Europeans looked at political associations,"[30] but it offered no political philosophy to describe or guide the implementation of its principle; it could shape political form but not bring that form into practical realization. The ancient political forms opposed the Church but could not resist it: "[T]he city is particularly inimical to the church because its civic passions bend the human heart toward human affairs, while the empire also is inimical to the church because it entertains (competing) universal claims. To summarize: our forebears had at their disposal three modes of human association, three political forms that could neither be reconciled nor made compatible."[31] But none of those three forms nor the combination of them brought the nation into existence. "The nation could come into being only through the action of the form itself, of what is the most formal in the form—that is, its unity. The entering wedge of the nation-to-be was the Christian king."[32] The implementation of the regimes of the nation form was left to man, and it came with the Christian kings, who would serve as the efficient causes of the nation.

A WORD ON THE CHURCH AS POLITICAL FORM

Before turning in greater detail to those kings, it is worth pausing to consider Manent's description of the Church as a political form. As we have seen, he acknowledges that it is an unusual form, a nonpolitical political

29 *Democracy without Nations?*, 96.
30 *Democracy without Nations?*, 96.
31 *Democracy without Nations?*, 97.
32 *Democracy without Nations?*, 97.

form. "To be sure, the Church cannot be placed on the same plane as the empire and the city-state. Organizing men's social and political life is not its raison d'être. But by its very existence and distinctive vocation, it posed an immense political problem to the European peoples."[33] On one hand, the Church resembles a political form in that men, those who respond to the Church's proposition affirmatively, seek collectively and individually the ultimate common good of salvation. But the Church does not provide, in conventional terms at least, a political association at the broadest level that seeks a common good in the human domain, though it is very, even exclusively, concerned with the good of souls. When it seeks the relief of material suffering, it does so in response to the command to love one's neighbor; while such relief is a good in itself, the Church acts principally for the sake of a good beyond the material. Its concern centers on the eternal salvation of souls. Its mission gave it "a right or duty to oversee everything that could place that salvation in peril."[34] It is interested in this world's politics only to the extent that earthly affairs affect salvation, and its ultimate common good lies beyond the good of earthly political forms and regimes. Occasionally, the Church in post-Roman Europe was dragged into more direct aspects of human governance where temporal authority had failed. But the sustained conflict between the Church and temporal government stemmed from the Church's interest in salvation and resultant "claim [to] the supreme power, the *plenitudo potestatis*"[35] to decide earthly matters where salvation was implicated—the ultimate power derived from the ultimate good, the power of the universal over the particular or the eternal over the temporal. The Church was both intensely interested in temporal governance and uninterested in it.

> The remarkable contradiction embedded in the Catholic Church's doctrine can be summarized in this way: although the Church leaves men free to organize themselves within the temporal sphere as they see fit, it simultaneously tends to impose a theocracy on them. It brings a religious constraint of a previously unheard of scope, and at the same time offers the emancipation of secular life. Unlike Judaism and Islam, the Church does not

33 Manent, *Intellectual History of Liberalism*, 4.
34 *Intellectual History of Liberalism*, 4.
35 *Intellectual History of Liberalism*, 5.

provide a law that is supposed to govern concretely all of men's actions in the earthly city.[36]

We have seen that in Manent's view of European history in the early centuries of the nation, there was not a strict separation of faith and governance but rather an ever-closer joining of the two in a "covenant between communion and freedom." The nature of the Church makes this covenant one of both distance and intimacy: "[T]he Christian Church is the only religious institution, indeed the only human institution, that presents itself as *produced by a purely spiritual act, the act of faith.* This independence is at once much more than a separation, because it opens up an infinite distance; and it is the opposite of a separation because it is the condition and the cause of an unprecedented union."[37] The Church is concerned with the infinite as it joins the finite, with the universal as it is decisive for the particular. As such, its pressure seems inevitably to lead to an "in-between form," the nation. "The great political problem in Europe was therefore the following: the nonreligious, secular lay world had to be organized under a form that was neither city-state nor empire, a form less 'particular' than the city-state and less 'universal' than the empire, or whose universality would be different from that of the empire. We know that this political form was absolute or national monarchy."[38] The force of the Church—not the Church itself acting formally—overcame the inimical resistance of city and empire by launching what would become the nation, or creating the conditions where the nation would launch itself.

We are left in no doubt of the power of the Church's proposition with its political effects. That power is singularly effective in propelling the movement of European political development as seen in the transition in political forms from city and empire to nation. But there is some doubt as to whether the Church should, by Manent's own account, be called a political form. It embodies a critical contradiction of being political yet nonpolitical, interested in and indifferent to earthly political regimes and outcomes. It is the source of a European manifestation of Manent's guiding theologico-political question, but in itself it does not answer that question. It moves toward the political vertex in Manent's triangle only insofar as its "home" position on the faith vertex demands. As a possible political form, the Church does not directly bear fruit in particular political regimes or

36 *Intellectual History of Liberalism*, 5.

37 Manent, *Beyond Radical Secularism*, 65.

38 Manent, *Intellectual History of Liberalism*, 7.

actualizations of its form, choosing instead where its interests are at stake to guide and, uneasily at times, ally with the regimes of another form, the nation. It would seem that it is best described as a supernatural political force in nature, or an apolitical form behind or above the political form of the nation.

THE CICERONIAN MOMENT: THE NATION AS THE POLITICAL FORM OF DISORDER

The nation emerges over the long course of what Manent labels "the Ciceronian moment," the extended era in Europe unfolding from the transition from city to empire in Rome through and long after the end of imperial authority. This moment of empire and its aftermath "redefines the political order in a way that distances us decisively from the ancient civic order, Greek or Roman."[39] It begins with Cicero's philosophical work and the Caesarism of the Roman empire, but it "is not limited to the last years of Cicero's life. It is only provisionally and imperfectly closed by the inauguration of the empire."[40] Rather, it

> endures and stretches until European political life finally produces its specific political form, the nation-state. The Ciceronian moment is characterized by an undetermined concrete political form; what defines it, one could say, is the indefinite character of the concrete political form and the need to formulate a rule of common life in the absence of this form. In this sense, what we call the Renaissance is the culmination of the Ciceronian moment and prepares its denouement.[41]

But the arrival of the nation-state will come only as its successor form, the modern state based on modern political philosophy, is already beginning its ascendance.

Manent chooses this "Ciceronian" description because during this period, there was little original political thought and, as already noted in the discussion on Cicero, his work was the only available intellectual resource to inform political rule and change. No new political thought, and

---

39 Manent, *Metamorphoses*, 143.
40 *Metamorphoses*, 143.
41 *Metamorphoses*, 143–44.

thus no political form determined or described by political philosophy, prevailed in Europe.

> [A]t least for many centuries, it is Cicero who gathered most intelligently and wisely all the usable elements of the pagan political tradition and transformed them, but still without being able to give them an operational form. He will be the source and resource of political thought for as many as fifteen centuries. . . . Looking at these centuries, the centuries that precede the crystallization of the modern order or the construction of the modern state, I realized that what best characterized these centuries politically was paradoxically the absence or indeterminacy of political order. I have suggested the term "Ciceronian moment" to designate this long period in which the political order is indeterminate. The political order is indeterminate because it has not found its political form. Neither the empire nor the city is capable of meeting the demands of the new situation. The regime is also indeterminate, because the received doctrine of the "best regime" is of little help when the political form upon which it is based is no longer available. The only political teaching that remains relevant is Cicero's.[42]

Cicero is an iconic figure for the in-between form, as he himself is an in-between man: Cicero finds "himself in a sort of no man's land between city and empire . . . [and] caught up between ancient notions . . . and the emergence of something new."[43] In the moment Manent names for him, the indeterminacy of political order and form characterizes these "fifteen centuries of Christianity [whose] distinctive phenomenon . . . is the power or authority of the Church and the diffusion of Christian mores."[44] This

---

42 Manent, *Seeing Things Politically*, 114.

43 *Seeing Things Politically*, 112.

44 *Metamorphoses*, 150–51. Charles McCoy describes this Ciceronian moment after the demise of the city-state in similar but distinctive terms:
Was it not Aristotle's opinion that in the milieu of empire men would live at random on the margin of society, contributing little or nothing to the common good, all readily victimized by the common slavery to which the whole of human nature is subject? It is in any case a most remarkable fact that this random freedom became the most characteristic expression of the philosophies of conduct that succeeded Aristotle [Stoicism, Cynicism, Epicureanism]. Far from introducing a loftier conception of the common good, the new concepts of world empire and world humanity were accomplished by philosophies that emphasized opposition between the common and individual good. The great empire spelled the end of active intimate participation in the life of the State [i.e., city or political community] that had defined man as a "political animal."

is, as explained above, one of the two indeterminacies that provide the conditions for the emergence of the nation. The Church's force, again, lacks a political principle that is concretely useful:

> [T]he power or authority of the Church, the ubiquity of Christian rituals, mores, images, and themes, must not conceal from us that Christianity, the Christian doctrine or proposition, plays only a very weak role in political elaboration during these so-called Christian centuries. By political elaboration I understand at the same time political action, the instrumental construction, and the discourse that justifies rationally, in any case in a convincing or persuasive way, doing this rather than that, choosing one alternative over another, preferring one regime to another, and so on. . . . Christian discourse, on whatever register, is not politically operational.[45]

Indeed, the only "authoritative text" on politics provided by Christianity was St. Paul's admonition in the Letter to the Romans, "Let every person be subject to the governing authorities," which carried "no determined political content whatever. Its political meaning depends entirely on the circumstances."[46] Again, the Church's relationship to earthly politics is both close and distant, but it never replaces Cicero's political thought (itself an extension and revision of ancient thought) with its own. "Christian discourse has its own mode and domain of operation and it is effectively discriminating in the community it orders, the Church, which is ontologically separated from political communities even though it is politically mixed with them."[47] The Church is in the world but not of it. The separation of Manent's vertices of his triangle—political, philosophical, theological—holds ontologically, even as the Church must exercise its divine mission by guiding politics for salvation without crossing

---

Charles N. R. McCoy, *The Structure of Political Thought: A Study in the History of Political Ideas* (New York: McGraw-Hill Book Company, 1963), 76. Aristotle's philosophy that joined the conduct of individual men to their political association was succeeded by philosophies that emphasized only the individual. The absence of political philosophy, a philosophy of forms that incorporate the common good as essential to man's nature, is the void of Manent's Ciceronian moment. The precedent for the individualism that will mark the modern state is also present here and will influence the modern philosophy that brings the Ciceronian moment to a close.

45 Manent, *Metamorphoses*, 150–51.

46 *Metamorphoses*, 151.

47 *Metamorphoses*, 151.

operationally to that vertex. Again, the vertices influence one another and react to one another while remaining distinct.

The nation, then, emerges within a new theological order and is seen during an extended period of political disorder, and that disorder is itself a cause of the nation.

> [I]t would be judicious to accord major importance to what I would call, in Aristotelian terms, the privation of order, or to the absence of order, or to the indeterminacy of the political order. My view is that it is important to begin by saying that during all those centuries, Europe was in search of its *political* order. . . . I see in this fact—the privation or absence of order—a *cause*. The historical cause or historical causality in this "Ciceronian moment" is the disorder of European politics, along with the effort to find some way of escaping it. If one prefers positive terms, we can say that the cause is the need or desire of human beings to be governed and, preferably, to be well-governed or not too badly governed.[48]

The nation's emergence responds to the indeterminacy of the Ciceronian moment without ending it. No political philosophy provides a basis for the introduction of political order; the nation is a form that emerges during disorder and without being described in theory before being introduced in practice, nor is it described historically until the modern project begins. The Church's proposition disorders the ancient order without replacing it, and no new political principle emerges to guide politics accordingly. Likewise, the indeterminacy of the Christian proposition of salvation remains throughout this moment as well; it calls ceaselessly throughout the era and must be answered whenever it calls.

Manent claims that the Ciceronian moment lasts until modern thought and its political form, the modern state, begin to provide a new sense of order from disorder. He does not specify which "fifteen centuries" he refers to as the chronological period of the moment, but his reference to the Renaissance preparation for the denouement of the Ciceronian moment is a reference to the sixteenth-century Renaissance thinker Michel de Montaigne. So the moment might be thought to extend very generally from the death of Cicero and the transition of Rome to empire form, through the spread of Christianity in the second century and the subsequent Roman adoption of the faith, through the Protestant Reformation

---

48 Manent, *Seeing Things Politically*, 116.

to the post-Renaissance arrival of the modern era in France and England beginning in 1715. The nation does not disappear abruptly at a specific terminus of the Ciceronian moment; rather, it begins to be eclipsed by the philosophy and the attitudes that will form its successor. Manent specifies that "the nations of Europe, after having mediated Christianity in the sixteenth and seventeenth centuries, will strive in the following centuries to mediate the new universal: humanity."[49] That effort to mediate humanity will become the mark of the modern state, so we can conclude that the nation reaches its fullest realization as the Ciceronian moment closes and the modern era begins. As will be discussed below, the Reformation plays a key role in bringing the nation to its fullest stature as a form and to its denouement. Contrary to the sometimes-prevailing view that the centuries Manent is describing passed during a period of Christian order, the "Middle Ages are thus a period of very deep disorder, from which it will take Europeans a long time to free themselves. . . . [P]olitically, what is decisive is that this was a time of disorder. . . . It is the Middle Ages that are disorder, and it is modernity that orders, and that orders very systematically with the construction of the modern state, and then with the construction of the homogenous modern nation."[50] We will return to the modern order and its homogenous brand of nation later. For now, we can know that the nation that Manent sees in the Ciceronian moment is the product of disorder that flows from centuries of political indeterminacy—indeterminacy whose conclusion only comes with the end of the nation and the rise of its successor form.

THE EMERGENCE OF THE NATION IN THE CHRISTIAN KINGS

The indeterminacies of the Ciceronian moment are not resolved until the modern state arrives to bring order from disorder. In the Ciceronian moment, as and after the authority of the Roman empire collapsed, the institution that proved more capable than city or empire in responding operationally to the indeterminacies was the Christian monarchy, which is the first look of the nation form. Why was the king superior to the earlier forms in coping with the political effects of the Church and responding,

---

49 *Seeing Things Politically*, 177.
50 *Seeing Things Politically*, 117–18.

again operationally rather than philosophically or theoretically, to the European theologico-political question? As we have seen and can now elaborate with the Christian king in mind, Manent begins by explaining the specific weaknesses of the city and empire when faced with the Church.

> City-states were ideologically weak: they were "particulars" facing two "universals," the Empire and the Church. Each faction within the European city-state tended to rely on the support of one of these universals (Guelphs and Ghibellines in Florence) or to rely also on some foreign monarchy. Furthermore, the city-states had an extremely intense, indeed tumultuous, political life. The interests and passions of the citizens were naturally turned toward worldly matters. The city-state thus tended to constitute an especially closed world, one especially resistant to the Church's influence. Finally, the natural position of its citizens was to assert their independence. On these three points, monarchy presented altogether different characteristics. Too inimical structurally to the Church's claims, the city-state was at the same time too weak to set up a political form capable of successfully asserting itself against the Church while acceding to certain of its demands.[51]

The "Church's strength was essentially spiritual" even in places such as Florence where the pope had a temporal political presence.[52] It is this spiritual power that the cities found overwhelming. The surveyable limits that define the city form turn out to work against it when faced with two entities that held universal aspirations. This conflict of form "had major consequences for all of European history. The mixture of structural hostility and intrinsic weakness in the city-state's relationship with the Church explains to a large extent why Italian city-states developed, and with such aggressiveness, the first truly secular civilization in the Christian world. The great literary assertions of the solidity, independence, and nobility of the secular world were born in Italy: those of Dante, Marsilius of Padua, Boccaccio."[53] Machiavelli would take up and transform those assertions with his attack on Christianity that would plant the early seeds of modern political thought.

---

51 Manent, *Intellectual History of Liberalism*, 6.

52 *Intellectual History of Liberalism*, 6.

53 *Intellectual History of Liberalism*, 6.

Like the city, the empire failed to answer Europe's theologico-polit-ical question. Its "actual performance (as distinguished from the prestige of its idea), was in a sense even more modest than that of the city-state."[54] Charlemagne and Frederick II demonstrate that the empire form did not fail "for lack of geniuses," or for leaders and personalities who in favorable circumstances might have brought the form into successful realization after Rome and in response to the disorder following its fall. Rather, "the intrinsic difficulty of the imperial venture in an area as geographically, ethnically, and politically divided as Europe has to be taken into account."[55] Such divisions present a risk to any empire with the distension of politics over diverse areas and people. Moreover, the universal pretensions of the empire form were, in the case of Europe in the Ciceronian moment, "preempted in a way by the Church."[56] A natural empire could not coexist with the supernatural empire of the Church. With city and empire unable to flourish in the Ciceronian moment, the nation had to emerge. The vehicle for that emergence was "the absolute or national monarchy."

The Christian kings assumed the in-between national form that could govern during the disorder of the Ciceronian moment. They were in between the city and the empire in the scope of their governance or their claim to universality, and they were in between the city and empire on one hand and the Church on the other in their claim to authority. In his particular relationship with the Church, the king "is more acceptable to the church than either the citizen-body of a city or an emperor. Citizens are carried away by their passions that make them forgetful of their souls, while the emperor aims at a *plenitudo potestatis* that necessarily rivals that which is claimed by the church."[57] Manent explains how the king found the middle ground where the Church could tolerate his temporal authority:

> Like the emperor, and unlike the city-state, the king was able to lay claim to "divine right" in accordance with the Pauline axiom: "All power comes from God." (The city-states did not because their magistrates, being a plurality, did not fill the first condition for being the image or lieutenant of God: unicity.) Yet in contrast with the emperor, the king did not in principle lay

---

54 *Intellectual History of Liberalism*, 6.
55 *Intellectual History of Liberalism*, 6.
56 *Intellectual History of Liberalism*, 6.
57 Manent, *Democracy without Nations?*, 98.

claim to universal monarchy, which limited the extent of the conflict with the Church's universality. Moreover, political life in a kingdom was much more modest than in a city-state, leaving men freer to dedicate themselves to matters of the other world. Finally, the natural position of a monarch's subjects was one of obedience, which suited the Church better. Because of these three features, monarchy was much more compatible with the Church than was the city-state. Simultaneously, and paradoxically, with the assertion of divine right the secular king was in principle radically independent from the Church: the king depended directly on God. The practical consequence was that kings tended to place themselves at the head of even the religious organizations of their kingdoms.[58]

Unlike the emperor, the king did not seek to resolve the theologico-political question by becoming a divinity himself, nor by mediating between his subjects and the divine; instead, he accepted the spiritual power and authority of the Church in a way that could acknowledge the Christian proposition while allowing men to govern themselves. He might sit in the front pew, but he would not be the priest. The Church saw an acceptable, even advantageous, combination of features in the king: the "Christian king bends the will of his subjects toward obedience, thus disposing them to obey the law of God and the injunctions of the church. At the same time, the extension of his power is confined within the limits of his realm, thereby conceding to the church her exclusive claim to universality."[59] This early nation form "permitted a broad acceptance of the Church's presence and, at the same time, possessed an extremely powerful force (the monarchy by divine right) for guaranteeing the political body's independence from the Church."[60] The king can thereby "defend the prerogatives of the secular domain against the encroachments of the church. He can do so much more efficiently than the republican citizen-body, which is always prone to agitation and disruption by the promises and threats of the church. He is also more effective than the emperor, whose unwieldy domain is even less susceptible to a rational government."[61] The king

---

58 Manent, *Intellectual History of Liberalism*, 7.

59 Manent, *Democracy without Nations?*, 98.

60 Manent, *Intellectual History of Liberalism*, 7.

61 Manent, *Democracy without Nations?*, 98. Manent's use of "rational" here recalls the relative decline in rationality (and philosophy) between the city—the first form in which men become rational and political simultaneously—and empire.

could thus invoke the active political principle of Christianity (that all power is from God) to keep the Church at bay and safely contained on the faith vertex of Manent's triangle, while he went about implementing self-government in secular affairs.

The kings filled the operational gap left by the absence of Christian political elaboration while leaving the essential Christian proposition intact and unchallenged. "The historical fortune of the monarchy in the Christian world stems in large part from the fact that this political form permitted a broad acceptance of the Church's presence and, at the same time, possessed an extremely powerful political force (the monarch by divine right) for guaranteeing the political body's independence from the Church."[62] Thus the force of the "form above the form," as the Church was characterized earlier, and the force of the form itself, the kings, achieved a certain balance or equilibrium, with both forces based on Christian principles. The two indeterminacies that mark the Ciceronian moment remain, with the monarchy operating in response to both. This operational nature of the monarchy is the feature that permits its success:

> Thus European monarchy had two sides. The first, a "static" one, can be described as the union of throne and altar. The king was a good Christian and submissive son of the Church, and the Church recognized him as king by God's grace and preached obedience to his power. The second was "dynamic": the king tended naturally to assert the political body's total independence from the Church and hence to claim even the religious sovereignty of his kingdom (for example, the nomination of bishops, control of religious orders, and even, in extreme cases such as England, participation in the definition of Christianity's dogmatic content). Whereas in the Middle Ages political bodies were enveloped or incorporated by the Church, every monarchy heading toward absolutism tended to incorporate the Church within its borders. The kingdom became the supreme political body, the human association par excellence. Once this superiority was permanently established, the kingdom became the nation.[63]

In Europe, then, the nation did not arise everywhere; it emerged only where the kings eventually established "the Church's complete subordination to

---

62 Manent, *Intellectual History of Liberalism*, 7.
63 *Intellectual History of Liberalism*, 7–8.

the body politic" in secular affairs.[64] As will be seen below, the Reformation will bring the Church's complete subordination in all domains.

This act of subordinating the Church also differentiates the nation importantly from the earlier forms of city and empire: "Thus monarchy appeared to be less a regime than a *process*."[65] The nation is a form in or of motion, visible operationally in its response to the Church's claims. This explains in part why the nation is so difficult for Manent to describe or to say anything about; motion is easier to see than to define or to describe. The king is a man of constant motion. He is unable to divinize himself or to embody the highest claims and propositions of his religion, as an emperor might have done; the king's legitimacy rested instead on earthly and secular activity. He "had to *act* continuously, and act on *his* society. . . . The king could not seize and retain the things most sacred to Christianity. . . . Instead he naturally took on the task of forming the political body as one whole, essentially distinct from the Church. He undertook the establishment of the secular city, the *civitas hominum*; he made it one as he himself was one."[66] This active motion responds to the restlessness of man discussed earlier in response to the theologico-political problem and to the two indeterminacies of the Christian proposition and the desire for self-rule. It also opens the way to the restlessness, the search with no end, that will characterize modernity.

> Monarchy broke the natural rhythm of political history in Europe, and only in Europe. The natural rhythm of a body politic can be roughly described as follows. In foreign policy, it fosters territorial expansion up to the point that this expansion threatens its defeat. In domestic policy it involves either conservatism, leading to a petrification of the regime, or a displacement traditionally described as "cyclical" among political forms, predetermined and constant in their essential characteristics: aristocracy, democracy, anarchy, despotism, monarchy. But European monarchy instead set in motion a political evolution leading to the incessant (and not at all cyclical) transformation of the internal constitution of states, one perpetually producing new

64 *Intellectual History of Liberalism*, 8.
65 *Intellectual History of Liberalism*, 8.
66 *Intellectual History of Liberalism*, 9.

political and social forms. Monarchy set history in motion, and we are still living with the consequences.[67]

As we saw earlier, Manent's project in the grandest sense is to bring both the ancient political cycle and the modern democratic cycle together under the principle that man is a political animal. The need for his project arises because the nation form as initially instantiated by the Christian kings broke the older cycle without changing the human nature that was its principle.

The nation form in its monarchical beginnings "sets history in motion"; Manent's later emphasis on the initial transformation of man as pre-political to man as political animal in the formation of the city might cause us to question that claim, but it can at least help us understand the importance of the king both in his own accomplishment in responding to the two powerful indeterminacies and in laying the operational ground-work for the modern form. The "Christian king appears as a historical agent of great magnitude. He can cooperate with the apostolic mission of the church (think of Alexander VI's 1493 Bull giving the Spanish crown an apostolic quality and mission in the Indies) while striving mightily to have his government freed as far as possible from its demands."[68] The king's limited scope of territory and his success in occupying the ground in between the Church and the secular permit the development of the later, more developed nation form in which European nations "are a kind of mean between the powerful localism of the city . . . and the imperial impulse to look toward unsubdued regions beyond the horizons."[69] This discovery of the mean between the two classical forms, a mean on display not in political philosophy but in Manent's path of tracing historical events (the papal bull mentioned here is a premier example), provides the basis for the soul of a fully developed Christian nation and its realization of "the national imagination" when infused with the Christian proposition:

> The national imagination has this singular character of being at once quite ample and neatly circumscribed, a reflection of which is to be found in our meticulously drawn national boundaries. In this connection I submit this thesis, or rather, hypothesis: this searching for the mean, this circumscribing of the national imagination, presupposed and built upon Christian qualities.

67 *Intellectual History of Liberalism*, 8.
68 Manent, *Democracy without Nations?*, 98.
69 *Democracy without Nations?*, 99.

> Because every human being is my neighbor, charity alleviates the pressure of those who are naturally close to me while it draws closer those who live far away; it weakens the grasp of localism while it assuages the vertigo of faraway domination. Again, I am not suggesting that charity as a theological virtue directly produced these political effects, only that whether the virtue was effective or not the perspective derived from charity informed the imagination of our forefathers and helped them discover a middle dimension between the little and the immense, thus preparing their souls for the nation that was then in formation.[70]

This passage provides an early description of the form, the nation marked by Christianity, that Manent will eventually prescribe for a Europe lost as the modern form fades. That nation emerged during the age of Christian monarchs, when "Christian kings and princes tried to enforce a more and more exact obedience, while the *corps* of their subjects, circumscribed more and more neatly, was feeling its way toward self-awareness—that is, toward *national* self-awareness. Then came the crisis, the contentious joining together of soul and body, of obedience and fellow-feeling. I refer to the crisis of the Reformation period."[71] The faith that shaped the early nation form would undergo a traumatic division, one result of which was the final development of the nation form.

THE REFORMATION AND THE NATIONAL APPROPRIATION OF CHRISTIANITY

The nation comes to the fullness of its form under the influence and effects of the Reformation. Although Machiavelli wrote the first lines of modern political philosophy just before the time of the Reformation, those lines had not yet had their eventual impact on what would become modern political thinking. The nation state continued to emerge in the disorder of the Ciceronian moment without a compelling, guiding, or describing political philosophy. Political events rather than political thought still steer Manent's path of inquiry into the nation.

The Christian kings succeeded in subordinating the Church in the secular realm while permitting its spiritual power to prevail in faith: the

---

70 *Democracy without Nations?*, 99.
71 *Democracy without Nations?*, 99–100.

Church could execute its salvific mission. The relationship was one of both resistance and cooperation. The Reformation

> appears as the period of the nationalization of Christianity—or, more precisely, of the national appropriation of Christianity. The translation of the Bible into several national languages served as the most revealing and effective instrument of this appropriation. The national appropriation of Christianity was necessarily a subjective appropriation. Only through the crystallizing of the nation can Christian liberty coincide with Christian obedience. At the same time, Christendom was broken apart and the "commonwealth of Christian subjects," the Christian nation, was born.[72]

Manent sees in the Reformation a resolution of Christian liberty and obedience wherein the spiritual power and authority of the Church, already subdued in the secular sphere by the kings, encountered resistance in its own sphere of the spiritual as men's subjective conscience came into conflict with Church teaching or practice. "The heart of the Reformation is undeniably its contestation of the mediating character of the Catholic Church. The Catholic Church offered itself as the necessary vehicle of salvation and the necessary mediation between man and God. . . . Luther attacks this mediation very directly and very violently, and the destruction of ecclesiastical mediation will bring about profound political upheavals."[73] The central question was who or what would mediate "the relationship of mankind to the divine," and that question will be answered in political, or national, terms.[74] Political form reflects theological and political human choices.

The equilibrium according to which the kings ruled their secular domains depended on their granting the Church the authority to mediate the relationship of God and man according to its teaching and mores. The king, unlike the emperor, did not attempt to divinize himself, nor did he claim to mediate between his subjects and God. The "fate of mediation in European history," and thus the equilibrium between the kings and the Church, meets its "decisive moment" in the Reformation. "The Reformation rejected the mediation of the Church as a separate and visible institution. Instead of being saved by partaking in the sacraments of the

72 *Democracy without Nations?*, 100.
73 Manent, *Seeing Things Politically*, 122.
74 *Seeing Things Politically*, 124.

Church, instead of being saved by being part of the Church, the believer instructed by Luther is saved by faith in the Word of God, by faith alone (*sola fide*), faith produced in the soul by grace alone (*sola gratia*)." [75] Luther's theology breaks the equilibrium of Church and king and ruptures as well the Church's authority of mediation.

> [F]or Luther the mediation of Christ, without the instrument or complement of ecclesial mediation, is accomplished by the gratuitous encounter between the justice of Christ and the injustice of the sinner, an encounter in which the two poles exchange their traits—justice against sin—while remaining what they are— the one just, the other sinful. In the Catholic ordering, one was more or less a good citizen of the City of God, that is, one was more just to the extent that one was less a sinner and that grace *really* transformed nature; in the Lutheran ordering, the Christian is always *simultaneously* a just person and a sinner. [76]

The Church's notion of mediation loses its place: the "crisis of the Reformation is not only of course the moment of the rupture of Catholic *unity* but also the moment of the rupture of the great Catholic *mediation*—the mediation between reason and faith, nature and grace, this world and the next, and also paganism and Christianity." [77] Luther's reordering and the elimination of Catholic mediation in Protestant places has political consequences.

> The break with ecclesiastical mediation in effect gives practically all power, including a certain spiritual power, to the temporal prince, since the Reformation strips spiritual princes or spiritual powers—the Church and the prelates—of their legitimacy. It is the community of citizens, if we dare refer to them already in this way, or the community of believers, that is henceforth the depository of religious authority; and since the community of believers is governed by temporal princes, it is the temporal princes who inherit the mediating power. Thus, the first political consequence of the Reformation is this: a considerable increase in the power and authority of temporal princes. [78]

75 Manent, *Metamorphoses*, 311.

76 *Metamorphoses*, 312.

77 *Metamorphoses*, 313.

78 Manent, *Seeing Things Politically*, 122.

The post-Reformation rulers, at least in Protestant lands, were stronger in the spiritual sphere, and thus even stronger in the temporal sphere, than their kingly predecessors who ruled in equilibrium with the Church.

Manent sees this change in the nation most visibly in Germany. Along with the strengthening of the temporal authorities, in the absence of a universal Church that mediates, "the sacred community, the Christian community, is [also] the community as defined politically and temporally. Now, the community defined politically and temporally is the national community. . . . [T]he Lutheran Reformation was a national revolution, . . . a German revolution."[79] The Reformation is thus a real spiritual revolution, in the sense of a change in "who rules" and where governing authority resides in spiritual affairs. This revolution, the "period of the nationalization of Christianity,"[80] intensifies the particularity of the nation form by depriving nations of the universal mediation and authority of the Church.

Manent turns to Max Weber to help understand the Reformation's political consequences as they appear most sharply in Germany.

> What happens when the entire ecclesiastical state is set aside, when it loses its mediating function? The spiritual ministry is appropriated by every Christian in what is called the "universal priesthood." All Christians now share in the priestly dignity; there is no difference among them other than the one born of *Beruf.* . . . The notion of *Beruf* unites and in some way fuses the religious sense of the divine calling or vocation and the secular meaning of office, function, or profession. In the course of the development of the reformed societies, especially the Calvinist, this notion will endow the secular professions with a religious quality. [This gives] the civil authority . . . a preponderant share in the universal priesthood. The gathering of Christians is relieved of ecclesiastical order only to fall under the hand of Lutheran princes. What begins with Luther is the replacement of the Christian Church with the German nation, the Christian German nation. The reformed ordering can only be held together by the mediation of the nation. . . . The nation is the mediator between the subjective freedom of the Christian and the sovereign grace of God.[81]

---

79 *Seeing Things Politically*, 122.
80 *Seeing Things Politically*, 123.
81 Manent, *Metamorphoses*, 319–20.

This nationalization of faith and mediation and the resulting intensification and particularization of the nation form represent a significant change in the nation, one that puts it on its way to becoming its successor form, the modern state, as we will see more fully in the next chapter: "[T]he break with Catholic mediation contributed to the strengthening of elements that will be decisive in the constitution of modern Europe, that is, the sovereignty of national princes and the authority or force of the national principle."[82] The finality of the nation form appears after the Reformation, as

> nations took their form or . . . the European nation took its specific form. Each nation was obliged to make a radical choice among the Christian confessions, and this choice decisively contributed to define that nation ever after. The nation's choice was more absolute than the will of the absolute prince. Kings fulfilled the wishes of their nations more than they commanded their nations to keep or to change their religion, as the histories of both France and England testify, though with opposite results.[83]

The choices of the nations in the spiritual domain brought about the demise of their political form.

Manent's path of inquiry into events reveals that the theological changes wrought by the Protestant Reformation carry the weightiest consequences for the political form of the nation. The nation becomes its most distinctive self, in ways that endure until today, in the denouement of the form that, prepared in the Renaissance, arrives with the Reformation. The most complete fulfillment of the nation form comes as it passes into modernity.

A SECOND WORD ON THE CHURCH AS POLITICAL FORM

The force of the Church is sufficient to forge the nation form where the city and empire had been unable to respond to the needs of the Ciceronian moment. But the Church cannot answer the question of a definitive political form that would resolve the disorder of the Ciceronian moment; it

---

82 Manent, *Seeing Things Politically*, 122–23.
83 Manent, *Metamorphoses*, 320–21.

leaves that unfinished business to modernity, which will attempt to bring order in part by extending the Reformation's deprivation of the Church's spiritual authority and subordination to the political sphere both in secular matters and in spiritual affairs. The Church's simultaneous interest and uninterest in political affairs provides it no basis for a final resolution of disorder. And the Church cannot resolve the disorder, in part because it is itself the source of the disorder in the Christian proposition; finally solving the theologico-political question would involve depriving Christians of the liberty to respond to the Church's proposition of salvation that is inherent to that proposition. Christians must choose. If the Church closes off that indeterminacy, it voids the basis of its own proposition. The genius of the nation was to permit the governance of secular affairs, the self-government in the national form that answered one of the determinacies, while leaving the theological question open. The Reformation, opening the way to the modern state, sought to close off the theological question by establishing the preeminence of the political order in spiritual choice.

But there is a second, related way Manent considers, in which the Church's pressure introduced tension into the political domain, and this way is directly relevant to the question of political form both because it shaped the citizen of the nation in conflicting ways and because, in doing so, it left modern thinkers looking for a new solution. The introduction of charity as a Christian principle brought, as we have seen, a "middle dimension" between localism and distance—the too-close neighbor and the too-far-away stranger—that prepared the way for the in-between nation. But charity also brings a problem. This problem is the relationship between pagan pride as the rightful outcome of a naturally virtuous life and Christian humility, embedded in what Manent calls the Christian critique of paganism. The Church's understanding of human virtue was largely in accord with the classical or pagan understanding. But there is an important divergence, and a passage we also saw earlier can now be understood in its fuller political implications in and after the Ciceronian moment:

> [W]hat drives European development as distinctively European lies originally in the intervention of Christianity. . . . [T]he essence of the Christian proposition understood as an historical factor is that it introduces something deeply troubling, a problem that proved insurmountable, in the practical framework, the arrangement of human virtues and motives. It addresses humanity with demands of unprecedented radicality. In particular, it presents a demand that endangers the natural framework of motives and

virtues, that is, the political association. It endangers the political framework of human life by requiring human beings to love
their enemies. [T]his exorbitant requirement ... represented a
radical modification of the relationship between the political
order and the religious order.... With the Christian Church, religion becomes entirely distinct from the political order; it leaves
behind the radical dependence that tied it to the political order
in order to attain an essential independence. It lives, henceforth,
from a principle that is not nature, in particular not man's political nature, namely charity, or obedience to the commandment
to love one's enemies.[84]

This divergence amounts to a highly important Christian critique of the
pagan order. We recall that early in his work, in his 1992 essay "The Truth,
Perhaps," Manent saw this Christian critique as a central question in
history. Throughout his work, Manent turns to Augustine as the emblem-
atic and authoritative agent of this critique. To the degree the Church is a
political form, it is "a novel human association, a novel political form. This
form is elucidated with the greatest breadth and precision in Augustine's
City of God."[85] Manent returns to this work frequently to understand the
implications of the Christian critique and its elevation of charity.

In *Metamorphoses of the City*, Manent devotes three chapters (entitled "The Critique of Paganism"; "The Two Cities"; and "The Stakes of
Mediation") to explaining this critique and its consequences. In so doing,
he unfolds not just a work of political philosophy in which political form
plays a central role, but a philosophy of history that is extraordinary in its
range and depth. Here, we can focus on the aspect of Augustine's critique
of paganism that bears on the form of the nation and its transition to the
modern, the division between glory and pride for the ancients, and charity
and humility for the Christian. "Christianity came to break and heal pagan
pride. This is the axis of *The City of God*."[86] The breakage would introduce
a division between the temporal and eternal communities or cities, and
within each person, mirroring the division between the religious and political orders and producing a disorder that could not be resolved in the
earthly city, or in time. The division between the two cities is a problem
for the philosophy of history. The division within each person is a problem

---

84 Manent, *Seeing Things Politically*, 204–5.

85 Manent, *Metamorphoses*, 230.

86 *Metamorphoses*, 249.

for politics that the Church as form, the form above the political form, introduces with the principle of charity—a principle that as Manent notes, never really becomes fully operative in the earthly city and is in competition or conflict with the natural principles of the pagan world.

We can focus on this question by examining another of Manent's formulations of the contest between Church and the earthly domain for the affection of men:

> In truth, human reason . . . commands actions only because it deliberates in and over a world it considers "sub ratione boni," under the aspect of good. The world of the good, the world of goods and evils, is certainly rich with uncertainties and complexities. In particular, the properly human goods are subject to the greater claim of the superhuman goods promised by religion, an uneven match that intimidates reason and crushes the will and is always pushing man back to the condition of immaturity that he wants to leave behind.[87]

St. Augustine provides an explanation of the Church's understanding of this choice whereby the earthly or temporal goods, which are in fact good when used and enjoyed within proper bounds and not taken falsely as final goods, must be ordered to their role as means toward the end of the supernatural good. St. Augustine delineates the Church's way through the "uncertainties and complexities of the world of goods and evils." The conflict or confusion of goods that Manent describes here is really one between the invisible and future goods of the City of God and the visible and immediate goods of the earthly city. On the one hand, there is the Christian invisible: "The new city, the City of God proposed by Christianity, is invisible, its laws and mores altogether different from those of the visible city and at times opposed to them."[88] On the other is the pagan visible: "The grandeur of paganism is visibility of strength and the exclusive legitimacy of the visible. Humanity wished to deploy itself wholly in the visible realm, to be entirely visible, that is, worthy of being seen—glorious."[89] This conflict is seen decisively in what we choose to love, whether we choose love oriented toward visible, natural, and temporal goods or love seeking invisible, supernatural, and eternal goods; the conflict is another manifestation of the two freedoms (the freedom to accept the Christian proposition

---

87 Manent, *City of Man*, 198.
88 Manent, *Metamorphoses*, 213–14.
89 Manent, *Seeing Things Politically*, 189.

and the freedom for self-rule) that the nation attempts to realize simultaneously. The Church's supernatural claim offers the prospects of eternal
salvation and eternal damnation, to be accepted on faith rather than on
the evidence of the senses. Such prospects are intimidating indeed, and
meant to be; they would overwhelm the reason that, on Manent's account,
arises in man as he becomes political and seeks visible, natural goods.
The supernatural can (and should, for the Christian) thus dominate the
political and natural. The equilibrium of the nation and Church rested on
the acceptance of the properly ordered relationship of the goods of the
two cities, between the good promised by faith and the good available
through reason in the earthly city, as reflected by the equilibrium of the
authorities governing their respective goods. This arrangement offered at
least the possibility of rightly ordered love.

    But the Church's order does not yield a final order in the earthly
city. The two Christian and secular freedoms cannot be realized perfectly
because the tension for human will and reason produced by the Church
remains active, and the two cities, while intermixed, remain opposed most
importantly in their two different loves: love of self or love of God. Manent
offers the following explanation:

> Let us turn to the final chapter of book 14 [of *City of God*]. There
> we find the most synthetic and most famous formulation of the
> difference or contrast, in truth, of the opposition between the
> two cities. We are told that "two cities were created by two kinds
> of love: the earthly city was created by self-love reaching the
> point of contempt for God, the Heavenly City by the love of God
> carried as far as contempt for self." Augustine goes on to expli-
> cate the opposition in these terms:
> • One city seeks its glory from men; for the other, God as witness
>   of its conscience is its greatest glory.
> • One city is dominated by the passion to dominate; in the other,
>   mutual service is rendered by charity, the rulers by ruling, the
>   subjects by obeying.
> • One city, in its masters, loves its own strength; the other says
>   to its God: "I will love you, Lord, my strength."[90]

The glory, domination, and strength of man are the source of pride;
humility demands deference to God and earthly rulers whose power
derives from him. Europeans in the age of the nation are taught by pagan

---

90 Manent, *Metamorphoses*, 276.

philosophy and history to pursue the pride of the earthly city; they are taught by the Church to embrace humility. "The Christian religion is essentially corrupting in that it divides man by adding to rational or natural motives—to properly human motives—other motives that claim to be supernatural or superior to reason. Man is thus compelled to 'see double' and no longer knows how to orient himself rationally in the world. In short, 'two worlds are too many, only one was needed.'"[91] These last words are those of Montesquieu, one of the first modern thinkers. The moderns will disrupt the equilibrium of authority that characterized the age of the nation in their effort to definitively leave behind man's immaturity and resolve the disorder and division that national man faced, restoring and raising to supremacy the rationality that the Church's supernatural claims of salvation and introduction of charity threatened. With its introduction of the principle of charity and the resultant conflict in human motives, Christianity retarded the action of men: "The Church was essentially a brake on human activity; it tended to dissuade people from doing whatever they might do in this world."[92] The moderns will seek to remove that brake. In political terms, this means liberal and modern thinkers will "institutionalize the sovereignty of the human will,"[93] as Manent claims in his 1993 essay on "Christianity and Democracy" and as will be explored in the next chapter.

THE THREE WAVES OF HISTORY

Manent's project of investigating political form, as indicated just now, fits within a larger philosophy of history that is most fully developed in his *Metamorphoses of the City*. The era of the nation is at the midpoint of that history, so the discussion of the nation presents a ripe opportunity to reflect on how the nation form in particular reflects the forms that came before and the form that succeeded it. This reflection also reminds us that Manent does not schematize history or politics neatly. The forms mix with and play off of each other.

---

[91] Manent, *City of Man*, 194.
[92] Manent, *Seeing Things Politically*, 123.
[93] Manent, "Christianity and Democracy," 99.

Manent sees a motion in European history that he characterizes as
three great waves: the pagan, the Christian, and the modern.[94] In each
wave, the agent of mediation between the human and divine changes.
Manent draws from Plato to identify mediation in the pagan wave. The
mediation that concerns Manent here is not that of the pagan gods of
Athens. Rather, it emerges from Plato's *Republic* and *Symposium*. Manent
recalls Socrates's instruction in the *Republic* that the guardians would hear
only stories that, contrary to Homer and the traditional myths of the city,
demonstrate the truth that the gods are good and do not change form. But
the Platonic Socrates's reform of the city's theology, as the city form gives
way to the empire, changes meaning when it is no longer understood in the
context "of the closed city but must be formulated in the open space of the
Greco-Roman empire."[95] The change of form produces a change in theological understanding; politics affects religion. This move in the context
of Platonic thought from the civic form to the imperial form produces a
"politically unmoored Platonism, [a] 'depoliticized' Platonism . . . that,
through a process whose shameful character Augustine unflaggingly
denounces at the same time he emphasizes its strange logical or even
ontological necessity, [means] the only mediators that can be envisaged
are the *demons*."[96] The empire is more distended, less politically concentrated than the city; Plato's theology is accordingly distended as it is placed
in the more distended, less politically pure form. The interpretation of later
Platonists, whose work Augustine read, will "inflect or 'concretize' the
understanding of the 'daemon' in such a way that Augustine will have no
difficulty in concluding that it is indeed a 'bad angel.' . . . [T]he Platonist
reform, in identifying the right idea of the true God or coming close to it,
induced a religion that adores the demons, with all the absurd or sordid

---

94 Leo Strauss identified "three waves" of modern thinking: Machiavelli's rejection of the
philosophical and theological tradition regarding moral nature and his reinterpretation of
virtue (followed by Hobbes's reinterpretation of natural right), Rousseau's notion of the
general will and its actualization in the historical process, and Nietzsche's "will to power"
and nihilism. See Leo Strauss, "The Three Waves of Modernity," in *An Introduction to
Political Philosophy: Ten Essays by Leo Strauss*, ed. Hilail Gildin (Detroit, MI: Wayne State
University Press, 1989), 81–98. With Manent's "three waves" thesis, he may be saluting
Strauss and simultaneously distinguishing his own work from Strauss's by extending the
decisive "waves" over greater swathes of time that include both the premodern and the
modern.

95 Manent, *Metamorphoses*, 307.

96 *Metamorphoses*, 308.

magical practices this adoration entailed."[97] This is the pagan notion of mediation critiqued by Augustine in *City of God*.

The three waves of European history, then, begin with this pagan mediation associated with the city and empire forms (originating in the former and deformed in the latter), followed by the Christian wave with the nation form, washing finally into the modern wave with the modern state characterized by "democracy or modern freedom."[98]

> Thus, in depoliticized or imperial paganism, mediation is "demonic," the demon being understood as the "erotic" dynamism of the human soul highlighted by Plato or, more and more, as a distinct spiritual substance. In Christianity the mediation is that of Christ, who is man and God, and the Church is mediating as "the body of Christ." In the modern order of human rights, so-called subjective rights, it seems there is no longer any mediation. Since the mediator is an intermediary between humans and gods or the divine and that the divine or relationship with the divine is no longer publicly acknowledged in our regimes— it is a private matter, *Privatsache*—one does not see where to look among us for the mediator or mediation. But if that is true, then an essential element of the human world, in any event an element that was essential during the two preceding waves of our history—the pagan and the Christian—has disappeared for us.[99]

Perhaps nowhere does Manent better explain the relationship between the human soul and the political form than in this explication of the three waves of mediation, which correlate to three eras of political form. Again, the nation is in the middle wave, in between the pagan and the modern. We might also add that the depoliticization of the pagan mediation at the time of the transition from city to empire occurs at the beginning of the disorder of the Ciceronian moment. Christianity cannot repair that disorder, as we have seen and see now in another light. The mediation of Christ takes place in the City of God both for those in heaven and for those in this life whose love of the eternal is properly ordered, not for those who insist on the love of the earthly city. This mediation sits alongside or above politics, leaving room for human action. The moderns, as we will see in the next chapter and as Manent has just said, ultimately seek to sweep

---

97 *Metamorphoses*, 308–9.

98 Manent, *Seeing Things Politically*, 192.

99 Manent, *Metamorphoses*, 310–11.

mediation off the board of politics; human action will be isolated from the divine, and on its own. Manent draws together his thinking on the three waves in *Seeing Things Politically*:

> I would compare the West to a succession of three waves, each emerging from the thrust and the failures of the preceding. This process involves succession and superposition, for each wave rests on the one that preceded it, the one it covers but that carries it along. It follows that, however modern we may wish to be, we cannot be content to allow ourselves to be carried along by the latest wave. We must . . . swim in deep waters, since beneath us lie in successive levels the distinct layers of pagan glory, Christian conscience, and modern rights. The wave that carries us must not make us forget the waves that carry it.[100]

The wave of the middle era, the era of Christian mediation and the nation form, washes into the modern wave beginning with the Reformation. Manent specifies that the modern began distinctly in 1715, but the end of the nation form and the introduction of the modern state are much less precise. The transition is evident in nineteenth-century France and Germany, with their respective foundations in revolution and historical identity.[101] "And there is no doubt that, at the end of the 19th century and still at the beginning of the 20th, Europeans, in different nations, had the sense of inhabiting the most fully developed political form and human association,"[102] the nation. We have seen as well that the references of the nation—language, faith, geography—remain visible and active today even if their force has been substantially weakened. Just as it took a long time for the nation to emerge in the Ciceronian moment, it has taken a long time for its successor, the modern state, to displace it. We will now turn to that form with its dismal effects and implications.

---

[100] Manent, *Seeing Things Politically*, 192.

[101] Manent, *Intellectual History of Liberalism*, 117.

[102] Manent, *Seeing Things Politically*, 145.

Chapter Five

THE MODERN STATE

MANENT RELIES HEAVILY ON ARISTOTLE AND AUGUSTINE in understanding the "what is" of past and contemporary politics, and he is not the first observer of politics to find the work of St. Augustine helpful in understanding the present moment. We can begin to examine his account of the modern state by turning to another thinker of classical and Augustinian bent who saw, in very similar ways, what Manent will find in the modern form. In his 1952 work *Les métamorphoses de la cité de Dieu*, one of France's leading minds, Étienne Gilson, saw around him an effort to defy Augustine and bring about the City of God on earth, in temporal affairs and by human means. Gilson did not use the language of political form, but his observations were clearly of a political as well as a philosophical or theological nature. He believed that some new form of human unity was indeed coming into being:

> The pains of the contemporary world are those of a childbirth, and what is being born at such great pain is a universal human society that will be for today's states what they themselves have become for the formerly divided peoples of which they are composed, as these peoples themselves seem to have been, still further back, in their families, clans, and tribes, which they completed by achieving unity. How is this ideal being born? And can it be realized outside the spiritual climate under which it originated? Such is the problem. . . . What characterizes these events to which we are witnesses, what distinguishes them from all that came before since the origins of history, is their global or . . . planetary character.[1]

---

1 Étienne Gilson, *Les métamorphoses de la cité de Dieu* (Louvain: Publications Universi-taires de Louvain, 1952), 1. The title in English is *Metamorphoses of the City of God*.
   Les doleurs du monde contemporain sont celles d'un enfantement, et ce qui naît à si grand'peine est une société humaine universelle, qui serait aux États

Gilson recognized that the notion of a new, universal political association that grows from and goes beyond the boundaries of the nation to encompass all of mankind was very much alive in post-World War II Europe. The roots of such a notion of a universal political community were present in Western thought as far back as Cicero, as developed in his *De Legibus*:

> And since right reason is Law, we must believe that men have Law also in common with the gods. Further, those who share Law must also share justice; and those who share these are to be regarded as members of the same commonwealth. If indeed they obey the same authorities and powers, this is true in a far greater degree; but as a matter of fact they do obey this celestial system, the divine mind, and the God of transcendent power. Hence we must now conceive of this whole universe as one commonwealth of which both gods and men are members.[2]

In Christian thinking, Cicero's universal commonwealth "of gods and men" becomes the City of God described by St. Augustine, intermixed with its distinct, temporal counterpart, the earthly city. Gilson remarks,

> When Augustine himself speaks of a "city," the term must be understood then in the figurative, or as he says, the "mystical" sense. There is on the one hand the society or city of all men who, loving God in Christ, are predestined to rule eternally with him, and on the other hand, there is a city of all men who, not loving God, are predestined to submit with the demons to eternal punishment. Augustine thus never conceived the idea of a single universal society, but of two that are universal at least in this sense that every man, whoever he is, is necessarily citizen of one or the other, predestined even to be of one or the other.[3]

---

d'aujourd'hui ce qu'eux-mêmes sont devenus pour les peuples autrefois divisés dont ils se composent, comme ces peuples eux-mêmes semblent l'avoir été, plus anciennement encore, en ces familles, clans et tribus, dont ils ont fini par assurer l'unité. Comment cet idéal est-il né? Et peut-il se réaliser hors du climat spirituel sous lequel il a pris naissance, tel est le problème. . . . Ce qui caractérise les événements dont nous sommes témoins, ce qui les distingue de tous ceux qui les ont précédés depuis les origines de l'histoire, c'est leur caractère mondial . . . ou . . . planétaire.

2 Cicero, *De Legibus*, translated by Clinton Walker Keyes (Cambridge, MA: Harvard University Press, 1928), 1.7.23.

3 Gilson, *Les métamorphoses de la cité de Dieu*, 49.

Lorsque Augustin lui-même parle d'une 'cité', c'est donc au sens figuré, ou même, comme il le dit, 'mystique', que ce terme doit être entendu. Il y a, d'une part, la société, ou cité, de tous les hommes qui, aimant Dieu dans le Christ, sont

Gilson does not object to secular progress toward universal understanding in all fields, such as science, letters, law, and philosophy, that can bring men closer together. His book is, rather, a warning against the temptation to seek to introduce the final, universal City of God on earth, using the means and motives of the earthly city. Like Manent in his path of studying political philosophy to understand political form, Gilson undertakes an investigation of the thinking that brought Europe to this temptation in the ashes of World War II, relying on the work of, inter alia, Dante, Campanella, Bacon, Leibniz, and Comte. He describes the problem:

> The worst error would be to imagine Europe, or even humanity, as a perfection of the notion of the universal church or as a veritable City of God. In whatever way they organize and unify, these temporal societies will never form anything other than a society itself temporal, more vast, but of the same nature. That this society has spiritual links, and that certain of these links are of a universal value, nothing is more certain. . . . But the amplitude of a society does not change the essence.[4]

And Gilson warns against the consequences of modern man's attempts, relying on purely human efforts without Christianity as mediator, to achieve the eternal universality that the Church, the form above or behind the form of the European nation in Manent's account, claims for itself:

> It remains, then, that . . . the temporal society of men will never realize [anything] other than an image of the supernatural and perfect [society] that is the City of God. The Church first proposed to men, through St. Augustine, the ideal of a society of children of God united to Him, and among themselves by the links of faith, of hope, and of charity. In effect, they [who would build the

---

prédestinés à règner éternellement avec lui, et, d'autre part, il y a la cité de tous les hommes qui, n'aimant pas Dieu, sont prédestinés à subir avec les démons un éternel supplice. Augustin n'a donc jamais conçu l'idée d'une société universelle unique, mais de deux, qui sont universelles au moins en ce sens que tout homme, quelqu'il soit, est nécessairement citoyen de l'une ou de l'autre, prédestiné même soit à l'une soit à l'autre.

4 *Les métamorphoses de la cité de Dieu*, 283.

La pire erreur serait d'imaginer l'Europe, ou même l'Humanité, comme un perfectionnement de la notion d'église universelle ou comme la véritable Cité de Dieu. De quelque manière qu'elles s'organisent et s'unissent, des sociétés temporelles ne formeront jamais qu'une société elle-même temporelle, plus vaste, mais de même nature. Que cette société ait des liens spirituels, et que certains de ces liens soient de valeur universelle, rien n'est plus certain. . . . Mais l'ampleur d'une société n'en change pas l'essence.

City of God without the Church] say, [such an ideal] is the only society worthy of the name, but we are going to do it ourselves, on this earth, with the aim of man and by his own means. We know the result, and moreover St. Augustine had foreseen it. It is called Babel, or confusion. It is the typical case of those ideas of which G. K. Chesterton said the world is full: a Christian idea become mad.[5]

This confusion, or madness, is the signal feature that Manent attributes to the modern state in its final and contemporary stage. Gilson, from an explicitly Christian philosophical perspective that sets him apart from Manent's determination to remain oriented in the philosophy-politics-religion triangle without committing to any vertex, describes the metamorphoses of the European understanding of the universal City of God that brought Europe to its mistaken attempt to create a final, universal political community on earth, without God or the Church—a secular effort to demystify the City of God. Manent traces the changes in European political form through poetic and political thought and events, from pre-political and pre-philosophical man to political man in the city, through empire and nation, to reach his account of the modern state as the effort to bring about a political form unifying all men in all places without reference to the divine. And, as with Gilson's Christian interpretation, Manent argues that the Christianity that separated the political and religious associations in the nation makes their rejoining impossible:

It is the figure of Jesus Christ that renders the ever-imminent reabsorption of the religious association into the political association impossible. It is the words he spoke that can be said to command the respect of the most powerful motives of nature, however little power they have to change the actual conduct of human beings. Joined to the sacrifice that seals them, these words guarantee that [all human enmity] has been overcome. In

---

5 *Les métamorphoses de la cité de Dieu*, 288.

Il reste donc que, dans la mesure où elle se ferra, la société temporelle des hommes ne réaliser jamais qu'une image de la société surnaturelle et parfaite qu'est la Cité de Dieu. L'Église a d'abord proposé aux hommes, par saint Augustin, l'idéal d'une société des enfants de Dieu unis à lui, et entre eux, par les liens de la foi, de l'espérance et de la charité. En effet, se sont-ils dit, c'est la seule société digne de ce nom, mais nous allons la faire nous-mêmes, sur cette terre, en vue de l'homme et par ses propres moyens. On sait le résultat, et saint Augustin l'avait d'ailleurs prévu. Il se nomme Babel, ou la confusion. C'est le cas type de ces idées dont G. K. Chesterton disait que le monde est plein: une idée chrétienne devenue folle.

> more immediately theological terms, the mediation of the Son,
> which is indispensable to reach the Father—the mediation of
> him in whom all enmity meets its death—prevents the Father
> from being enlisted in the service of the city and prevents Chris-
> tianity from producing a "political theology."[6]

Christianity makes impossible a universal political association that mediates all humanity without the Church; to achieve such a universality, the
modern state will have to exclude God, which will prove to be a disastrous
and futile effort. Gilson's metamorphoses of the understanding of God's
city, and Manent's metamorphoses of the city into other forms, converge
in the modern moment that both observe acutely.

    This convergence points us back to the premodern view of man that
is shared by Hellenic philosophy and the Church, the view that accepts
a common moral nature according to which man must act. The modern
state is opposed to, and will seek to flee or escape, the limits that this
nature supposedly imposes. Aristotle looked around and saw the city
and people acting in the city. He sought a science of politics and human
action to describe those phenomena. Manent looks around and sees the
modern state, and he seeks a science of that state and human action, or
inaction, within it. He finds in the modern a rejection of the possibility
of a classical science of the human and of politics, and he pursues an
inquiry that will permit a renewed understanding of the human. Given
the constant of human nature as political animal, that inquiry must necessarily account for how the modern state came to be after the forms that
preceded it—how it came to be from the natural forms of city and empire,
through the nation under the pressure of the Church. All of Manent's work
points to this account of what he sees around him in Europe today, to the
"what is" of the politics of our moment. His two paths of investigation of
political thought and political events come together in the modern form;
unlike the nation, which arose and endured in a time lacking original
political thought, the modern state rests on a vast body of thought that
shapes the events that lead to the moment he and Gilson observe. Unlike
the nation, which governed in a period of disorder, the modern state
achieves order after extended, and sometimes critically contradictory,
intellectual effort. Manent devotes much of his work to explaining how
modern political thought produced the modern state, but four particular
books stand out: *An Intellectual History of Liberalism*, *The City of Man*, *A*

---

6 Manent, *Seeing Things Politically*, 206.

World beyond Politics?, and *Metamorphoses of the City*. His most recent book-length work, *La loi naturelle et les droits d l'homme*, recapitulates some of his earlier thinking in a specifically Christian context. Much of this chapter will be devoted to a book-by-book exposition of these five works. Before turning to those accounts, we will present a summary of the modern state form as Manent sees it, drawing from several sources including his *Democracy without Nations?* What emerges is a picture of a political form that, as Gilson warned, seeks to encompass all of mankind in a universal association on man's terms, without God, a form that fails man in every important respect.

THE MODERN STATE

As seen earlier, Manent's inquiry is shaped by his interest in the "modern difference." Europeans want to be modern—a decision they made at a particular moment in the late seventeenth and early eighteenth centuries—though what "modern" is remains to Manent a mystery only partly resolved. To be modern is to be governed by reason alone, without faith, yet the same era of philosophy that taught this precept has also told us that reason is wrong or unreliable. The modern does not seek a principle of nature by which to act, but rather, with Montesquieu, finds in whatever comes along the factual truth of history with no reference to nature. Nature is no longer the source of "what is," freeing the human mind to determine reality at any moment in history, freed of the tension between the particular and the universal that was always present in nature. Classical notions of law and virtue are now seen to be confining rather than liberating, and modern man "has become a runner and will go on running until the end of the world":[7] running from the constraints of nature and law and seeking not the good but only an escape from the evils around him. The natural relationships of family and city are part of the nature that must be fled. Moderns are conscious both of the ancient understanding of nature and of the modern rejection of it. Only History can accommodate this conflict, and History discards the Being of nature and law; historicism replaces metaphysics and ontology. This brief summary conveys the modern difference that the modern political form will reflect.

Early in his investigation, Manent identifies the main features of the modern state: "One can agree without too much difficulty as to the

---

7 Manent, *City of Man*, 48.

principal elements of the modern regime, namely, liberal democracy (they are legible in our institutions as well as books). All legitimacy is founded on individual or collective consent; men possess equal rights; law is sovereign; the state is distinct from society and is the latter's representative instrument."[8] Manent refers here to the modern "regime" that we can see and that we live under, but these are also the characteristic of the modern form that "wants to institutionalize the sovereignty of the human will."[9] The modern project to "establish political legitimacy on the will of the human individual has been led to its completion."[10] This feature of the dominance of will is common to all modern regimes and thus to the modern form.[11] The modern form recognizes

> only free and equal individuals, [with] no legitimacy except that founded on their will. . . . Not only does it say nothing about God, but it says nothing, or very little, about the world and even about man. However, by positing that the political body has for its only rule or law the will of the individuals who compose it, it deprives the law of God of all political authority or validity, whether the latter is conceived as explicitly revealed or solely inscribed in the nature of man. It refuses all authority to that which has by definition, naturally or supernaturally, the highest authority.[12]

The modern form has no place for the authority of nature or God, exactly the situation foreseen also by Gilson. Thirty years after his own early claims regarding the attributes of the modern state, Manent continues to argue in very similar terms: "[T]he modern political framework, a framework within which the great notions by which we interpret and organize our lives are deployed with an extraordinary authority: man is determined by society, man is a historical being, man is a being who has rights."[13] This

---

8 Manent, "The Truth, Perhaps," 36.

9 Manent, "Christianity and Democracy," 99.

10 "Christianity and Democracy," 101.

11 This aspect of the modern form explains the fact that all modern Western regimes, and those derived from modern Western thinking including communist and fascist regimes or those established in the wake of Western decolonization, purport to be elected or otherwise legitimized by elections or expressions of the popular will. Such claims from regimes on every continent over the last century suggest the global effects of modern political thought, though obviously with widely divergent degrees of authenticity and rootedness.

12 "Christianity and Democracy," 99.

13 Manent, *Seeing Things Politically*, 89.

is the anthropology of the modern political form, in which man's nature under divine or natural law plays no role.

As with the nation, Manent describes the modern state without precisely defining it. Its existence emerges from the nation, which as a form remains active. There is no precise "tipping point" from nation to modern state, and at times Manent will describe the form as "nation-state" in its later existence after modern political thinking has taken effect, as "modern nation," or as "modern state." The modern state's roots are in the nation, with a nationalism accelerated by the Protestant Reformation, and decisively shaped by the modern thought that sought to bring political order and close the centuries-long Ciceronian moment. In all cases of this form, the prevailing characteristics of the modern state and its modern inhabitants are those described above, to a greater or lesser degree depending on time and place; as with the nation, we know the modern state when we see its features dominating a political association in ways distinct from the earlier forms.

The most prominent feature of the modern state is "democracy." As democratic practices replaced monarchies, "the democratic idea justified and nourished the love each people naturally has for itself."[14] Democracy supported the particularity of the nation. But ongoing democratization reversed that effect. "But now, in the name of democracy, this love is criticized and mocked. And what future can human *association* have if no particular group, no 'communion,' no people is legitimate any longer? What becomes of us if only human *generality* is legitimate?"[15] This fate is the urgent question that we are left with as the modern political form has democratized away from the nation, and to which we will return below.

To help place the modern form historically within the progress of democratization, which in the terms of Tocqueville is "a movement toward an ever-greater equality of conditions,"[16] and to clarify that the motion of political form is not a step-by-step or linear historical system, Manent proposes a consideration of two dates and three concentric circles. "The two dates most generally acknowledged to have structured or punctuated the development of modern European democracy are separated by more than a century: 1848 and 1968."[17] The year 1848 marks roughly 150 years

---

14 Manent, *Democracy without Nations?*, 9.
15 *Democracy without Nations?*, 9.
16 *Democracy without Nations?*, 11.
17 *Democracy without Nations?*, 12.

from the early eighteenth-century origins of the modern that Manent has identified in France: "1848 was the year of the *Communist Manifesto* and those bloody June days in Paris when the National Guard crushed the Paris workers' uprising—one the closing of the national workshops had provoked. In short, 1848 was the initial explosion of *the social question*, the declaration of class warfare, and the establishment of class struggle."[18] The year 1968, with student riots in France and elsewhere, marked "the last burst of the torch that had first been lit in 1848. . . . From 1848 to 1968: it seems to me that axial core, the inner circle—the magma, one might say—of our modern history. Then, *the* problem of democracy was called 'the social question,'"[19] the question posed most acutely by Marx. The social question involved what to do about the inequalities in society in the context of the then-recent beginnings of democratization.

But as Manent explains, 1848 was not the first moment of democracy. "Democracy . . . did not come into existence in 1848. . . . The greatest book ever written on democracy was published in 1835 and 1840." [20] Tocqueville's *Democracy in America* both compared the French and American versions of revolution and democracy, and the democratic age with the aristocratic age that preceded it. Both of those ages, of course, operated with the form of the nation. Democracy appears with American independence in 1776, and it is institutionalized differently in America than in revolutionary France in 1789. The period between 1776 and 1848 of contending means of democratic institutionalization precedes the period of the social question, and Manent labels this a "Tocquevillian period."[21] But while the social question suspended the Tocquevillian period of consideration of democratic institutions, it did not conclusively finish it. The Tocquevillian critique emerges again after 1968 in the form of a critique of the totalitarian states. This reassertion of the Tocquevillian critique, according to Manent, "was 'an explosion of mildness' or 'softness,' an explosion of what Tocqueville called 'democratic mildness.' Thus, it also marked an upsurge of democratic sentiment par excellence, that of 'human resemblance.'"[22] Manent's insight here explains what Gilson saw in postwar Europe's universalist aspirations, which awaited

---

18 *Democracy without Nations?*, 12.

19 *Democracy without Nations?*, 12.

20 *Democracy without Nations?*, 12–13.

21 *Democracy without Nations?*, 13.

22 *Democracy without Nations?*, 14.

the demise of the social question as the dominant European intellectual motif in order to emerge fully. That demise opened the way to the later stages of the modern state, or as we will see shortly, the democratic empire.

Manent identifies the attacks of September 11, 2001, as a major milestone that marked the end of the reasserted Tocquevillian critique that began in 1968 in response to the totalitarian experience. He leaves this claim somewhat mysterious, though as we will see shortly it is a date that appears to usher in a new divergence between Europe and the United States, whereby Europe will seek a path of democracy disconnected from its national roots. The year 2001 is the end of an era, and Manent now has the historical resources necessary to place the modern nation-state in its full context. To visualize Manent's understanding, he invites us to

> imagine three concentric circles arranged on a temporal axis. The first circle is that of the social question, its diameter running from 1848 to 1968; the second circle concerns the sovereignty of the people, with its diameter joining 1776 and 2001; finally there is the third circle, that of the sovereign nation-state. Its diameter runs from approximately 1651—the year Hobbes published *Leviathan* and sketched the architectural plan of the modern state to a date we cannot as yet give. But that state will become apparent when the nation-state gives way to another political form—if indeed that moment ever comes.[23]

Thus we can now understand that, chronologically, the modern form, coming out of the acceleration of nationalization after the Protestant Reformation, has an intellectual starting point with Hobbes (with Machiavelli as a critical precursor); moves through and is shaped by the subsequent thought of the moderns such as Montesquieu; and sees definitive events in 1776 and 1789, 1848, 1968, and 2001. The era of the modern state is some 350 years old and still underway.

Democracy provides the means by which the modern state realizes the imposition of human will under the auspices of "individual or collective consent." Manent characterizes the contemporary stage of modern state democracy as "democratic empire," a label he can apply to both Europe and the United States, though with different emphases and results. In the European instantiation, democratic empire follows from the weakening of the nation with its particular claims and characteristics:

23 *Democracy without Nations?*, 15.

The weakening of the European nations weakens [the] framework in which the similar and the different [within and among
nations] can be recognized and take on meaning. It is not surpris-
ing, therefore, that we seek refuge in a vague idea of human
unity, an imminent unity that would resolve by a kind of internal necessity the problem of human order we no longer know
how to state. This idea takes rather different forms depending on
whether one looks at "old Europe" or its cross-Atlantic progeny.
But if European quietism presents a vivid contrast to American
activism, the two are nonetheless versions of what one might
call "democratic empire." Both sides propose such an empire
with equal conviction and even obstinacy.[24]

The form of empire, to recall its description, seeks to bring as much as
possible under its rule; it aspires to the universal in contrast to the defining
limits of the city. In the case of the United States, "one central nation, the
model and guardian of democracy, encourages all peoples, whoever and
wherever they are, to establish a democratic regime and cultivate democratic mores."[25] The American modern state, more than Europe, retains
an interest in the value of the nation form, while seeking the universal
advancement of democracy. Its version of "democratic empire is characterized by a harmonious mixture of older elements, such as the maintenance of nations and willingness to take recourse to force, with newer
elements. The primary newer element is the vision of a united world in
which collective differences will no longer be truly meaningful or significant."[26] Europe, on the other hand, substitutes for the American central
notion of democracy promotion,

---

24 *Democracy without Nations?*, 6. Manent is writing here around 2005 to 2006, in the
wake of the American invasions of Afghanistan and Iraq that produced considerable
transatlantic tension, especially between the United States and what Secretary of Defense
Donald Rumsfeld called "the old Europe" of Western European nations, particularly France
and Germany. President George W. Bush's second inaugural address in January 2005
proclaimed his "freedom agenda" with a strong claim that global democracy promotion was
both in American and Western interests and in accord with "America's ideal of freedom":
"So it is the policy of the United States to seek and support the growth of democratic
movements and institutions in every nation and culture, with the ultimate goal of ending
tyranny in our world." George W. Bush, "Second Inaugural Address," January 20, 2005,
NPR, transcript, https://www.npr.org/templates/story/story.php?storyId=4460172. The
American tradition of such universal claims goes back to the Declaration of Independence,
and they became more active as operational principles around the time of the Spanish-
American War, followed by the presidency of Woodrow Wilson.

25 Manent, *Democracy without Nations?*, 6.

26 *Democracy without Nations?*, 6–7.

a central human *agency*. This agency was born . . . on either side of the Rhine. But it soon detached itself from any particular territory or people and is now occupied with extending the area of "pure democracy," . . . democracy without a people—that is, democratic *governance*, which is very respectful of human rights but detached from any collective deliberation. The European version of democratic empire distinguishes itself by the radicality with which it detaches democracy from every real people and constructs a *kratos* without a *dèmos*. What now possesses *kratos* is the very idea of democracy. The European empire, however, has one thing in common with the American version: it too is animated by a vision of a world in which no collective difference is significant.[27]

This last phase of the development of the modern state produces, in both Europe and the United States, "an explosion of human unity [that] makes both groups less capable of actually seeing the present state of the world. Occupied with building our twin towers of Babel, we no longer appreciate the fact that separations between and among human groups cannot be entirely overcome."[28] Thus, as Gilson feared, Manent sees in the desire for a universalism that seeks the City of God without God (substituting democracy for the divine and for nature) the Babel and confusion of the modern state.

The modern state, then, is, at least in Europe, the democratic nation that has traded its decisive nationhood for a pure, unpeopled democracy that installs human will as *kratos,* even as rump nations remain a part of the lives of their peoples. Manent's central investigation into the movement of political form aims to explain how this came about from the earlier forms that Europe had seen. Manent's allusion to the placement of *kratos* in the "very idea of democracy" provides an important key. One distinction above all underlies Manent's view of the modern state: city and empire, the natural political forms, "developed spontaneously, that is, in the absence of any prior idea or conception."[29] It can be described as

---

27 *Democracy without Nations?*, 7.

28 *Democracy without Nations?*, 7. Again, writing in the first decade after the attacks of September 11, 2001, Manent's allusion to the "twin towers" of Babel perhaps also alludes to the twin towers of the World Trade Center, which symbolized global or universal economic aspirations.

29 Manent, *Seeing Things Politically*, 109.

a science, as Aristotle and to some degree Cicero did, but its development did not follow a philosophical prescription—"unlike the modern state."[30]

> [I]n Greek politics and the science of politics, experience and the interpretation of experience came to light together, or at least in proximity and intimacy that were never to be found again. Modern political science—the one that is not Greek—will on the contrary always find itself confronted with the necessity of *deliberately* joining these two aspects that in Greece were joined *naturally*. It must be elaborated in a world where *there already is* an authoritative political science, that of the Greeks, especially Aristotle's. Modern political science will thus necessarily have a very deliberate and "constructed" character. I seek in vain for the proper adjective to give an idea of this specific effort that modern political science must make to bring together science and experience. In any case, this effort necessarily encounters the alternative of whether to bear more (or first of all) upon science or more (or first of all) upon experience. Of course, the choice between the two ways is not arbitrary. It is conditioned in every epoch by the relative situation of science and experience.[31]

Manent's investigation of modern thought thus examines "two great versions of modern political science, . . . one that emphasizes science and one that emphasizes experience."[32] In both cases, the adjective that Manent is seeking here to describe modern political science is supplied by Francis Slade: the modern state is the form that is "thought into existence" or constructed intellectually before manifesting itself in a place or time. Slade writes,

> Modern political philosophy created a unique new political form, the state, one unassimilable to any of the well-known regimes because the state is intended to replace them all. It is a form that supplanted, one might say dissolved, all previous political forms in the West and which has been exported throughout the world. As Hegel puts it, "The state is universal in form, a form whose essential principle is thought." Modern political philosophy achieved this by constructing an understanding of government as such, something entirely different from the regimes, or

---

30 Manent, *Democracy without Nations?*, 7.

31 Manent, *Metamorphoses*, 21.

32 *Metamorphoses*, 21.

forms of political rule, which had been the concern of premodern
political philosophy. . . . Modern political philosophy reduces all
regimes to government, for government is what every regime is.[33]

Existing in thought as the creation or construction of political thinkers
who seek comprehensively to fill the philosophical void of the Ciceronian
moment, the modern state is thought and not seen. Manent has insisted
on the visibility of the ancient city; Slade agrees and draws the distinction
with the modern form: "The state as a political form is not visible, as the
regimes are, in the obvious, the almost inevitable, the almost natural articulations of a large society. The state does not 'appear.'"[34] It is, as Manent
says, an idea that develops in the deliberate joining of prescriptive science
and experience. It thus joins two vertices of Manent's triangle, philosophy
and political events, seeking to found itself entirely on reason (in philosophy) and to control events (in politics) while excluding the third vertex
of religion.

Manent's work in the five major volumes to which we now turn
explains how various aspects of this idea of the modern state came to be,
and what it means. Of the five works considered here, the initial volume,
An Intellectual History of Liberalism, is the most important for understanding Manent's science of the modern political form. Liberal ideas
were the intellectual elements of the modern state, and liberal thinkers
developed these elements and constructed the modern form in their
minds before modern people adopted it as their political association. The
main elements of the modern state are thus captured in this first work,
especially in Manent's appraisal of Machiavelli and Hobbes, to which he
returns constantly in his later work. After *An Intellectual History of Liberalism*, Manent's work begins to enlarge toward what might be described as
a philosophy of history. This philosophy, though, is not one of the "historicisms of *almost* irresistible plausibility" mentioned earlier in discussing
Manent's rejection of such historicism. Manent's philosophy of history is
not about a *Geist* that realizes itself in historical logic or a schema of class
warfare—as we saw in chapter 1, Manent had rejected Marxism early in his
academic career. What he has said he is seeking, rather, is a philosophy
of the "what is" of politics as seen in political form and its movement,
and it is the science of action and politics under the principle of man
as a political animal. His philosophy is an alternative or competitor to

33 Slade, "Two Versions of Political Philosophy," 242.
34 "Two Versions of Political Philosophy," 243.

the philosophies of history that, as we will see below, flow from liberal thought. And it is a philosophy always returning to the visible movement of political form in which man is the principle. This book will remain focused on Manent's work on political form, and his work beyond that exceeds the scope intended here, but it is useful to keep in mind that political form is both important in itself for what it teaches about politics and, in a sense, as his means to his political science and philosophy, his window into his larger understanding of history and man.

AN INTELLECTUAL HISTORY OF LIBERALISM

Drawing on the extensive research for his comprehensive anthology of liberal writing in his 1986 *Les Libéraux*, Manent opens his 1987 (original French edition) *An Intellectual History of Liberalism (Histoire intellectuelle du libéralism)* with his intention "to present the main themes and the decisive moments of the history of liberalism. For almost three centuries liberal political doctrine constituted the principal current of modern politics in Europe and the West. Thus I have felt it necessary to begin by sketching out an interpretation of European history prior to liberalism, so as to make the development of liberalism itself intelligible."[35] Manent thus pursues his two avenues of investigation of political events and political philosophy, though he presents the pre-liberal sketch of political events only as a "scale model of this history, a summary of its major articulations."[36] He asserts the key distinction regarding the modern era of politics:

> A singular feature of the present historical situation is that political thought and political life are, in modern times, intimately linked. This is something new. The political history of Greece or Rome can be related without referring to "ideas" or "doctrines."
> ... It was from the experience of life in the Greek city-state that Plato and Aristotle elaborated their interpretations of human life, which constitute the matrix of all subsequent philosophy. But these interpretations emerged *after* the great cycle of Greek politics occurred. The case of modern political philosophy is completely different. One is tempted to say that it was conceived

---

35 Manent, *Intellectual History of Liberalism*, xv. There are wording differences in some places between the original French edition's *avant-propos* and the preface to the English translation cited here. There are, however, no substantive differences in the two versions for the points discussed in this section.

36 *Intellectual History of Liberalism*, xv.

and chosen *before* being implemented. It was at dawn that the owl of liberalism took flight.[37]

This "rise in the political power of the 'theory'"[38] holds on all points of the spectrum of modern political thought, from the republicanism of the American founders to Marxism. Manent immediately introduces as an example of a modern intellectual theoretical construct one "of the principal ideas of liberalism, . . . that of the 'individual' . . . who, because he is human, is naturally entitled to 'rights' that can be enumerated . . . and attributed to him independently of his function or place in society and that make him the equal of any other man."[39] Manent will develop throughout his work the claim that this rights-bearing individual becomes the modern version of, or the modern replacement for, the ancient citizen. This has profound implications for the possibilities of human action and, as we will see shortly, the human soul.

> As familiar as this idea [of individual rights] may seem, it really ought to strike us as strange. How can rights be attributed to the individual as individual if rights govern the relationships between several individuals, if the very idea of a right presupposes an already instituted community or society? How can political legitimacy be founded on the rights of the individual if he never exists as such, if he is always necessarily linked to other individuals, to a family, class, profession, or nation? However, it is on this idea, so obviously "asocial" and "apolitical," that the liberal body politic was progressively constructed. What is an election with universal suffrage, if not that moment when each person strips himself of his social or natural characteristics—income, profession, even sex—to become a "simple individual"? It is that moment when the body politic peacefully breaks up, becoming a "state of nature," only to reconstruct itself immediately afterward. Nor is there any doubt that this individual, so obviously "imaginary," has tended more and more to become reality. The inhabitants of Western democracies have become ever more autonomous, ever more equal, and have felt

37 *Intellectual History of Liberalism*, xv.
38 *Intellectual History of Liberalism*, xv.
39 *Intellectual History of Liberalism*, xv.

themselves progressively less defined by the family or social class to which they belong.[40]

The modern "body politic," or the modern political form as the denationalized democracy, is peopled by autonomous individuals who live contrary to their nature as political animals. This form grows out of the transformation of the nation form by the liberal political thought that theorized the modern form into existence.

The denationalization of democracy follows the intensification of the nation form in the Protestant Reformation. The liberal thought that would produce this denationalization began in earnest with the onset of the modern some three centuries ago. Developing from its antecedents in Machiavelli and Hobbes, it "is not our past; it is our present. . . . Our present political regime remains determined, in its generating principle, by this origin. Its singularity still dwells in us because we continue to feel the consequences of the solemn decisions taken three centuries ago."[41] These decisions, Manent claims, produced the triumph of liberalism over Christianity as a political force. Such a victory was not a process of secularization that held onto liberty and equality as essentially Christian "'biblical values' . . . shaping civic life."[42] It was, rather, an overthrow of and separation from Christian political authority that formed the essence of the modern, liberal political project.

> It is widely believed that the originality of European political history stems from Christianity, and that the development of modern politics can be described as a process of "secularization." . . . The thesis was born and acquired its credence just after the French Revolution. It had the merit of reconciling proponents and opponents of the "new freedom": there were those who thought that the hour of human maturity had arrived and those who remained attached to the old religion. The former saw in Christianity the first expression of human liberty and equality, hidden under the veils of grace or hampered by the swaddling clothes of alienation. The latter celebrated modern freedom as the last conquest of the Gospel. We must remember, however, that this reconciliation (which in France took more than a century to be achieved) came about just after the

---

40 *Intellectual History of Liberalism*, xvi.
41 *Intellectual History of Liberalism*, xvii.
42 *Intellectual History of Liberalism*, xvii.

> Christian religion had been totally stripped of all political power
> for the first time. . . . The decisive question then is the following:
> must the Enlightenment's war against Christianity be seen as
> the expression of an immense misunderstanding, for which we
> must seek to grasp the "historical reasons"? Or does this period
> give us the meaning of the modern political venture, and thus
> of liberalism, much more clearly than the subsequent period of
> reconciliation?[43]

Christianity becomes not a power authoritatively informing rule but merely
one opinion among many of equal value. The modern form is determined
or shaped not by Christianity, as in the nation, but by the absence of any
such determining moral judgment. The result of the liberal triumph is
that modern regimes are vulnerable to—indeed founded upon—a division
between a guiding opinion and the power or legitimacy of the regime.
"[N]othing guarantees that this disjunction between power and opinion,
which we take for granted and which our regimes reflect, is founded in
nature; it may simply be the founding prejudice or a particular opinion of
our regimes."[44] For some, this modern indeterminacy may "explicitly institute the disjunction between power, knowledge, and right that is essential
to freedom."[45] The triumph of liberalism would represent a better, more
free resolution of the tension between the Church and the nation. "Or
does it rather bring to light the paradox of a state which, having wished
to close itself off from Christianity's power, from the power of one particular opinion, is endlessly obliged to deprive any opinion of power?"[46]
Depriving opinions of power would, of course, render powerless those
with distinct opinions who would seek to rule. The self-governance of citizens of diverse opinions, visible in the natural political forms, is replaced
by the theorized sovereignty of the state.

Manent introduces the theologico-political question as it became
central in Europe during the reign of the national Christian kings; this question has already been explored extensively in earlier chapters. Manent then
turns to a thinker-by-thinker discussion of the key liberal political philosophers, beginning with the two principal antecedents to liberal thought and
the two fathers of modern political thought, Machiavelli and Hobbes. Of

---

43 *Intellectual History of Liberalism*, xvii.

44 *Intellectual History of Liberalism*, xvii.

45 *Intellectual History of Liberalism*, xviii.

46 *Intellectual History of Liberalism*, xviii.

the liberal thinkers whose work Manent recounts in this volume, these two are the most significant for the modern political form because they provide the break with the classical understanding of man and politics necessary to think that form into existence, and Manent's account of their thought will thus receive the most thorough exposition here.

Machiavelli will succeed in articulating a political science that would provide an alternative to a "Europe dominated by the idea of Christian salvation."[47] Those who earlier might have sought to oppose the Church lacked the intellectual tools to do so during the long Ciceronian moment with its dearth of political thought. That began to change around 1300 in Italy when "the first major attempt to emancipate man's political nature took place, [as] the rediscovery of Aristotle's works, thanks to their translation into Latin, had its full effect. This great intellectual event was also a great political event.... [T]he natural, or secular, world found itself potentially emancipated from Christian categories."[48] Dante and Marsilius of Padua challenged the power of the papacy. Their efforts were stillborn as efficacious political science, for two reasons. First, they favored political empire as a political form, but as discussed in the previous chapter, this form was no longer suitable for Europe. Second, the work of Aristotle could be used both to challenge and to support the Church's claims. "Aristotle interpreted human life in terms of *goods* and *ends*, all organized in a *hierarchy*."[49] While Aristotle wrote in the context of nature rather than the Church's supernatural understanding, his work was essentially consonant with the Church's view and "vulnerable to the Christian claim that the good brought by the Church is greater, the end it reveals higher, than any merely natural good or end."[50] This potential complementarity between Aristotle and the Church was most fully developed by St. Thomas Aquinas, demonstrating that Aristotle's work could be used both to oppose and to support the Church. To resolve conflicts between the ends of nature and the ends proposed by the Church, Thomas invoked "prudence, heightened by faith."[51] This most reasonable answer was no help to those who sought to place Aristotle's natural thinking in opposition to the Church, and it

47 *Intellectual History of Liberalism*, 10.
48 *Intellectual History of Liberalism*, 10.
49 *Intellectual History of Liberalism*, 11.
50 *Intellectual History of Liberalism*, 11.
51 *Intellectual History of Liberalism*, 12.

thus did not answer the theologico-political question definitively. Aristotle had been rediscovered only to be appropriated by the Church.

Machiavelli went far beyond Dante and Marsilius. His "political thought became a full participant in the political situation. Henceforth, it was impossible to understand political history without having previously grasped the broad outlines of the history of political thought."[52] It was Machiavelli, then, who necessitated Manent's two tracks of inquiry into political thought and political events, and it is with Machiavelli that we might first conclude that in terms of political form, ideas (not merely description) have consequences. "In Machiavelli modernity found an expression of itself that determined the orientation of the European mind, and hence of European political history, from that moment on."[53] Machiavelli initiates the awaited emergence from the Ciceronian moment. The modern form will have to be thought in the European mind before it can be instantiated, and Machiavelli breaks with the past to begin that thought.

As a Florentine, Machiavelli's "'experience of the modern things' was the experience of political life in a city-state," in the residue of the earlier form that no longer suited its European political circumstances and had now become "particularly unfriendly toward the Church and particularly vulnerable when dealing with it."[54] Manent attributes to Machiavelli's Florentine "situation of a quite powerless hostility" toward the Church, the origins of "the idea of radically excluding religion from the city-state, of closing off completely the city-state from religion's influence."[55] Such an exclusion was both the cause and the result of Machiavelli's "realism," which taught that "'evil' is politically more significant, more substantial, more 'real' than 'good.' "[56] This shift to an emphasis on evil, rather than the classical notion of a search for the good, produces one "of the most deeply rooted traits of the modern soul, . . . doubt of the good, the smile of superiority and mockery, the passion for losing one's innocence. To understand how modern politics was set in motion and developed, one must have previously grasped the change in what has to be called *the status of the good*."[57]

52 *Intellectual History of Liberalism*, 12.
53 *Intellectual History of Liberalism*, 12.
54 *Intellectual History of Liberalism*, 13.
55 *Intellectual History of Liberalism*, 13.
56 *Intellectual History of Liberalism*, 13.
57 *Intellectual History of Liberalism*, 14.

The consequences of this change from a search for, to a suspicion of, the good are profound. The city-state in Machiavelli's thinking is "an artificial island constructed by violent means. It is not open to anything beyond itself; it is intelligible only in relation to what it brings about."[58] The city has lost its natural character in the ancient sense and fled its telos to become a human construct. It is no longer open to a greater good that religion, particularly Christianity, might seek. Christianity's introduction of the softened stricture of "love your enemy," in Machiavelli's view, weakens the bonds of self-preservation between the city and its inhabitants, where any real "public good can only be brought about by the power of violence and fear."[59] Christianity's notion of good is thus a political problem to be overcome at all costs. Machiavelli's emphasis on evil reshapes the essential nature of a political form: "the political order is now a closed circle having its own foundation within itself, or rather below itself. To assert the necessity and fecundity of evil is now to assert the self-sufficiency of the earthly, secular order."[60] It will be centuries before the modern state brings this resolution of the theologico-political question to bear in actual political form, but its intellectual origin is present in Machiavelli's thought.

Machiavelli further identifies two groups in this city's politics, the nobility and the common people. The first have a political aim, to oppress the commoners—an aim that is concrete and achievable but not a good in any classical sense. The common people seek only to avoid oppression—a negative rather than a positive aim. Whatever good Machiavelli accepts in politics is in the common people with their rejection of oppression, and this is a passive good.

> If political action is not organized in view of a good—or, more generally, if no human action has an intrinsically good end— then all the goodness of the world belongs to the innocent passivity of those who ordinarily do not act in political terms, to the people. . . . [W]e see a new spiritual mechanism that is going to act powerfully on the development of modern politics and, more generally, on modern sensibility: the discrediting of

---

58 *Intellectual History of Liberalism*, 14.

59 *Intellectual History of Liberalism*, 15.

60 *Intellectual History of Liberalism*, 15.

the idea of the good, coinciding with the elevation of the idea
of the people.[61]

Machiavelli, then, sets the intellectual stage for the exclusion of a morally
non-neutral good, or an active and positive good—and thus the Church—
from politics, as well as for the political form that will institute the legitimacy of the will of the people, democracy.

The other father of modern political thought, Thomas Hobbes,
also merits extended consideration. As Machiavelli saw in the people's
aspiration to avoid oppression his only real if weak notion of the good,
Hobbes claims

> the people themselves—not as part of the body politics distinct
> from the elite, but as all those wishing to live free from fear—...
> are going to take the political initiative. The basic needs of all
> individuals—security, peace—are going to be the foundations
> of the legitimate political institution. The men whom Borgia's
> exploits leave *satisfatti e stupide* [as Machiavelli approves of
> Borgia's brutality] are going to want to be satisfied, and they
> are going to know how this satisfaction can be obtained. To be
> satisfied, they are going to become intelligent.[62]

Manent points here to an inherently democratic basis for the new political
form. Hobbes writes from the perspective of his experience of the English
Civil War, for which he identified two causes: a secular cause in the universities who provided the education of the elites; and a religious cause in
the Presbyterians, or Puritans, whose influence is extensive among the
people. The combination of the universities' reliance on classical Greek
and Roman models that praised freedom, and the Puritan demand that
each person must obey individual inspiration, "conspire to foment the
spirit of disobedience"[63] that threatens or obstructs the prospect of peace
and security from fear. These "doctrines existed in England only as opinions" that could be used to justify any policy or violence; the bases of one
in classical nature and the other in Christian grace were shown in the war
to be incapable of providing a political way out of insecurity and toward
political unity. They must be overcome or channeled to open the way
for Hobbes's political project: "The only possible response was obvious:

---

61 *Intellectual History of Liberalism*, 16.
62 *Intellectual History of Liberalism*, 20.
63 *Intellectual History of Liberalism*, 21.

art. . . . The foundation, stronger than all opinion, of the new political art will be this passion: *the fear of death.* . . . The principle of this new order would not be the good one was seeking, but the evil one was fleeing."[64] This "fleeing rather than seeking" is, as we have seen, one of the key aspects of the modern difference that Manent identifies.

Hobbes also gives rise to a second aspect of the modern difference: the modern form's exclusive reliance on reason. From Hobbes's state of nature in which life is a war of all against all, reason will provide the political means to escape the fear of death. "Human reason, observing the absurdity of this war, is going to seek a means of peace. More precisely, what one calls reason is born from this necessity, which is experienced and recognized through passion: it is the faculty of inventing means or producing effects. The new political art will be the good use of this faculty."[65] Reason's primary function is no longer to discern the reality of nature and make speech and choice conform to that reality: it is, rather, to devise the political means to escape the passionate fear of death. Those means are, of course, the construction and maintenance of the Leviathan, the state or political form to which all will sacrifice their unlimited "right over everything [in the state of nature, to avoid death] and will transfer it to the one to whom he entrusts sovereignty. . . . The right of the sovereign, individual or collective, is necessarily unlimited. . . . The Leviathan . . . is that 'artificial man' or 'mortal God' who will ensure civil peace."[66] The Leviathan protects us from death and frees us from fear. The essential nature of "freedom" is thus detached from the classical notion of "free to do what is right."

Manent finds in Hobbes two founding principles or categories of liberal and modern thought. The first, just touched on, is the rights of the individual. The foundation of the state's sovereignty is the transfer to the state of the individual's right to self-preservation, to escape death. This upends the Aristotelian telos of the city, to live well and to seek a common good: "Men must no longer be guided by goods or by the good, but by the right that is born from the necessity of fleeing evil. In the moral and political language developed by Hobbes, and which is still ours today, the

64 *Intellectual History of Liberalism*, 22–23.
65 *Intellectual History of Liberalism*, 25.
66 *Intellectual History of Liberalism*, 25.

right [of the individual] replaces the good."[67] This tectonic shift in political thought provided an enduring fundament of the modern form.

The second foundational and enduring principle is that of representation. To derive this principle, Hobbes begins with a notion of equality in the state of nature that is the most basic attribute of human relations: each man is capable of killing another, regardless of their relative physical prowess, intelligence, virtue, or other qualities. This, in Manent's understanding, produces a second shift from the classical view of politics as natural: "If men are essentially equal, if their equal powers are neutralized, then the political power that binds the body politic is not natural."[68] There is no basis in weaker or stronger, more virtuous or less virtuous, for obedience to a political rule. Manent seems further to claim here that the neutrality of the state of nature means that there is no natural force, no Aristotelian political like-mindedness or friendship that could offer a basis for politics. "If it [the binding political power] is not natural, then it is artificial. But an artifact is made entirely by the artisan. . . . Political power incorporates and represents the intention and determination of artisans, who are men in the state of nature desiring peace."[69] Men must use reason to think through their political form, and then fabricate it. The substance of that form is the equality of men in their capacity to kill one another and their incapacity to avoid being killed, and thus the equal powerlessness of men to escape the fear of death. These equal and powerless men constitute a "civil society" whose political aim is overcoming the fear of death. "Civil society is the locus of equal rights, and the state is the instrument of this civil society that ensures order and peace."[70] Rule and society are thus disjoined. The notion of representation is what connects society, or the ruled, to the ruler. One of several problems produced by this version of the ruler-ruled distinction is that the necessity for representation both demands the consent of the ruled and divides the will and the actions of the individual:

> If men are equal in the state of nature because the weakest can always kill the strongest, there is no reason why one man rather than the other commands. If obedience cannot be based on nature, but if it is necessary for civil peace, it can have its source

67 *Intellectual History of Liberalism*, 25.
68 *Intellectual History of Liberalism*, 26.
69 *Intellectual History of Liberalism*, 26.
70 *Intellectual History of Liberalism*, 26.

> only in *convention*. It can be legitimate only when founded on
> the *consent* of the one who obeys. More generally, according to
> Hobbes, every obligation necessarily has its source in an action
> taken by the individual who obeys. . . . [In Hobbes's state, the]
> individual has consented in principle to what the sovereign
> orders him to do, since he is the Author of his Representative's
> actions. . . . There is a basic identity between the subject and
> the sovereign. Still, such an expression is misleading. Hobbes
> excludes any transfer of will, any representation of one will by
> another: will belongs to the individual. Certainly, the subject
> recognizes all the sovereign's *actions* as his own, but that does
> not at all signify that the subject recognizes his own will in the
> sovereign's *will*.[71]

Each subject wills the existence of absolute sovereignty for the sake of the
peace and for the absence of fear that it brings. But in Hobbes's scheme,
the will of the ruled as individuals and the state's particular political
program of action remain disconnected: "Hobbes decisively prepares the
democratic idea, but remains no less decisively short of it."[72] There will
be few, if any, actual instantiations of the Leviathan as Hobbes theorizes
it. But the modern form will incorporate his fundamental notions of individual rights, consent, and representation while extending democracy
in an effort to join the will of the ruled (or at least a majority of the ruled
measured by counting votes) to the actions of the state.

Manent extends his treatment of Hobbes's break with the classical
understanding of politics in an important way. "Hobbes creates the political order from human impotence; Aristotle created it from human capac-
ities or strength. Unlike Aristotle's city-state, the Hobbesian body politic
does not compose and adjust forces (virtue, wealth, freedom); it relieves
weaknesses. Leviathan heals, at least in part, the ills of the 'natural condition of mankind.'"[73] Man retains something of a political nature under
Hobbes, but it is the nature of a powerless creature, and the political art
of such a creature in the end completely changes the relationship of the
divine and the political from what it had been under the nation form:

> The device of representation is supported by a conception
> of man's nature that extends beyond the idea of rights. The

---

71 *Intellectual History of Liberalism*, 27.

72 *Intellectual History of Liberalism*, 27.

73 *Intellectual History of Liberalism*, 31.

"artisan" of absolute power is capable of fabricating that power because, in his being, he too is power, or rather desires power. In this sense, the Hobbesian individual remains something of a political animal. This individual greedy for power is powerless in the state of nature. . . . So as to make a certain power from his impotence he constructs an absolute power above himself. The traditional religious interpretation of royal power signified that the king linked himself directly with God, that he was accountable only to Him, that he was his lieutenant or representative, and that consequently he participated in the omnipotence or sovereignty of God. But the case of the Hobbesian absolute power is completely different. It is no longer an almighty being who gives existence and the meaning of existence to absolute power. On the contrary, it is powerless beings who create Leviathan to remedy their weakness. Absolute power is no longer God's representative, but mankind's; its transcendence no longer has its origins in God's strength but in man's weakness.[74]

This explication of the modern political project finds in Hobbes the intellectual historical basis for the metaphor of the Tower of Babel (with its subsequent confusion) used by Gilson and Manent, and it delivers the Hobbesian resolution to the theologico-political problem.

Leviathan's power is therefore such that men cannot imagine a greater one. . . . St. Anselm's . . . God (a being such that a greater one is inconceivable) . . . [according to Hobbes] does indeed exist, . . . it actually organizes the human world, but . . . it is fabricated by men. The political institution is the human device permitting men to make effective and efficient this "idea of the greatest power" that in their impotence they are naturally led to imagine. There is no more subtle way of suggesting that the construction of Leviathan reproduces the genesis of the idea of God.[75]

Hobbes as father of modern political thought thus thinks into existence a political form that is itself godlike in scope and power; the roots of the modern political project's tendency toward and desire for a universal form are thus already present in the Leviathan. Manent hints as well at the exclusively human efficient cause of the Leviathan, where men

---

74 *Intellectual History of Liberalism*, 30.
75 *Intellectual History of Liberalism*, 30.

construct their state with themselves as the efficient cause and no need for regard for a final cause. This removal of the final cause marks the broader modern project. Moreover, Hobbes effectively demolishes classical political thought with its distinctions among regimes by reducing the classical choice among regimes to a binary question where "political discussion faces only clear-cut alternatives. Either the body politic exists and citizens live in civil peace, or it does not and citizens tear each other to pieces. . . . This means that the comparisons between the respective merits of different political regimes seems altogether pointless to Hobbes. . . . [T]he inflexible rule is this: that each citizen must consider the regime under which he lives as the best one."[76] Further, each state, regardless of regime, "is essentially democratic. The foundation of every regime is based on each citizen's consent."[77] Whether rule appears to be by the one, the few, or the many, the modern state is a democracy; classical regime analysis is *dépassé*.

Finally, Manent details further Hobbes's resolution of the theologico-political question. Hobbes sees men as torn between obedience to the religious authorities and obedience to the human city, each of which offers competing goods. Manent argues that this choice of obedience, of whom each individual's conscience tells him to obey, while always present in politics, is raised in a newly intense way with Hobbes. While the Greeks asked what the best regime was and who was to command, Hobbes asks whom we are to obey. He seeks in effect a third world beyond the Church and the city.

> If peace is at last to be achieved, a *third world* must be constructed, one where the conflict will lose all urgency because it will lose its meaning. . . . The [old worlds of Church and city] do have something in common. This common ground, the locus of their conflict, is man himself. Not man as member of the human city (since the church claims him), nor man as faithful member of the Church (since the human city claims him), but the man who belongs to neither of these two cities. This man's name is already known to us: he is the *individual*.[78]

Manent points out that this neutral individual of pre-Christian, pre-city greyness does not actually exist, as real men were already of the Church,

---

76 *Intellectual History of Liberalism*, 31.

77 *Intellectual History of Liberalism*, 31.

78 *Intellectual History of Liberalism*, 35.

of the city, or of both. This "individual 'exists' insofar as he hesitates in his obedience and is considered 'prior to' his choice of obedience. . . . It can be objected that this is a purely abstract point of view, leaving the reality of the conflict intact. But if, starting from this idea of the *individual*, I succeed in conceiving of a viable political *institution*, then this inexistent individual will come into existence as citizen or subject of this institution."[79] Hobbes thus begins not with a visible example of an Athenian or an Englishman but with an abstract notion of a man who must be brought into existence through political theory, through the conceptualization of the state. In Athens, we recall from Manent's account of the poetic sources of the city, man became political as he became rational, through his own thought in the context of the real city in nature with its conflicts and limits. In Hobbes's Leviathan, the individual citizen comes into existence as the state is thought into existence. Both man as political actor and the political association are constructions of the mind of the political philosopher, not creatures of nature. This radically alters both the classical and the Christian orders. "To fulfill its function, this new political institution by its very constitution must prevent the individual from being claimed by either the old city or the old Church. The obedience to which the individual will be subjected must be invulnerable to the criticisms and claims of the former candidates for power."[80] Modern philosophy in Hobbes thus thinks its way beyond St. Augustine's choice between the City of God and the earthly city by means of an indisputable obedience to the state that subsumes both old forms. "Of course, one will continue to hear the old claims, those of the rich, the poor, the wise, the priests. But their impact will be blunted by the absolute character of the obedience founding the new city. They will be *neutralized*."[81] We can infer, then, that as with Machiavelli, the classical and Christian notions of good are neutralized as claims on man. This newly existent individual must choose to obey the state rather than any natural or supernatural claim to good. Like the features of the rights of the individual and the consent of the ruled, the moral neutrality effected by Hobbes endures in the modern form. It is the fruit of the elimination of good as a political concern by Machiavelli; with Hobbes, it claims to relieve the fear of death and the powerlessness of the individual.

While more than footnotes to Machiavelli and Hobbes, the remaining liberal thinkers treated by Manent essentially build upon

79 *Intellectual History of Liberalism*, 36.
80 *Intellectual History of Liberalism*, 36.
81 *Intellectual History of Liberalism*, 36.

the break with the classical introduced by the first two modern political philosophers. They will accept the key elements of this break even while differing with their predecessors regarding the means to proceed with politics in accord with modern thinking. The Leviathan as detailed by Hobbes never becomes political reality or an actual regime, at least in Western nations. John Locke, on the other hand, moves liberal thought from its Hobbesian theoretical origins to the realm of the practically realizable. Much of Manent's work on Locke connects him to Hobbes. In particular, on Manent's reading, Locke will alter the Hobbesian state of nature in a way that will establish the individual as a more secure "vehicle" or bearer of rights, and thus a stronger basis for a political science based on rights.

Hobbes's individual in the state of nature "is not the independent individual as such [because] it is the war of all against all that gives him birth. In other words, the individual exists only through a kind of negative sociability, that of war. The unlimited right he has [to protect his life] is only an effect of this war. Consequently, the individual does not truly have this right; it appears only when he is threatened by death."[82] To rephrase Manent, it is the condition of fear, rather than the nature of the individual himself, that supports the rights of the individual. Locke will modify Hobbes to give individual rights a more stable basis to support an actual political form:

> Thus one sees how Hobbes elaborates, with an extraordinary power of suggestion, a new idea of the body politic: power is an ingenious device constructed by powerless individuals for protecting their rights. He does not succeed, however, in carrying out this idea completely. Individuals in the state of nature are not truly individuals entitled to rights intrinsically belonging to them, and power constructed in this way is not really a protector of their rights since it can protect them only insofar as it threatens them. The program of what later became liberalism is thus laid out. It will entail giving the Hobbesian idea of political power its full scope by modifying its beginning and its end. The individual in the state of nature will acquire intrinsic rights, and power will be limited to the protection of individual rights. This will be Locke's approach.[83]

82 *Intellectual History of Liberalism*, 40.
83 *Intellectual History of Liberalism*, 40.

Locke, like Hobbes, relies on fear as the primary motivation of political action. But he changes the proximate cause of that fear: man's "first need and therefore fundamental right is that of preserving his life. But what threatens his life? Locke answers: not other individuals, but rather hunger. This is the original difference between Locke and Hobbes."[84] Lockean man "is more Hobbesian than Hobbes's man. The [Hobbesian] one who is driven by the desire for power is driven by the desire for a specifically human good; the [Lockean] one who is driven by hunger is driven simply by the desire to flee from evil. In simplifying Hobbes, Locke makes him more coherent."[85] Locke "will simply erase rivalry"[86] for goods or power in the Hobbesian sense. This permits Locke to isolate the individual almost hermetically in the state of nature, strengthening the independence of the notional individual. "If man fundamentally is hungry man, he is radically separated from his fellow man; his only relationships are with his body and with nature. If Locke succeeds in basing individual rights solely on hunger, on the relationship of the solitary individual with nature, he will have shown how human rights can be an attribute of the lone individual."[87] This lone, hungry individual becomes the subject of Locke's labor theory of property, which Manent sees as the basis both for a notion of society and then for the political form that serves the society of fundamentally lone individuals. Contracts permit the exchange of goods between individuals whose exchanges germinate society:

> Thus one sees being born from nature a *society*, a series of regulated relationships among individuals. In Locke's interpretation, "society," or at least its essential elements, is born before the political institution. . . . [Hobbes's] "civil society" is originally founded on a negative sociability, that of war. Prior to the political institution, it is essentially unbearable. With Locke, it becomes bearable. Society becomes the series of economic exchanges into which men enter as laborers and owners. The Lockean state of nature is both more individualistic and more social than that of Hobbes. Rights, in the form of the fundamental right to property, belong to the solitary individual, and this individual builds up positive relationships with others.[88]

---

84 *Intellectual History of Liberalism*, 40–41.
85 *Intellectual History of Liberalism*, 42.
86 *Intellectual History of Liberalism*, 41.
87 *Intellectual History of Liberalism*, 42.
88 *Intellectual History of Liberalism*, 44.

Locke's views of political form and political institutions, as adopted in liberal thought, are founded on "the development of economic society from its modest beginning in the hungry individual. . . . In this hungry individual lies the primordial basis of human life. One sees why the liberal program, once completely elaborated, made the right to property and the economy in general the foundation of social life. . . . The right to property was recognized as *the* fundamental right."[89] This identification of property as the fundamental right provides a high degree of clarity and certainty in answering the question of what justice is: "Justice is *always already realized*, as long as property is guaranteed and protected."[90] Thus the preservation of the property right becomes the end of government, the equivalent of the "living well or finely" of the Aristotelian city. "[E]conomic activity became the dominant activity in liberal societies, more precisely . . . the erection of the 'sovereign state' above 'civil society' corresponded to the liberation of economic activity and, soon, its dominant position in society."[91] This opens the way for another characteristic of the modern form to emerge, namely, the authoritative neutrality of science. Economic activity replaces the politics of the ancient city without fulfilling man's political nature; with Locke, according to Manent, nature (something that must be overcome to escape the fear of hunger) becomes man's opponent in an unprecedented way, and science emerges as man's morally undemanding "friend" and most powerful tool:

> The same movement that brings the sovereign state to forbid men to exercise personal power over each other is going to lead the members of society to turn progressively away from each other, to avoid encounters in which they experience mortal dangers. They are going to seek a neutral ground for their actions, one where they do not meet their fellow men and where they do not encroach upon sovereignty. Up to the constitution of the sovereign state, the primary object of each person's activity was the other man. Henceforth, that object will be *nature*. Men turn away from men and instead turn themselves toward nature so as to understand and control it. Science is neutral and its conclusions are imposed on everyone. . . . The economy, closely linked with science, tends to become the arena par excellence of human activity because in its finality, the economy is directed toward

89 *Intellectual History of Liberalism*, 45–46.

90 *Intellectual History of Liberalism*, 46.

91 *Intellectual History of Liberalism*, 46–47.

nature and not toward other men. The development of absolute sovereignty within the framework of the state, and the development of science and economy within the framework of civil society, have the same motivating force.[92]

In the modern form, politics cedes its status as human action par excellence (its rightful place, according to Manent, as seen earlier) to economics, or to a new political economy; the contest among men over the question of who rules the city, which marked with subdued violence the politics of the Greek city, is replaced by the contest between isolated individuals whose contest is with nature and whose means is a triumphant and neutral science.[93]

From this explication, it is a short step to Locke's prescription for political institutions. Such institutions must exist because there is always a tendency to fall from Locke's relatively benign state of nature, in which fear of hunger is the concern rather than the threats of other men, into a Hobbesian state of war: "The state of nature always ends up becoming a state of war. This is the Hobbesian 'moment' of the Lockean doctrine. And any doctrine of the state of nature and the social contract (even Rousseau's) necessarily has a Hobbesian moment, since only an unbearable state of war, an intolerable evil can explain why men agreed to leave a state where in principle their rights were flourishing."[94] Political institutions exist "to preserve property endangered by the inevitable disorders of the state of nature. . . . [I]t is necessary to institute a 'supreme power' that has the right to demand obedience."[95] That supreme power, in turn, must also be constrained by being subject to its own laws so as not to violate the property right. In Manent's understanding of Locke, only a "representative and sovereign legislative body fulfills this double condition, and only as long as certain precautions are taken."[96] One such precaution is that the legislature not be in continuous session in order to avoid its becoming isolated from the society's interest. This precaution necessitates an

---

92 *Intellectual History of Liberalism*, 47.

93 Manent does not make the point explicitly here, but the Cartesian (and Baconian) influence on liberal politics seems clear in the focus on the manipulation of nature for the material improvement of mankind's condition. We need not consider an immaterial final cause or a telos of the political association to have Locke's politics; we need merely protect the right to property.

94 *Intellectual History of Liberalism*, 48.

95 *Intellectual History of Liberalism*, 48.

96 *Intellectual History of Liberalism*, 48.

executive power that can apply the laws continuously, with the authority
to deal with contingencies not anticipated by the legislative power. But the
executive prerogative to enforce the law exists by definition only within the
body politic whose representatives authorized the law. Thus there must
be, in theory, a third power to deal with relations beyond the political
association—matters of war and peaceful foreign relations not subject to
the legislature's contractual authority—which usually resides, for conve-
nience, in the executive power.

The legislative power, in Locke's scheme, is supreme, and "no
political will, no constituted power has the right to oppose [it]. . . . As
such, this power is as 'absolute' as Hobbes's Leviathan."[97] This absolute
status of the legislative power leaves the executive with "the problem of
the modern executive. Its meaning and legitimacy are uncertain" in the
face of the Leviathanic legislature.[98] This power is "a radically new notion
in the history of political thought. . . . Aristotle's 'executive,' so to speak,
is a plural power [of ruling magistrates] while the modern executive is
essentially an indivisible power. . . . The mystery of the modern executive
is the mystery of its unity."[99] This mystery at the heart of Lockean liberal
thought will remain unresolved in the modern form. In theory, the legislative power "is the direct extension of the individual's desire for self-preservation" and must indeed prevail over the executive, "because it directly
expresses the desire for preserving property, the origin of the political
institution."[100] Both forms of power exist in Locke's state of nature. But
the executive power to preserve property, shared by all before political
institutions arise, is supposedly completely abandoned to those institutions, yet "this total abandonment proves in fact to be impossible: the
individual retains the natural executive power insofar as the law can never
be completely effective."[101] The legislative power can be based on representation as that power transitions from the state of nature to the civil state,
but because the law of civil society can never anticipate every contingency
or deal with every circumstance—the very problem that creates the need
for the executive—the executive power cannot make the same transition
from natural to representative civil authority. This difference between the

97 *Intellectual History of Liberalism*, 49.
98 *Intellectual History of Liberalism*, 49.
99 *Intellectual History of Liberalism*, 49.
100 *Intellectual History of Liberalism*, 50.
101 *Intellectual History of Liberalism*, 50.

executive and legislative powers "reveals the difference between man's natural and political conditions . . . by showing the inadequacy of law [and thus the executive power, and] indicates the rupture between the state of nature and the civil state."[102] The executive is formally subordinate to the legislative, but insofar "as it does not represent individuals in their 'natural' condition, it will be able to 'represent' them in their political condition. The executive will be able to say, for example, that whereas the legislative body represents the 'interests of society,' it represents 'the greatness of the nation.'"[103] Legislative deliberation can produce a general sense of unity and perhaps a few broad strains or tendencies of agreed direction from among the diverse interests it represents, but because "the modern representative body confines itself to the law and leaves action to the executive, its deliberation is always radically incomplete. The immediate link between deliberation and action is a necessary condition for political action, and more generally for all human action. And since the unity of deliberation and action cannot reside in the legislative body, it will come forth in the executive power."[104] The implications for Manent's Aristotelian understanding of human action as resulting from deliberation are clear. The modern state's placement of the highest deliberative political legitimacy in the legislature that chooses the laws for those it represents, which as a representative body it cannot then truly act upon, severs political deliberation and action. The executive, theoretically inferior to the legislative, will join deliberation and action again and thereby restore, or achieve, the unity of the political association. It will thus be the true locus of unity in the modern form. Representation renders impossible a natural politics like that of the city and opens the way for an unnatural concentration of power that Locke himself never intended.

Montesquieu is the liberal thinker who will attempt to cope with this possibility of concentration of power. Montesquieu stands both in continuity with, and in contradiction to, his liberal predecessors.

> Montesquieu's political intentions remain essentially the same as those of Hobbes and Locke, but the means chosen for realizing them, and the language in which they are described, are radically different. The political intention remains the same: the end of the political institution is to ensure the *security* of persons

---

102 *Intellectual History of Liberalism*, 51.
103 *Intellectual History of Liberalism*, 51.
104 *Intellectual History of Liberalism*, 52.

> and goods. . . . But the need for individual self-preservation is
> no longer strictly speaking the foundation of political legiti-
> macy. . . . Montesquieu abandons [the] language [of absolute
> rights] and reestablishes on new bases the flexibility of ancient
> politics.[105]

The problem for Hobbes and Locke had been, in Manent's view, that in
creating a neutral power that would be superior to the interests that drive
fearful men into war, the sovereign political power would also threaten
war on its subjects. If the sovereign turns against its subjects, their only
remedy is rebellion. Montesquieu, observing the English system of rule
from afar, will attempt instead the remedy of separation of powers. Manent
claims that Montesquieu can achieve this by "forgetting" the principle of
legitimacy and, in effect, divorcing the principle of popular legitimacy,
which enables the practical possibility of separation of powers, from that
separation itself:

> [D]emocratic legitimacy, the condition for liberal institutions in
> the framework of the English monarchy, could in other circum-
> stances become their enemy [by turning against the people].
> Thus Montesquieu's thought represents that unique, exquisite
> moment of liberalism when the question of legitimacy could
> be forgotten, a pause between the active sovereignty of kings
> (which comes to an end with the English revolution) and the
> active sovereignty of the people (which begins with the French
> Revolution).[106]

Montesquieu is working, then, at a moment of transition, as seen in the
movement from the active principle of the premodern national monarchy
to the modern, democratic form. "By seeing the heart of the political
problem in the conflict between *power* and *liberty*, Montesquieu determines the definitive language of liberalism. In so doing, he reverses
Locke's point of view, so as to carry out the latter's intention more effectively. Instead of starting with the right that founds liberty, he starts with
the power that threatens it; instead of pondering the origin of power, he
ponders its effects."[107] The Hobbesian quest for power is not part of man's
nature, in Montesquieu's estimation; it only arises in a dangerous form "if

---

105 *Intellectual History of Liberalism*, 53.

106 *Intellectual History of Liberalism*, 55.

107 *Intellectual History of Liberalism*, 55.

the individual is in a social or political institution already endowing him with a certain power. It is born thanks to institutions."[108] We need not find a regime or form that controls or defeats man's nature, which is "sufficiently flexible, sufficiently plastic, for its behavior to be largely determined by the institution in which it lives."[109] We must simply allow institutions or political powers to offset one another. The two powers of principal concern are the legislative and the executive; the third power, the judicial, is important and powerful—and will become increasingly so in the later stages of the modern form—but largely invisible. And, again, Montesquieu will invert Locke in order to get the relationship between power and liberty as right, as enduring, and as possible. In Locke's thinking, the legislature that is formed to represent the people must remain essentially in continuity with them. For Montesquieu, the "faithfulness of the representatives to the electorate is valuable only if they also know how to be unfaithful; one has the feeling that the principal merit of representation is to prevent the people from taking 'active resolutions,' 'something of which it is entirely incapable.'"[110] The people may or may not be able to select representatives competently, but they assuredly cannot deliberate well. Deliberation then becomes a function of the representatives conducted without decisive reference to the electorate itself and, as we have seen, without the capacity to act upon the results of the deliberation.

We can infer from Manent's account that Montesquieu thus widens the gap between the ruling and the ruled. Legitimacy of power is one thing, but this is of secondary and largely historical importance (and thus relegated to hazy memory); operationally, the use of power and the surety that one power would check the ambitions of the other, become the foci of concern. Where there is a need to act and a disagreement between the legislative and the executive powers (the latter being, in Montesquieu's thought, a monarch), necessity would force agreement and action. Such necessity governs to a greater degree than the two powers, and the views of the citizens are seen in whom they support yet also mediated by the relative independence of the legislature and the executive. Citizens "have a twofold interest: that the power serve their interest, *and* that it not weigh too heavily on society. They also have a twofold feeling: that the power they favor 'represents' them, *and* also that it is different from them—that it

108 *Intellectual History of Liberalism*, 55.
109 *Intellectual History of Liberalism*, 55.
110 *Intellectual History of Liberalism*, 57.

does not understand or will betray them."[111] The governed are thus subject both to a desire for identification with their representatives and with a fear of and alienation from them. Again, the citizen of the modern liberal form is a divided person. And the divided person is, in a sense, powerless because with the division of powers, he can do little to other citizens; likewise, the powers, vulnerable to the possibility of losing support from the citizens, share the impotence of those citizens. This condition in which the "impotence of citizens and power condition each other ... is ultimately what Montesquieu calls liberty."[112] The problem of power and liberty becomes, operationally, the problem of impotence and liberty. "We have thus fulfilled the original program of liberalism by reversing the order of the factors. The representative regime initially was the ingenious device making it possible to leave a state of nature that was essentially (Hobbes) if not even necessarily (Locke) unbearable. It became the ingenious device making it possible to live in an essentially satisfying state of nature."[113] But that better state of nature does not mean that Montesquieu has salvaged a natural politics for the modern representative state, because the citizen of that state remains "*radically divided*: the dividing line between the natural man and the citizen is now within us."[114] Deliberation and action are removed from the citizens; politics as human action par excellence is not their domain. For the citizens and the powers, there is a profound tension between the alienation from and the need for one another that each experiences. Montesquieu does not return us to Aristotle. He only ameliorates the most onerous (and thus the most implausible) aspects of the Leviathan of his liberal predecessors, and by doing so he advances the movement of political form that they began.

Manent turns next to Rousseau, whom he labels a "critic of liberalism." Rousseau's France was a place where the de jure rule of the king had been replaced by the de facto power of opinion, and Rousseau was interested less in the imminent revolution, which he considered inevitable as a result of this displacement, than in what would follow. The opinion that mattered, the one that assigned position and credit to men, was that of society. Society "is inequality. [It was] not characterized by powers attributable to persons or institutions, but by an inequality relating only

---

111 *Intellectual History of Liberalism*, 59.
112 *Intellectual History of Liberalism*, 60.
113 *Intellectual History of Liberalism*, 63.
114 *Intellectual History of Liberalism*, 64.

to itself, with no content or meaning other than itself. . . . The relationships of power had become simply that, 'relationships.' They were relationships of inequality. Therefore, the spirit of society was inequality."[115] This observation is the basis of Rousseau's contribution to liberal thought. He will critique Hobbes and Locke with regard to political form but, according to Manent, will ultimately serve their cause not in thinking about political form but in describing the modern man who will occupy that form.

Manent recalls that "the foundation of liberalism is the distinction between civil society and the state: the latter is the representative instrument of the former. Civil society tends to be self-sufficient. Within it, members are governed neither by political power nor by other members; each of them is the source of his actions."[116] But each citizen depends on others for his business and recreation; their relationship is one of both dependence and independence (Manent does not draw the comparison, but such a view mirrors Montesquieu's understanding of the relationship between the citizens and the ruling powers). Citizens in this condition of dependence and independence will, according to Rousseau, relate to each other by comparing themselves, a form of relationship that brings invidious results. Manent writes here not just of Rousseau's day, but of our own:

> Comparing oneself to others is the misfortune and original sin of men in our societies. The misfortune is that the man who compares himself with others is always unhappy. There will always be someone richer than me, and even if I am the richest, I will not be the most handsome or the most intelligent. The sin is that the man who compares himself is always corrupted or on the point of being so. Not only does the desire to be first lead him to commit the everyday mischief that the moral code condemns, it also obliges him to give others a pleasing image of himself, to flatter himself and flatter them. His exterior will never be in harmony with his interior and his life will be a permanent lie. . . . For the man who lives by comparison is the one who, in his relationships with others, thinks only of himself, and in his relations with himself thinks only of others. He is the *divided* man.[117]

Again, modern man is divided. Rousseau's contribution is to see that such a man is typical not only of France but of modern Europe as a whole; this

115 *Intellectual History of Liberalism*, 65.
116 *Intellectual History of Liberalism*, 65–66.
117 *Intellectual History of Liberalism*, 66.

comparing and divided man is the inhabitant of modern European society. The inequality that fosters the comparing tendency may be more visible in one place than another, but "fundamentally, the behavior was that of *modern* man in *modern* society: it was the same in Paris and London, Edinburgh and Naples. Modern man had become a *bourgeois*; he had ceased to be a *citizen*."[118] The division of civil society from political rule thus hastened (and perhaps made inevitable) the movement from classical citizen to modern man. Regardless of differences in regimes between, for example, absolutist monarchical France and the liberal English regime, "the motivating spirit of social life was identical in the two nations. The same human type tended to prevail: the bourgeois, the man who by withdrawing into himself distinguished his own good from the common good. But to find his own good, he needed others, on whom he was dependent while seeking to exploit them."[119] The separation of private and public interest that we saw earlier in Cicero and the Roman empire with the institution of the magistrate comes into its fullness as observed by Rousseau in modern Europe with the separation of civil society from the state in the liberal form, producing "the homogeneity of what [Rousseau] calls the 'modern peoples.'"[120] In Manent's terms, national distinctions now matter less than the common modern type. England went through a period of real citizenship and institutional arrangements influenced by Locke en route to the triumph of the bourgeois; France, rather, developed consistently along the lines forecast by Hobbes. But in both cases, and across Europe, liberalism produced the self-divided bourgeois replacement for the integrated human citizen.

Rousseau is displeased with his conclusions about the results of inequality. "For him, modern society makes men nasty and unhappy; but it is unnatural for man to be nasty and unhappy. Therefore, this society is unnatural. The good society can only be one that conforms to man's nature. Thus, the true nature of man has to be discovered: this is Rousseau's great investigation,"[121] and it will carry important consequences for modern political history and thought. Rousseau concludes that there is only one solution:

---

118 *Intellectual History of Liberalism*, 67.

119 *Intellectual History of Liberalism*, 67.

120 *Intellectual History of Liberalism*, 67.

121 *Intellectual History of Liberalism*, 72–73.

> to remove one by one the veils that human convention and
> artifice have draped over the true face of man, to isolate the
> simplest operations of the human soul. . . . Since any society
> implies conventions and artifice, one has to consider man prior
> to conventions, artifice, or society: the original solitary indi-
> vidual. And since man develops his faculties only through the
> development of society, this original solitary individual will not
> be a man, but rather a kind of animal endowed with perfectibil-
> ity, that is with the capacity to become a man.[122]

This creature of complete potential is not the social or political animal
of Aristotelian politics. Rousseau's search for this solitary man extends
Hobbes's search for the individual who existed before choosing between
ecclesial and political authorities. But just as Hobbes was searching for
an imaginary individual who would be the basis for his theory, Rousseau's search "reaches an end only when the original man ceases to be a
man. This is the point reached by Rousseau,"[123] with major political consequences. No society could ever shape man into his happy, natural self.

> We have already seen that society is corrupt and man is unhappy
> when the individual is divided; man in nature is happy and good
> because he is *whole*, because he is self-sufficient. The good polity
> ought to preserve this individual unity, integrity, and self-suf-
> ficiency. It is obviously impossible to do that. What might be
> done, however, is to succeed in identifying each individual with
> the polity itself; in that way, no member of the body politic will
> any longer distinguish his own being from the common being.
> He will be whole because he will be one with the body politic.[124]

The contradiction, as Manent explains, is obvious: the state is based on the
preservation of the individual whose nature is solitary and whole, but the
state subsumes the individual entirely; the individual must change nature
from whole and solitary into whole as part of the collective. The liberal
social contract remains, and individuals come together as proprietors to
protect their property; in that sense, they become liberal bourgeois. But
they then become identical with the state in order to retain or regain a
natural wholeness. The individual thus "becomes more rigorously *citizen*

---

122 *Intellectual History of Liberalism*, 73.
123 *Intellectual History of Liberalism*, 73.
124 *Intellectual History of Liberalism*, 74.

than the most hardened Spartan."[125] This reveals the paradox in Rousseau's thought: "On the one hand, society is essentially contrary to nature; on the other, it comes near to conforming to nature only insofar as it imposes the greatest unity possible on its members, identifying each person with everyone and the whole—in short, only insofar as it changes man's nature."[126] Why is this not a fatal contradiction? Because "it is natural for man to change his nature because man, at bottom, is not nature but *liberty*."[127] Rousseau's freedom, then, is the freedom not to be natural in a fixed sense, or to flee any constraint of nature. Liberty begins in a plastic human nature and consists in man's forming that plasticity as he wishes: "liberty is that power by which man gives orders to his own nature, or changes his nature, or is a law unto itself. . . . Rousseau's antiliberal thought is going to provide content to the hypothetical being on which liberalism constructed itself, the individual. . . . With Rousseau, freedom becomes immediate to the individual, it is a feeling, both experienced and required, of *autonomy*."[128] This feeling, in Manent's account, becomes the existential principle of liberalism, the feeling of autonomy "by which the individual becomes aware of himself, by which man feels himself to be free to, or tries to be, an individual."[129] This sublime feeling demands a sublime political motive, which can only be supplied by revolution. And since the modern man of comparison and internal contradiction is the modern type across Europe, this autonomous impulse will take root beyond France, though its playing out will vary with the circumstances.

The necessity of revolution brings "modern political thought . . . [to] its ultimate expression and complexity. It turns against liberalism only because it has carried through its original impetus and logic to the end: constructing an indivisible body politic from supposedly radically independent individuals. . . . The French Revolution will follow in its very evolution the rhythm of Rousseau's thought."[130] France will ultimately reject the perfect equality for which the Revolution stood. But the effects of Rousseau's thought will endure in very fundamental ways for the modern form.

---

125 *Intellectual History of Liberalism*, 75.
126 *Intellectual History of Liberalism*, 77.
127 *Intellectual History of Liberalism*, 77.
128 *Intellectual History of Liberalism*, 77.
129 *Intellectual History of Liberalism*, 77.
130 *Intellectual History of Liberalism*, 78.

By raising itself above all the determinations of nature, the revolutionary act opened up an indeterminate "possibility" that no
politics would henceforth be able to forget or fulfill. This possibility, which is impossible, casts man's political nature into a
new element, that of an elusive, uncontrollable, and sovereign
history. And for controlling history, the Revolution bequeathed
to Europe an extraordinarily active and powerful figure of political unity: the *nation*. . . . Nature ceases to be the criterion, the
reference, or the model [for politics]. Two other criteria are going
to take its place: history and liberty. All political considerations
and theories after the French Revolution will develop within
philosophies of history and will be subordinated to them.[131]

As we have seen, modern man is a being of history rather than of nature,
an autonomous being who can reject nature and fashion himself, and
Manent now makes clear that this being arises definitively with Rousseau. This also marks a supremely important moment in the movement
of political form in Europe. The nation form, not itself a natural form but
also not anti-natural, with its energy and strength, is now brought under
the modern yoke and turned to the pro-autonomy and anti-natural uses of
modernity. The nation becomes the modern nation-state, or the modern
form in its early stages.

Manent considers three other liberal thinkers—Constant, Guizot,
and Tocqueville—each of whom is important as an observer and philosopher of political history. Tocqueville, in particular, considers the new
equality of his age and concludes, in Manent's summary,

that what liberalism considered the presupposition of a legitimate political order must in fact be sought, created, constructed.
The state of nature is not the beginning of man's political history,
it is rather its completion or perhaps its prospect. The liberal
plan, because it wants to found itself on "natural" equality,
essentially opens up a history: the history of man's efforts and
progress toward artificially establishing through sovereignty the
"natural" equality from which he will be able to construct the
legitimate political order in a fully rational or conscious way.
Since nature never tires of producing inequalities, influences,
and dependencies, this "first moment" never disappears. . . .
This "first moment" gives democratic man the feeling of living

in "history" since it makes him live within a project of which man is both the sovereign master and obedient subject.[132]

But with Rousseau, the elements of thinking that will permit modern man to think the modern form into being are in place. The theologico-political question with which Manent began and that so occupied Machiavelli and Hobbes is, after the efforts of the French Revolutionaries to erase Christianity entirely, handled by subsequent liberals in a softer but effective way. Human rights become the means or language by which the Gospel is most fully realized, so the oppositional nature of Christianity and the wants of secular rulers are reconciled, and religion can be slowly excluded as a threat to the polity. Yet the completion of liberal thinking leaves much unresolved: "The motivating force of modern history thus appears to be twofold: the natural desire to escape from the political power of revealed religion; the no less natural desire to escape the mechanism man conceived to satisfy the first desire."[133] In finding a political arrangement that could resist and subdue Christianity and permit him to escape the constraints of nature, modern man raised a force he finds equally oppressive. And after the disasters and totalitarianisms of the twentieth century,

> civil society and the state find themselves back in naked conflict, without the protection of king, revolution, or nation. . . . The Christian religion from which they tried to protect the polity is just as weak today as civil society and the state. But even in its present weakness, that religion still leads us to seek a separation of nature and law that it once forced us to desire. *Vis a tergo* that pushed the nations of the West toward a society without religion, it still remains sovereign in its apparent exhaustion, as if, in three centuries of "accelerating" history, nothing had happened.[134]

Liberalism issued into the modern state, but it produced only exhaustion on all fronts, not the decisive closure to the theologico-political question that drove its preeminent thinkers. This exhaustion will be a hallmark of the contemporary modern state as Manent assesses it throughout his work. Liberalism did not overcome nature or faith in politics. It only produced a failed political form.

---

132 *Intellectual History of Liberalism*, 112–13.
133 *Intellectual History of Liberalism*, 116.
134 *Intellectual History of Liberalism*, 117.

THE CITY OF MAN

The title of *The City of Man* offers a double reference, first to St. Augustine's *City of God*, to which the earthly city of man is the unfortunate opposition, and second to Leo Strauss's *The City and Man*. Both, as we saw earlier, are important influences on Manent, and some aspects of *The City of Man* were considered there in the context of understanding Manent's project. Augustine provides the "framework" of the conflict between the Church and the polity that drives the movement of earthly politics, specifically of political form in Europe. Strauss considers three classical thinkers—Aristotle, Plato, and Thucydides—in his own project of returning to classical political philosophy both on its own merits and as a way to better understand modern philosophy. Manent's title aptly acknowledges these influences.

Manent's concern in this work is to understand how modern people came to see themselves as they do: as historical, or living in history; as inhabitants of society and thus the subjects of sociology; and as utilitarian materialists in the economic sphere. It extends directly from his treatment of philosophical history in *An Intellectual History of Liberalism*. As noted earlier, in Manent's view, we all see ourselves as modern in this way, and it produces a "glorious" feeling.

> The consciousness of being historical is the central and perhaps also the strangest aspect of the modern experience. Modern philosophy is convinced that the experience of history is the most profound and decisive experience. [In this book] I shall study the paths modern philosophy took to arrive at this conclusion. I shall examine more generally how the consciousness of being modern has modified the consciousness of being man and whether it has increased or obscured our understanding of man. My concern will be first to describe and then to evaluate the main aspects of the human phenomenon according to the modern difference.[135]

Manent, in addition to alluding to his phenomenological influence, informs us immediately that this work is about an understanding of man, modern man in particular, as a being not of nature (and not as a political animal by nature) but of history. He organizes this material thematically, rather than by thinker, and divides the themes into two broad categories:

---

135 Manent, *City of Man*, 7–8.

the self-consciousness of modern man and the self-affirmation of modern man. The central question in this book is not the modern political form itself but what kind of man peoples it. We will dip only briefly into these themes to understand the features of modern man that directly relate to his modern political form.

In the modern, as we have seen, history is authoritative. Manent begins by developing ideas that he has raised previously regarding the modern difference and the internal division of modern man. Relying largely on Montesquieu and folding in the importance of commerce as understood by Constant and Adam Smith, he writes,

> Until the eighteenth century, European men essentially lived under the regime of virtue and law, either civic or Christian, that enjoined a man to risk his life or mortify his nature. But more and more they tend to live under the regime of commerce and liberty that was set into motion and maintained by the desire and the necessity of avoiding death and misery. They place themselves more and more under the authority of the modern experience. . . . [But] the regime of liberty cannot be said to be strictly speaking "in conformity with nature." It cannot be the unifying element of the different possibilities.[136]

Modern man is divided against himself. He knows of the classical view but sees traditional life with its natural relationships of family and city as a regime of law that called on him to exhibit virtue and constrained his nature to be free, to flee danger, and to seek comfort. The traditional man sought good, though the precise nature of that good was obscure and subject to corruption, while the modern man flees constraint and pain. In this change of kinds of men, of apparently different natures of men, and of the politics they pursue (of seeking good versus fleeing evil), modern man recognizes "the succession and incompatibility of two moral attitudes, two directions of attention and intention, [and] he concludes implicitly but irresistibly that there are two successive and incompatible humanities, the ancient and the modern. Self-consciousness, the consciousness of being modern, is thus the consciousness of this division."[137] Modern man, because he can survey two distinct humanities and contrast them without detecting why one would be superior to the other, concludes that neither nature nor law is really the "core" of what it is to be human. We are instead

---

136 *City of Man*, 46–47.
137 *City of Man*, 48.

bound "by the mother and sum of all successions, which is History."[138] To be human is to be historical, to know the succession or progress of which one is an example. "Modern consciousness negates the ancient regime of life under the law in the name of nature and at the same time it negates nature in the name of liberty."[139] Modern man is thus above law, nature, and all those who came before him, self-affirmed as superior, but never satisfied with the commerce he has enjoyed, the freedom he has achieved, or the security from evil he has sought.

The man who is modern is also, as we have seen, a member of society, itself a modern entity that is distinct from the polity. Manent claims that society embodies the modern phenomenon of historical conscious-ness: "While Greek man came into contact with and came to know his nature through the political regime of his city, it is by means of society that modern man comes into contact with and comes to know his new element, history."[140] This entity must have its own science and sociology and must carry its own sociological viewpoint. The "sociologist's analytic scrutiny separates the state from society and from the church. The body politic that the ancient law held together is dismembered into three great parts, each one subject in turn to further subdivisions."[141] The state is divided between powers, the church among diverse sects, and society among different groups. "From now on life will be lived in the 'age of separations.'"[142] Man and city are no longer unified in themselves or with each other. As a result, the study of politics is no longer the study of the whole human association, much less the science of governing souls, but one among several sciences. Politics becomes the study of political law or legislation. With Christianity's authority in decline after the Reforma-tion (a decline that steepens after the French Revolution but brings no replacement by another religion) and with sociology concerned with the mores of this moment in history, "Europeans witness something unheard of in the chronicle of humanity. An essential part of their life [religion] is in the process of breaking away from law because, in becoming purely political, the law raises itself irresistibly above the contents of life."[143] In

---

138 *City of Man*, 48.
139 *City of Man*, 49.
140 *City of Man*, 50.
141 *City of Man*, 82.
142 *City of Man*, 82.
143 *City of Man*, 84.

Europe, political law is now rarefied from the life of the people it rules. At the same time, it is only one of the many mores or influences in society that command its subjects. "One can say, in the language of command, that different sociological parameters govern men. One can also say, in the terms of matter subjected to necessity, that the political law is one social 'thing' among others. Many things govern men."[144] Sociology's affirmation of history affirms this manifold command. We can infer that among these fragmented forces or powers of governance, one would not find nature with a common good to be sought, nor a faith that offers a higher good.

After affirming the historical and sociological viewpoints as decisive in modern society and polity, Manent turns to a domain he rarely addresses: economics. He relies mainly on the work of Adam Smith, and his concern is not principally with economic institutions but with the kind of man who typifies economic modernity. This man is *homo oeconomicus,* "the thinnest of all beings."[145] This man suffers in particular from an impoverished power of imagination, which, imbued with the labor theory of value inaugurated by Locke, is reduced to utility:

> Once labor appears as the measure or cause of value, the imagination as a universal human faculty capable of reaching beyond the merely useful and embracing the Whole of the world departs from the scene, leaving behind it the insubstantial aura that goes with the products of the Useful and that advertising seizes upon with marvelous ease. Then the "economic viewpoint" confidently settles in, which is in no way a "conception of the world"—with its advent the imagination renounces the world—but rather the vital principle and untiring motor of the commercial society. In the new society, the objects of the imagination and the objects of labor blend together in such a way that the two overlap in an ever more exact manner. The one great object the imagination retains is precisely the harmonious system of production and consumption, the system of commercial liberty governed by the marketplace. Man as economist is the pure spectator of man become *homo oeconomicus.*[146]

The task of the modern state is to preserve this elegant and well-tuned system of commerce and markets so that modern man can use his now

---

144 *City of Man,* 85.

145 *City of Man,* 88.

146 *City of Man,* 102.

sadly constricted imagination to ponder new, never-ending projects of utility. Manent's description of this poverty of imagination is moving:

> [It] no longer seeks to embrace as in the past the Being which is "greater than which nothing can be conceived," nor even the lesser divinities. . . . It has ceased to build temples or erect statues of a beauty worthy of their greatness. It conceives the new ideas that . . . will allow the human condition to become better and especially to bring the system of labor to fulfillment. It is still the same imagination. . . . But . . . bent on our sphere, it . . . has lost all sense of glory.[147]

The skyscrapers of Manhattan are a poor substitute for the temples of Athens or the cathedrals of medieval Europe.

Modern man is historical rather than natural in orientation, lives in a society distinct from the polity, and imagines only materially useful outcomes. Manent now arrives at the essence of the modern man in his relationship to others and to his polity: "Man is the being that defines himself by the fact of having rights. Whatever being he has can and must be forgotten in the affirmation of his rights. . . . [M]an and the rights of man form a perfect and self-sufficient circle that contains the promise of an absolutely unprecedented liberation of man, who is now impenetrable to Being."[148] History replaces Being and historicism replaces ontology. "Man has the rights of man. And so one escapes the necessity of the presence, even the fleeting presence, of the verb that affirms and connects. . . . Man can in all honesty forget Being."[149] Man as bearer of rights need not concern himself further with what he is, with what his nature might demand, and thus with what a good life for him would be; he is not constrained by nor concerned with metaphysics. His possession of rights is all he knows and all he needs to know. The modern state has the task, therefore, of affirming and protecting rights and thus protecting the essence of the modern version of the citizen. The telos of man and his political association ceases to be of interest to philosophers or their readers. As we have seen repeatedly, in the political association, the modern form that grew out of the nation replaces telos with the rational human will and institutionalizes that will: "[I]f he considers the institutions of modern democracy inasmuch as they realize the principle of the reasonable will,

---

147 *City of Man*, 108.
148 *City of Man*, 138.
149 *City of Man*, 139.

modern man . . . is necessarily satisfied. Politically, he desires nothing else but what he already has. . . . In willing democracy, the will wills itself."[150] Modern man, the individual democratic man, *homo oeconomicus*, wills his rights and the political form that protects them in lieu of any serious concern for a common good. He eschews his own nature and the law that governed that nature. Guided by modern philosophy in his understanding of himself and of politics, he thereby "surrenders to the most bombastic illusion that has ever enslaved the thinking species."[151]

With *An Intellectual History of Liberalism* and *The City of Man*, Manent has largely accomplished his investigation into the modern difference; he traces the thought that led to the emergence of modern man, as distinct from his premodern counterpart, and that man's new political form. He will subsequently add to this investigation without changing its substance, always returning to the central notion of political form.

A WORLD BEYOND POLITICS?: A DEFENSE OF THE NATION-STATE

The French title of this work, *Cours familier de philosophie politique*, suggests a series of lectures on a variety of topics related to political philosophy. Published originally in 2001, it was written after *An Intellectual History of Liberalism* and *The City of Man* and before *Metamorphoses of the City*. As such, it describes Manent's considered conclusions after the labor of his major works on the development of modern thought, but before his grandest effort in *Metamorphoses*. Manent begins *A World beyond Politics?* by expanding on science as an authority in modern life—an authority that along with the historical sense produces divisions in modern man. Manent relies on Weber:

> The major separation in [Weber's] view is the separation of science and life: between science that has no meaning for man and does not tell him how to live, and life that has no unity, that is shot through with and so to speak defined by the conflicts of values, by the "war of the gods," in which each man must *choose*, without any rational warrant, his god or demon. This separation between science and life is solidly linked to the

---

150 *City of Man*, 160.
151 *City of Man*, 204.

constitutive separation of the political order between the public and the private: science rules the public domain, it is the only value effectively accepted in the public realm; life, authentic life, is to be sought in the private realm, authentic life is private life. Thus we are strangely divided: we have faith in science, we make it sovereign in the public forum, that is to say, we join together the two strongest ideas in the mind of man, the idea of truth and the idea of the Republic, and at the same time we decide to live so to speak apart and elsewhere: outside the public sphere, in the private; outside science, in values. . . . Modern man, democratic man, wants first to create the framework of his life, the most neutral and even the emptiest framework, in order then to live all the more freely. He affirms science in order to better affirm liberty. Of course, he can only affirm each by affirming their separation.[152]

Modern man chooses—not rationally, that is to say, not with deliberation—the "value" of non-value or morally neutral politics, replacing the moral content of political deliberation with a science that has nothing moral or compelling to say about what is a good life, and thus need not be obeyed in the private life. A moral science, or knowledge of what is beyond ourselves in a nature that has moral content, is impossible. If such a natural morality even existed, we could not know it; thus, claims about right and wrong, good and bad, lie entirely in the private sphere. Such is the regime of liberty that liberal thought, joined to the ideas of history, sociology, and utilitarian economics, has yielded. It is a world of divisions that mark the democratic form as it developed in Europe.

Manent identifies six categories of divisions that are present in, and indeed central to, the modern democratic form: separation of professions, or division of labor; separation of powers in government; separation of church and state; separation of civil society and the state; separation between represented and representative; and separation of facts and values, or science and life. All of these divisions have been explored earlier, with the addition of the science-life division just now. These divisions overlap with one another—Manent, as always, does not pretend to have an airtight schematic diagram—and "all of them [are] imperatives [in the modern democratic form]. These separations *must* be put into effect, and thereafter they *must* be preserved. Why? Because these separations are

152 Manent, *A World beyond Politics?*, 8–9.

necessary for liberty. Better yet, they define liberty as the moderns understand it. Modern liberty is founded on an organization of separations. The modern regime institutes its separations for the sake of liberty. Modern liberty is inseparably linked to these separations."[153] Further, these separations are distinct to the modern form: "[T]his concern for separation is specific to the modern era; inversely, it is alien to earlier, . . . predemocratic societies [where] the accent is explicitly, emphatically, at times obsessively placed on social unity, on concord."[154] The division before the modern form is the distinction between those who rule and those who are ruled, but this distinction actually assures unity because it clarifies the location of authority and minimizes discord and the drift toward disorder. On the other hand, "modern politics was set up to abolish or at least get around the command-relation that was the pivot of ancient politics"; the division of representation is a way of allowing citizens to authorize themselves to act or not to act, rather than be told what to do.[155] It accommodates all of the divisions to ensure liberty.

The effects of this accumulation of divisions play out in the modern form in a profoundly inhuman way, a way that produces a sense of powerlessness that ultimately leads to hatred. Manent explains,

> To function well such a system requires a rigorous and efficacious separation between the majority and the opposition. Thus it needs a certain vitality of partisan spirit. Such a system excites the partisan spirit it needs in order to function. At the same time, it forever frustrates partisan passions since it is organized to prevent their having an open field and being able to achieve what they desire. In psychological terms, one could say that this organization of separations excites the desires and wills of the members of society in an extreme way and frustrates them in a way that is just as extreme. Wills are mobilized since they form the link between the citizens and the party they favor. . . . At the same time, the party members know, or at least they come to know, that their wills will have very little effect and that their desires will not be satisfied. Thus such a system nurtures a will that wants to be partisan and knows that it is powerless. . . . A

---

153 *A World beyond Politics?*, 13. Manent uses "regime" here (*le régime moderne* in the original French text, p. 28), but I believe it is clear that he intends to include all regimes of the modern form.

154 *A World beyond Politics?*, 13.

155 *A World beyond Politics?*, 14.

society so organized tends to present a very specific mixture of agitation and immobility that wears souls down all the while it discourages great undertakings.[156]

This passage offers one of the first instances of Manent's view of the exhausting effects of the modern form on the human soul. Modern man has escaped nature and law in pursuit of liberty and autonomy, which are necessarily supported by an organization of separations. Man thus separates himself from all that provides him the chance to be fully human, to do great and divine things, to join deliberation and action in accord with nature in a political form that is suitable to his being as a political animal. His determination to be an individual is closely linked: "what [democratic people] feel first is their individuality as subjects [rather than bonds to other people or to the polity]. . . . In a democratic society, men are irresistibly tempted to forget that they are political animals."[157] Man's enthronement of his will as an ersatz telos brings only disappointment and weariness that he, not knowing himself, cannot fathom.

Throughout *A World beyond Politics?*, Manent begins to develop the notion of the modern form as a universal empire of humanity, with a nonpolitical humanity itself as the essential political principle. Unlike the original empire form, which sought to bring as much as possible under its political association without opposing the political nature of man, this modern empire would seek to escape that political nature. The "idea that humanity tends irresistibly toward unity spread in Europe at the beginning of the eighteenth century and won over nearly everyone in the following century."[158] Gilson noticed the tendency toward this aspiration after the catastrophic wars of the twentieth century. Manent begins to examine how such an empire, ruled by a morally neutral law as arbitrated by increasingly powerful tribunals and judges, would seek to constitute "a new metapolitical humanity that has overcome or transcended its political condition,"[159] where a universal understanding of human rights provides the guiding source of authority—an authority that remains morally neutral beyond those rights. At this point, Manent can begin to think more carefully about the modern political form, its failures, and the implications of

---

156 *A World beyond Politics?*, 18.
157 *A World beyond Politics?*, 112–14.
158 *A World beyond Politics?*, 125.
159 *A World beyond Politics?*, 186.

that failure for philosophy of history. We will remain focused on political form as we turn again to *Metamorphoses of the City*.

METAMORPHOSES OF THE CITY

Metamorphoses of the City, perhaps Manent's magnum opus, is an extraordinary attempt to fulfill his task of bringing together the ancient political cycle and a new, different, modern political cycle in a single history under the principle of man as a political animal. This history, as already noted, amounts to a descriptive science or philosophy of the "what is" of human action in politics. We have already referred to this work extensively in understanding Manent's project and his work on the forms of city and empire. By the time of writing this book, Manent has available all of his thought on the modern state that we have just discussed, and his comments on the modern form can briefly focus on particular aspects as needed to develop his broader investigation.

Manent begins by explaining that in our contemporary condition, we are in danger of abandoning politics and its forms altogether. The quest of the modern state toward a universal form, now exhausted, has had the effect of undermining the notion of form itself. We saw earlier that the modern form, the denationalized democratic nation, is marked by the authority of a neutral science that tells us nothing about good and bad but produces powerful technology. At the same time, we tend toward an "empire of law" governed by morally neutral judges and tribunals. The effects are radical, and it is worth quoting Manent's description of our moment at length:

> With the end or weakening of the representative regime that articulated actions and words in the national framework, the modern political order nears the end of its course. The sciences and technologies continue to run in their sphere, but they are more and more detached from the framework in which they found their meaning and their usefulness, when the modernization of national life in all its aspects was the evident and common task. We are witnessing a more and more profound divorce between the process of civilization and the political structure. The ever more complex and constraining order of ordinary life, the ever-tighter network of the rules we obey with ever-greater docility, must not blind us to the growing uncertainty, that is to say, the growing disorder of the form of common life.... It seems that we are on the way to returning to a situation

of political indetermination comparable in one sense to the one that preceded the construction of modern politics. . . . We observe not the excess but the dearth of political forms. At least in Europe, its native land, the form of the nation is discredited, delegitimized, without there being any other form in the process of being elaborated. Not only that, but the authoritative, if not unique, opinion has been hammering at us for twenty years that the future belongs to a delocalized or global process of civilization and that we have no need of a political form. Thus the necessity to articulate words and actions politically has been lost from view. The technological norm and juridical rule are supposed to be enough for organizing common life.[160]

The modern form, which Manent took decades to understand, has played itself out. Its pretentions to a morally neutral and thus anti-natural form of politics that would be universally valid, which rested on a radical equality, laid the foundation for its demise.

The modern political cycle took up, broadened, and profoundly transformed the Greek political cycle. In both cases, to be sure, the vector of political history is a vector of democratization. But in the modern European nations, unlike what took place in the Greek cities, the confrontation between the many and the few was decisively mediated by the one, that is, by the State, which was at first royal and later republican, but always "monarchical."[161]

The monarch of the Christian nation, whose powers were transferred to representative bodies that assumed sovereignty, was replaced by the kingly sovereign state. Manent continues,

This active interposition of the State has very deep consequences that are not yet exhausted. The people ceased to be the many to become simply *all*. In the eyes of the One, all became the people, all were equal. The modern State signifies, by imposing it, this *plane of equality* on which we have been living for two or three centuries—the plane of equal human rights, the plane of the equal or similar human condition. Henceforth, the few as few no longer have any admissible claim. Any political or moral

---

160 Manent, *Metamorphoses*, 13.
161 *Metamorphoses*, 99.

argument, any human argument, is acceptable only if it can be generalized, or universalized. Henceforth democracy is the only legitimate political regime.[162]

The motion of the modern political cycle is not from one form to another. It is from one form to the formlessness that results from the denial of the particularity of the nation form; without some particularity, on Manent's reading, no real form is possible. This cycle is from the natural (or at least not anti-natural) and political toward the anti-natural and the apolitical, and it issues in an essentially inhuman result in the modern state as envisioned by Hobbes with his attempt to subordinate both political and religious choice and loyalty to Leviathan:

> [T]he modern state represses almost equally the two divergent movements of the soul: not only does it severely circumscribe the public expression of religious convictions and affects—religion is henceforth essentially a private thing—but it makes and is organized to make the "ancient freedom," that is, the direct expression of civic commitments, impossible: citizens can act only through their representatives. The modern State thus rests on the repression, in any case the frustration, of the two most powerful human affects: on the one hand the passionate interest in this world as expressed in active participation in the common thing, and on the other the passionate interest in the eternal and the infinite as expressed in the postulation of another world and participation in a community of faith. . . . [W]ith these two fundamental movements of the soul repressed or frustrated, the soul no longer recognizes itself, and thus observers conclude that we have entered a postcivic as well as a post-Christian era.[163]

As before in *A World beyond Politics?*, Manent's inquiry into political form yields a judgment about the modern form's effects on the soul: political philosophy, philosophy of history, and philosophy of man come together. The modern form renders impossible any serious human activity in two of the domains of Manent's triangle—faith and politics—the latter, again, being the visible arena of human action par excellence. The modern form— the form that is constructed in thought or philosophy and elevates reason above all—thus breaks down the distinction between faith and politics

---

162 *Metamorphoses*, 99.
163 *Metamorphoses*, 217.

by removing the possibility of both. Philosophy triumphs by destroying Manent's triangle and thereby crushes the human soul itself.

Manent allows that analyzing the state of souls is a risky and uncertain business, but he is clear on his view of the effects of the modern state on the soul, producing a continuous state of "timidity or indecision." He cites Francois-René de Chateaubriand, an early-nineteenth-century Catholic Romantic, who perceived the modern soul's problem "with a clarity we have become incapable of."[164] Chateaubriand describes the human soul, still as near-divine as nature would have it, thrust into the modern condition: "The imagination is rich, abundant, wonderful; existence is poor, dry, and disenchanted. One dwells with a full heart in an empty world."[165] Chateaubriand thus foresees the outcome of the modern political cycle. In Manent's words, we are deprived of both a "great political existence" and a "religious life devoid of timidity, by their absence or rather their presence in the state of demoralizing traces of possibilities of life that one feels incapable of either embracing or forgetting."[166] We retain a vague sense of what we are by nature, but in an anti-natural political form we cannot live according to that nature. Hobbes's effort to resolve the theologico-political question, to reconcile the City of God and the earthly city, to bring together the Church and secular authorities under the modern State, has made man miserable, but it has not changed his nature as a political animal.

Manent returns in *Metamorphoses of the City* to an extensive discussion of St. Augustine's *City of God* to understand the fundamental problem of the modern form: its aim at universality. We have already seen this tendency and can limit ourselves here to a final observation of how Manent joins political philosophy, based on the movement of political form, to philosophy of history. Like Gilson, he believes that humanity as a whole cannot provide a basis for a universal political form, and that the attempt to achieve the universality of the City of God on earth in a universal form embracing all of humanity is a catastrophe. His reasoning is straightforward: a good politics requires the limits that make possible a common political operation to create a common good that did not exist before.

> If there is a universal human community or association, it is the framework and instrument of some action; it "does" something. The city is the framework and the instrument of a

---

164 *Metamorphoses*, 218.
165 *Metamorphoses*, 218.
166 *Metamorphoses*, 220.

specific action—chiefly "self-government." The Church is the framework and the instrument of a specific action—the "life of charity," "sanctification." But what about humanity? Well, in spite of what Dante advances with so much assurance, it is difficult to conceive what this operation would be; and thus it is difficult to maintain that humanity constitutes an effective political community. These remarks help us to account for the way philosophies of history beginning in the eighteenth century were deployed as though they were self-evident and necessary. The operation of humanity as a whole that must be postulated and situated somewhere was supposed to come to sight in the movement of history that . . . leads to a goal on which all or nearly all of them agree: the unification of humanity. . . . But it could be said that the philosophies of history run aground when reaching the harbor. For, if the moving principle of history is the effort to attain unity . . . what happens when we have achieved the unity of humanity, that is, once we have reached the end of history? What then does humanity do? This is where the philosophers of history do not know what to say, or they utter childish nonsense. But if united humanity has nothing to do, then it does not exist or it no longer exists.[167]

The limitless ambition to capture the whole of humanity under a political form fails because it removes the possibility of a common operation that can only take place within a particular people with a particular common good. The usual name for the project of the modern state is "utopia," which in Manent's view turns out indeed to be a place that is nowhere, or at least a place with no meaningful politics.

LA LOI NATURELLE ET LES DROITS DE L'HOMME

In chapter 1, we saw that Manent is a theoretical philosopher interested primarily in knowing the "what is" of politics, man, and history. With *Metamorphoses of the City*, Manent's theoretical work on political form is largely complete. His subsequent works rely on this theoretical, descriptive base to begin to deploy prescriptive thoughts on issues ranging from the European Union to the implications of Islam in France, all tied to his

---

167 *Metamorphoses*, 299–300.

understanding of the centrality of political form in human life. We will touch on these prescriptive ideas in the conclusion.

In 2018, Manent published a book-length treatment of the relationship of natural law and human rights in the context of the modern state that illustrates his willingness to draw prescriptive conclusions from his theoretical investigations of political thought and political events. He breaks no new ground on political form in this work but returns to his previous work on man as exclusively a "bearer of rights," representation, the modern project's attempts to escape the command of nature and law, and the anti-natural character of the modern state. Here is one example: "This practical primacy of command has been lost from view in the conditions of modern *society* and *liberty*, where the irresistible power of the sovereign State imposes the . . . equality of rights, and then proposes and promises a life that ignores, it must be said ostensibly or apparently, command as obedience, this life that we call 'free' where each is occupied night and day pursuing the mirage of 'autonomy.'"[168] The book was based on a series of six lectures Manent delivered for the Catholic Institute of Paris, illustrating another change in Manent's work that will be considered in the conclusion: as Manent becomes more prescriptive, his writing also becomes more openly Christian.[169]

THE MODERN STATE: FINAL ASSESSMENT

The modern political form has arrived at the point of having nothing to do. Its citizens exist in the shadows of their religious and political nature. Modern humanity conceived as a political form "is devoid of political significance; it does not constitute an effective political resource. . . . [It] can only protect what is and prohibit what could be."[170] The modern form exists merely to protect human rights and preserve the system of *homo oeconomicus*. Manent's theoretical work on political form leads us to conclude that the modern form offers nothing of the human grandeur

---

168 Pierre Manent, *La loi naturelle et les droits de l'homme* (Paris: Presses Universitaires de France, 2018), 129. "Cette primauté pratique du commandement a été perdue de vue dans les conditions de la *société* et de la *liberté* modernes, où la puissance irrésistible de l'État souverain impose . . . l'égalité des droits, et donc propose et promeut une vie qui ignore, faut-il dire ostensiblement ou apparemment, le commandement comme l'obéissance, cette vie que nous disons «libre» où chacun est occupé nuit et jour à poursuivre le mirage de l'«autonomie»."

169 These lectures were sponsored by the Institute's Étienne Gilson Chair.

170 Manent, *Metamorphoses*, 326–27.

of its predecessor forms. It has run its course with no successor in sight. Manent's own philosophy of history, owing much to Augustine and following Aristotle's method, consists in describing what is, and what is in the modern condition is insufficient for the men who comprise humanity. The motion of political form that drove political history in Europe has paused, or ceased. If history has ended, it has ended not in a final, universal political association that elevates man in reason, but in stasis, paralysis, and a haunting dissatisfaction that we are barely capable of acknowledging, much less understanding. The modern state has returned to the pre-political condition, where the common good is not imagined. If men become rational as they become political, they must in some sense lose their reason if and as they lose politics. As Gilson feared, the de-Christianized modern state that proposes a political form for universal humanity has become the confusion of a Christian idea gone mad.

Chapter Six

WHAT MANENT HAS TAUGHT US—SO FAR

INCORPORATING A BROAD RANGE OF SOURCES from poetry to philosophy to history, Pierre Manent investigates political thought and political events to develop an Aristotelian philosophy of politics within an Augustinian philosophy of history. The City of God is the only true human universal association, the only human association that can have an operation of humanity as a whole in its telos, individual and collective, to worship God. The earthly city or political association is its own domain of action in which man is the principle and must seek to discern, and to act according to, the command and the necessity of nature, which is to act in the here and now with an understanding of the authority of a final cause that man does not create and cannot ignore. The human political association, to be truly political and thus natural or at least not anti-natural, is limited to a particular place and people wherein human action and being human are visible phenomena. The divine and human domains are distinct but intermixed. Human attempts to make the two identical or reduce the two to one, either through attributing to the earthly city no order or telos of its own aside from its eschatological end in the City of God (i.e., faith denying the natural significance of human reason and the production of a common good), or through the elevation of human reason to exclude any claims of the City of God (i.e., reason denying the proper claims of faith), are catastrophic. Modernity with its political form of the anti-natural modern state is one such catastrophe. This conclusion will be a brief attempt to raise and tentatively answer a few questions about Manent's project and to suggest how the work of two other thinkers, Francis Slade and Robert Sokolowski, complements and completes Manent's.

HAS MANENT SUCCEEDED
IN HIS GRAND PROJECT?

Has Manent succeeded in his grandest and most sweeping effort? This is the attempt to show that the ancient and modern political cycles and the period between them, which appear different both in events and in the political philosophies that described or drove them, in fact belong together in a single "reasoned history" under the unifying Aristotelian principle that man is, by nature, a political animal.

It is impossible for Manent to demonstrate such a claim analytically, of course. But his invocation of a wide range of Western sources gives his science a rigorous plausibility that easily settles into comprehensive persuasiveness. Perhaps the most convincing element of Manent's work lies in his constant reference to the motion of political form. European man has thus far not arrived at an enduring political form. But all evidence suggests that he constantly seeks such a form, a form that will permit him to act rationally both for his own good and a common good. As one form fails to satisfy him fully and decays, another develops. This motion occurs in times of plenty (the modern) and in times of want, suggesting that material comfort is not the principle of nature that would bring the motion to a good rest. The need that drives the motion is a spiritual need of the soul. And while it is a spiritual need, it is a need of man in the human domain that Christianity does not answer in this domain, having little to say about political arrangements. Man must use his reason to meet this need.

In *Metamorphoses of the City*, as we saw, Manent comes to believe that while the difference between the modern and ancient views of man and politics is significant, that difference pales in comparison to the movement from the pre-political condition to the city, or the political condition. Man becomes rational at the same time he becomes political—Aristotle described man as both political and rational by nature—and his nature is thus formed or brought to realization at that moment. Manent's investigation aims to bring together all of human history in a science of human action from that moment of our first becoming political. Political form is the broadest category that captures both man's rationality (Manent seeks a *reasoned* history) and his political nature, as form makes visible both man's logos and his search for a common good. For this reason, a science of political form is the most likely possibility to succeed in Manent's effort to recover a full science of man's action and politics.

One question immediately arises: if political form is the arrangement for political action, or human action par excellence, and human
action is the visible outcome of deliberation and choice, is political form
itself chosen? Or does political form have some status above or beyond
human action as a result of nature, history, or both, in which case man
would be the principle of action within the form but not of the form itself?
One can see with Manent that the city came into being when the virtuous
few or rich began to see, with their logos, the possibility of a good larger
than their own interests and brought the many along into a common operation that, while fraught with various conflicts, overcame at least inter-
mittently the division or war between the rich and the poor. One can see
how Rome in its decay from the virtues of the Republic turned outward
in a search for imperial glory. One can see how Europeans under kings
chose not to arrange their politics in either city or empire and thus introduced a new form, the nation, that could hold the secular ground while
bending to the Church's claims for salvation. One sees in the constitutions
of modern nation-states a choice of certain political arrangements. But
with the exception of this last form, the deliberation and choice of political form does not come in one clear instant. Manent claims that only the
modern form is thought or theorized before it exists. But the choice of form
in all cases is the result of many smaller acts of deliberation and choice
that occur in particular circumstances over time and whose results, even
in the case of modern democracies, are only visible in retrospect with
careful historical reconstruction. Man is still the principle of political form,
in smaller and less grand choices that "add up" to a collection of choices
from which political form emerges.

Aristotle had the advantage of examining one political form, the
city, with different regimes that were in close proximity over a relatively
short period of time. The concentration of the city's political energy within
its limits made the politics described by Aristotle vivid and visible. Manent
faces a much larger challenge: over two thousand more years of history
and political thought, from a more expansive area with different peoples
and distended forms; and the introduction of a religion (which Manent
shares) that purports to elucidate the final "philosophy of history" in the
Incarnation of the one God who promises the possibility of an eternal
salvation that transcends the human domain—a religion that greatly
influences politics without proposing a program for the resolution of the
questions man must consider in seeking a common good. Manent's great
success lies in seeing that the essential principles of man's rational and
political nature identified by Aristotle hold across the history of the West

and throughout the history of the earthly city and the political association in all its forms. Only Christianity and salvation history will ultimately
collapse Manent's triangle of politics, philosophy, and faith into a unified,
single whole. In the meantime, we find again and again that our attempts
to do so ourselves, attempts driven by the desire to leave aside our political
and rational nature, are hazardous to our souls.

MANENT'S PREFERRED FORM:
THE NATION OF A CHRISTIAN MARK

Like his friend and mentor Raymond Aron, Manent is interested in considering contemporary problems and using his descriptive understanding of
political form as the basis for prescriptive thinking about those problems.
Two areas of particular concern to Manent are the rise of Islam in France
and the pretensions of the European Union to be a universal political form
embodying the religion of man, to be the completion of the modern state
with the erasure of the underlying nation.

   Manent tells us that as the modern form displays its anti-natural
character, it fails the souls under its sovereignty and grinds to a halt: human
action beyond the assertion of rights and the search for material comfort
is paralyzed within the modern state, and the motion of political form is
suspended. "European democratic universalism shades into nihilism; it
is the fulfillment of nihilism. It consists in saying: Europe is nothing other
and wants to be nothing other than pure human universality. It cannot,
then, be anything definite; in a very real sense, it wants to be *nothing*, an
absence open in every way to the presence of the other."[1] This absence of
political form in any articulated way means that the "European Union is
not political; it does not mediate: it *blends* in its own eyes with humanity
as it moves toward unification. Today, the religion of humanity, which is
Europe's religion, prevents the question of humanity from being posed."[2]
If Europe is not political, it cannot ask the fundamental question, What
is man? If we do not ask that question, we do not see that man is political
and rational, and the possibilities for action in common are lost. Manent

---

1 Manent, *Seeing Things Politically*, 188.
2 *Seeing Things Politically*, 188.

puts it bluntly: "the modern nation's trajectory ends in the self-destruction of Europe."[3]

Manent knows that no supranational political entity such as the European Union or the United Nations can suffice as a political form itself or issue a new form to replace the modern state. The modern state is incapable of even considering the question of political form, and no political philosopher is in sight to theorize a new form. What then do we do? In *Metamorphoses of the City*, Manent does not answer the question, noting only that, in the common European opinion, "the nations are exhausted" and, in his own view, the modern state has emptied itself of political significance.[4] In *Seeing Things Politically* and *Beyond Radical Secularism*, Manent does not change his assessment but finds the only possible resources available to be those that sustained Europe before the modern state, that is, the nation and the Christian faith. Without suggesting how to realize his alternative to the modern state, he identifies what he considers the only possible favorable alternative: the "nation of a Christian mark," the nation "stamped" by Christianity, and, in the particular case of France, Catholic Christianity.[5]

This form is, first, a nation that looks toward Christian teaching for its historical and moral orientation while governing itself primarily as men and citizens should strive to do by nature. It is not a theocracy (as in a government of priests) or a "Christian form" but a *human* political form whose understanding of the common good and the actions needed to achieve that good is shaped by man's reason in accord with the authority of Christianity. It is not morally neutral but resembles the nation after the Reformation, at a time when each nation was known by its choice of Christian confession, before the religious neutralization of, and the exclusion of Christianity from, the modern state. In *Metamorphoses of the City*, Manent wonders whether this nation form retains any energy; he seems to answer in the negative, although he allows that such a conclusion is "in the realm of what is not certain and cannot be verified."[6] We have seen earlier that the nation remains, in his view, present in the language and traditional references of contemporary European countries. In *Seeing Things Politically*, Manent reminds us that "the phases of the past, those we have left

---

3 Manent, *Metamorphoses*, 325.

4 *Metamorphoses*, 326.

5 Manent, *Beyond Radical Secularism*, 19.

6 Manent, *Metamorphoses*, 326.

behind, never simply disappear. They have reached their limits but they remain present and active."[7] He hopes that such a presence can somehow regain political force without falling into the idolization of the nation-state in the "blood and soil" nationalism that drove the "thirty years war"—the two world wars and the interwar era—of the early twentieth century.

Christianity also remains potentially active as a power to mark a nation. As we saw earlier, Manent concludes *An Intellectual History of Liberalism* by noting that after three hundred years of liberal thought that sought to exclude the Church completely from politics, the Church is decidedly weaker but "remains sovereign in its apparent exhaustion, as if, in three centuries of 'accelerating history,' nothing had happened."[8] In the case of France, post-revolutionary secularization succeeded in detaching the polity from the Church and "accomplished . . . the weakening of the social power of the Church by bringing to an end the Church's role in the State."[9] But the end of the former political and social power of the Church nevertheless leaves it in a position possibly to put its stamp on a nation of pluralistic religious camps. The Catholic Church

> establishes a relationship with each of the other great spiritual forces [Judaism, Protestantism, Islam, or the religion of human-ity and human rights]. . . . [B]eing alone capable of nourishing a meaningful and substantial relationship with all the other spiri-tual forces, it is the center or the pivot of a configuration in which we have to live and think. It is thus the mediator par excellence . . . in a sense that is less defined spiritually, but very meaning-fully politically. The Pope has put down his tiara and the Church no longer claims to gather humanity under its rule. Still, given the spiritual fragmentation that affects the Western world, it is a fixed point that is concerned to relate itself intelligently to all the other points, and to which the other points can try to relate.[10]

Manent searches for a renewed political form framed with the resources of the nation form and of Christianity. He does so in response to the imme-diate demands of Muslims in France, and in response to the longer-term problem of the modern state's reaching its limits of action.

---

7 Manent, *Seeing Things Politically*, 192.
8 Manent, *Intellectual History of Liberalism*, 117.
9 Manent, *Beyond Radical Secularism*, 19.
10 *Beyond Radical Secularism*, 105.

With respect to the problem of Islam, Manent seeks an integration of Muslims, which requires something other than the nihilism of the modern state in order for them to see something into which they might integrate. That something requires that society rid "itself of the immanence of rights and of their now exclusive authority and . . . succeed in reviving representation, the consciousness and the will of a common life, the feeling that it is desirable to participate in a form of life."[11] Despite the problems of separation between society and the polity, between the ruler and the ruled, that representation as developed in liberal thought produced, Manent sees it as preferable to the universal aspirations of pan-European government: "It is urgent to recover a representative regime beyond the already tired illusions of European governance. A representative government presupposes a people to represent."[12] Such a people must be more than a collective of individuals whose principal concern is the rights that protect their private autonomy. Such a people must want to engage in a common operation for a common good. Renewing the nation marked by Christianity, Manent argues, demands the active participation of French Catholics. That participation is urgent, because while the immediate crisis of the rise of Islam might or might not instigate such a renewal, that crisis is a symptom of the dissipation of the modern state and signals that "a long period of calm is coming to an end. A period of trial is beginning."[13] This trial will be decisive for Catholicism and, one senses in Manent's words, for the West.

But Manent does not despair, at least not publicly. He writes that the nation and the Christian faith that are the core of European history leave us "not without resources, both old and new. In a certain sense we experience an embarrassment of riches that we do not know how to set in order. These are the various spiritual forces that I have tried . . . to relate to one another, without, I hope, losing sight of the great indeterminacy of our moral and political landscape."[14] Man is still the principle of action who must make his choices in the two indeterminacies of the political form and the Christian proposition. But having surveyed the modern scene and found it severely wanting, Manent allows and perhaps increasingly emphasizes that while faith and politics are still on different vertices of

---

11 *Beyond Radical Secularism*, 80.
12 *Beyond Radical Secularism*, 88.
13 *Beyond Radical Secularism*, 102.
14 *Beyond Radical Secularism*, 113.

his triangle, they are integrally linked in the "what is" of man and nature. One cannot eliminate the distinction—that is the task of salvation history— but, again, losing sight of one to privilege the other, which is the modern project, yields only the loss of everything. That is the loss foreseen by Gilson and Manent.

In calling for the nation of a Christian mark, Manent might be accused of addressing only the particular case of France with its history of Catholicism, revolution, *laïcisme*, and later Muslim immigration from the former empire; the original title of *Beyond Radical Secularism* was *La Situation de la France*, and Manent is plainly writing for a French audience. But at the end of the book, he makes clear that he imagines the nation of a Christian mark to be the form proper to all of Europe and the West. In doing so, he clarifies the importance of the link between the City of God and the earthly city.

> There is no future for Europeans, either on the side of autoch-thony, even if one is necessarily born in some place, nor on the side of rootlessness. . . . We have confined ourselves to this deadly alternative because we have established ourselves within immanence as the true place of humanity. If we are but terres-trial vegetables, in effect we are left with only the choice between being rooted and being uprooted. And yet the history of Europe . . . is unintelligible if one does not take into account a very differ-ent notion, a notion elaborated by ancient Israel, reconfigured by Christianity and lost when the European arc was broken [in modernity]. This notion, without which the history of Europe is unintelligible, has itself become unintelligible to contemporary Europeans. In their eyes, this is simply foreign or contrary to reason. Whoever mentions such things by this very act leaves beyond the domain of rational communication and, one can say, democracy itself. I am speaking, of course, of the Covenant.[15]

The Covenant, treated by moderns as a nonsensical notion in their version of logos, was what permitted man to act as man, so long as he remained within the boundaries of the Covenant without closing himself off to the other party of the Covenant. The Covenant

> is a certain way of understanding human action in the word and in the Whole, of understanding at once its greatness and

---

15 *Beyond Radical Secularism*, 113.

its precariousness. "God" is here the one who gives victory, but who also chastises lack of measure. . . . In brief, as great as man is in his pride as a free agent, his action is inscribed in an order of the good that he does not produce and an order of grace upon which he ultimately depends. . . . Let us simply say, for present purposes, that the Covenant opens up a history of freedom, that it authorizes and so to speak motivates the greatest human enterprises.[16]

Here Manent beautifully summarizes the philosophy of history found in St. Augustine. The pagans knew of the natural order that included moral goodness and commanded or forbade certain actions, but they lacked the Jewish and Christian God of the Covenant, originally revealed to the Jews and by grace later extended as an offer or possibility for all mankind. The "European arc" is ultimately the carrying forward of the Covenant in the earthly city; that is the meaning of European political history, a meaning of inestimable significance now forgotten in the modern state. "It is up to Christians to renew the meaning and the credibility of the spiritual communities that make up European life,"[17] Manent exhorts us. This renewal can only take place within an articulated political form that draws upon European and Western spiritual resources. The Jews have shown the way in our day with the establishment of the State of Israel as their particular national form, a form they drew from Europe. Europe must follow suit. "To declare or even to guarantee the rights of human beings is not sufficient to bring men together. They need a form of common life. The future of the nation of a Christian mark is a cause that brings us all together."[18] Europeans must reassemble the collapsed triangle of faith, politics, and philosophy and understand the natural and authoritative relationships among the three vertices. Whether the citizens of the modern West can or will make the choices and take the actions that might restore the "European arc" to its movement of the centuries, halted with the modern form, is *the* question of the moment. Manent's exhortation aside, there is little in Aristotle or Augustine or Manent to suggest a clear path forward, only the constant ends that we must seek if we are to be human, and that we forget if we are modern.

16 *Beyond Radical Secularism*, 113–14.
17 *Beyond Radical Secularism*, 114.
18 *Beyond Radical Secularism*, 115.

We saw in chapter 1 that Manent is concerned about recovering an understanding of the heterogeneity and genuine diversity of human action. While Manent's "nation of a Christian mark" suggests a common form of political arrangement, it is also his response to the need to recover the heterogeneity of political action. However he makes his living or spends his recreation time, modern man is essentially of one type, the bearer of human rights whose only purpose or end is the maintenance and expansion of those rights and the autonomy they ensure. The ancient city was different. It emerged from the conflict between the virtuous or rich few and the poor many, and the war between the two parts was barely sublimated to the possibility of a common good. Before the modern state, politics was an intense and difficult activity of bringing together into a common operation people with different purposes and ends, citizens who were diverse not just in appearance or physical characteristics but in how they saw their own lives and purposes that were at variance with others. Economic differences were important but were not the only differences that had to be accommodated in the polity. The modern state degrades that diversity by reducing each citizen to his status as an individual with rights vis-à-vis the state and other citizens. The same homogeneity of the modern individual applies to regimes of the modern form.

> What, in effect, is the modern state, the sovereign and liberal state, if not this extraordinary instrument that both tends to strip the diversity of regimes and of political forms of all relevance and to insert itself between man and God, or to make itself God? It tends to deny the relevance or importance of the question of the regime or political form because, by guaranteeing members of society the enjoyment of their rights, it seems to dispense them from having to govern themselves. It inserts itself between man and God, or it makes itself a God, because, by abstracting itself from the society where human beings live, and by offering itself as the sovereign author of the human order, it assumes the high ground and arrogates to itself the task reserved to divine Providence.[19]

The modern state was only able to accomplish this democratic separation of society and politics because it drew from the resources of natural politics, from "peoples' seeking the best means to govern themselves in

---

19 *Beyond Radical Secularism*, 86.

obedience to divine government."[20] Once it had used those resources to empower itself, the modern state shed the deference to "divine government," leaving it positioned to "be successively and sometimes simultaneously impartial master and furious tyrant, intelligent servant and blind slave."[21] Again, the modern state collapses Manent's triangle by removing the vertex of faith, with despotic results for the souls within the form. The nation marked by Christianity holds the possibility of restoring the triangle and with it the human heterogeneity that fosters "the diversity of common things produced by humanity [that] is the object of wonder and admiration," when men are free to respond in deliberation, choice and action to the double indeterminacy of political form and the Christian proposition.[22]

A BRIEF COMPLAINT: WHERE IS HAPPINESS? WHERE IS FRIENDSHIP?

Manent succeeds in bringing European political movement into a visible reasoned history under the principle that man is a political animal. That is, of course, a tremendous achievement. But Aristotle did not say only that man is a political and rational animal. He specified as important for what it is to be human, that all men seek the good and especially the final good for the sake of which all other goods are means—happiness. Politics is the science of human good and of this "chief good" that is "among the most godlike things; for that which is the prize and end of virtue seems to be the best thing in the world, and something godlike and blessed."[23] Aristotle, then, is concerned with happiness as man's telos, the telos of the political and rational agent, the telos that is part of man's nature and closely related to his political and rational characteristics. Man's political nature would seem to mean little if it is not considered in light of his telos, his happiness.

Likewise, Aristotle discusses friendship and affection. In the political context, Aristotle describes a form or characteristic of friendship that prevails in a good city—concord. Concord consists in agreement about

---

20 *Beyond Radical Secularism*, 87.
21 *Beyond Radical Secularism*, 87.
22 *Beyond Radical Secularism*, 86.
23 Aristotle, *Nicomachean Ethics* 1.2.1094a23, 1.9.1099b14–17.

actions to be taken for the common good. "Concord seems, then, to be political friendship, as indeed it is commonly said to be; for it is concerned with things that are to our interest and have an influence on our life."[24] Aristotle's example of concord is agreement among the rich and the poor that the best should rule.

Yet Manent rarely discusses happiness or friendship.[25] As man's happiness is an activity that is in accord with virtue, and the literature on virtue and eudaimonia is already vast, perhaps Manent simply has other work to do. But there is another possible explanation. Aristotle allows that the happiest life is one of contemplation of the "noble and divine," but that such a life is "too high for man."[26] What is possible, as a kind of secondary way of life that produces some measure of happiness, is a life of virtuous action and justice toward one another, which is to say a life of virtuous political action. The contemplative life transports us from this human domain to the divine domain, but such transportation, Aristotle insists, is not really possible for men, as it is too divine and demands the most of the divine within us. Perfect happiness for the rational, political animal, despite the fact that it is our telos, is apparently unavailable in the human domain.[27] We must make do with politics, and Manent focuses his attention on our domain, which is the possible, the political.

Moreover, Manent is working with a resource unavailable to Aristotle: the Christian faith. Christianity teaches, of course, that man's full and final happiness will only be realized in the next life. To reach that life of perfect happiness in knowing and contemplating God, and to gain some share of it now, we must order our faith and our actions in this life to God. For Manent to proceed further in the "happiness quest" would require him to enter theology rather than political philosophy, and to cross from his politics and philosophy vertices to the vertex of faith. He is ultimately prepared to do so in some sense, as we have seen in his plea for the nation of a Christian mark that highlights the placement of his science of politics within the Augustinian understanding of history. His science

---

24 *Nicomachean Ethics* 9.6.1167b2–4.

25 In a conversation in May 2018, I asked Manent why he wrote so little about happiness. He was surprised and answered that no one had asked him that before, and that he would have to think about it.

26 *Nicomachean Ethics* 10.7.1177a15, 10.7.1177b26.

27 Man seems, according to Aristotle, to be the one being in nature who cannot realize his telos in nature. This oddity cries out for an explanation, which might conceivably be supplied by the doctrine of original sin whereby man's fall prevents his fully knowing and realizing his telos in this life. This revelation was also unavailable to Aristotle, of course.

itself, though, maintains its separation among the vertices. Yet his science would be more complete, more thoroughly Aristotelian, if he enlarged it to treat more explicitly the relation between politics and happiness, between political action and the final human telos.

The same holds for friendship and affection. Manent stresses the conflict among the parts of the natural city and the diversity of clashing human ends that must be brought into concord to seek a political common good. The political friendship that Aristotle describes is, in a sense, a weak form of friendship, just enough concord to allow the city to thrive in the midst of its differences and quarrels. But Aristotle's notion of friendship occupies two chapters in the *Nicomachean Ethics* and is a sine qua non for politics to unfold. Aristotle argues in the *Politics*,

> [T]he city is the community in living well both of households and families for the sake of a complete and self-sufficient life. . . . It was on this account that marriage connections arose in cities, as well as clans, festivals, and the pastimes of living together. This sort of thing is the work of affection; for affection is the intentional choice of living together. Living well, then, is the end of the city, and these things are for the sake of this end. . . . This, we assert, is living happily and finely. The political community must be regarded, therefore, as being for the sake of noble actions, not for the sake of living together.[28]

Friendship is not the telos of the city, but it is necessary for the city to realize its telos of noble actions, or the common good beyond one's private interests. Manent's potential contribution on friendship, on how citizens can come to see a common good in the midst of their authentic diversity and heterogeneity, and on how civic friendship is related to the rationality that arises simultaneously with the political condition, would deepen his science of the "what is" of politics within the framework of all of Aristotle's natural relationships. It would further secure his effort to bring European political history under the principle of man as political animal.

IS MANENT'S POLITICAL FOCUS A LIABILITY?

At a broader level, Manent's focus on the political may incur weaknesses in trying to see the whole of the human person as a political, but not

---

28 Aristotle, *Politics* 3.10.1280b33–1281a4.

exclusively political, animal. As we have seen throughout, Manent considers political action to be the defining exemplar of human action, of what it is to be human. In chapter 1, we heard his claim that he does not "see political things as a subset of the human things that interest me. . . . Political order is what truly gives human life its form. Political things are the cause of human order or disorder."[29] This view of politics as preeminent in human experience risks excluding other, equally (or more) important aspects of human existence from the answer to the question of what it is to be human, or at least minimizing those aspects in a way that distorts the whole of human existence.

For example, St. Augustine asks, "As far as this mortal life is concerned, which is spent and finished in a few days, what difference does it make under what rule a man lives who is soon to die, provided only that those who rule him do not compel him to do what is impious and wicked?"[30] Augustine analyzes the Roman empire in depth, and he comments that living under a benevolent Christian ruler is better than living under a tyrant. But as we saw in chapter 2, he refuses to undertake a rigorous study of the merits of particular political regimes or forms. He seems relatively indifferent to political form, which is not the determinant of a good life in his understanding. Something else is at the forefront of Augustine's notion of the human person: the person's choice to love the eternal rather than the temporal, using the latter to seek and reach the former. Political form would seem to be a temporal matter.

In chapter 1, we compared Manent's project on political form to the work of Alasdair MacIntyre. While there are important convergences, MacIntyre sees the political form as a framework for human life as it proceeds in various practices and activities that shape the thriving human. His preferred political form is the city, with its limited size and common language, culture, and traditions of practice. But what seems more important to MacIntyre are the activities that occur within the form. The political form is not the central feature of human history, as Manent claims. Rather, it permits the person to engage in the full range of work, leisure, educational, family, religious, *and* political choices and actions that comprise a truly human life.

Russell Hittinger describes a different approach to understanding the fulfillment of the social and political nature of man that rests on Aristotle and places politics in an important but not predominant place in

---

29 Manent, *Seeing Things Politically*, 1–2.
30 Augustine, *City of God* 5.17.

the good life. He does so by returning to Pope Leo XIII's 1891 encyclical, *Rerum Novarum*. Pope Leo identifies "three 'necessary societies'—that is, societies necessary for human happiness. They include domestic society (marriage and family), polity, and Church, . . . 'distinct from one another and yet harmoniously combined by God, into which man is born: two, namely family and civil society, belong to the natural order; the third, the Church, to the supernatural order.'"[31] This "structure" of human memberships in distinct but related communities displaces politics as preeminent but recognizes its crucial place in human life. It also moves the Church to the status of the supernatural, not a temporal political form as Manent had described it (keeping in mind Manent's qualification that Church is a strange political form). Hittinger sees three common properties to the three societies. "Their respective forms and ends are not purely voluntary," meaning they cannot be simply reshaped according to transient whims and wishes.[32] Polity is the most variable of the three in form, as there are different legitimate forms that could permit the realization of the ends of politics, but family and Church have only one legitimate form. Second, the societies "are not disposable platforms for lifestyle. We are to dwell, or to live in them," and to participate in them.[33] This mark of the societies is very much in accord with MacIntyre's view of the city, and it would comport with Manent's understanding of the grounding importance of enduring (if not permanent) form in human life. Finally, "the societies are subsidiary to one another. . . . The different orders need each other. . . . It is not sufficient for human happiness to dwell in only one society."[34] The whole human being needs the political community as it exists under a political form, but he or she needs more than the political to be human.

SLADE AND SOKOLOWSKI

Many critics of liberalism and the distinctively modern political form that is the state are available to supplement and reinforce Manent's work. Two in particular, Francis Slade and Robert Sokolowski, whose work has been referred to earlier, know and share a particular sympathy with Manent's

31 Russell Hittinger, "The Three Necessary Societies," *First Things* (June 2017), accessed June 15, 2023, https://www.firstthings.com/article/2017/06/the-three-necessary-societies.

32 "The Three Necessary Societies."

33 "The Three Necessary Societies."

34 "The Three Necessary Societies."

ideas and can complement and help complete his work on political form. I wish to call attention only fleetingly to these complementarities, all of which flow from the Aristotelian understanding of man as political and rational by nature.

Some readers of Manent may consider his science of political form to be overly focused on France, Germany, and perhaps Great Britain; in other words, his science, especially in treating the modern state, might be seen not as one of a broad political form but as one narrowly confined to one or a few specific regimes. The work of Francis Slade testifies to the broad validity of Manent's formal understanding of the modern state. Slade is especially acute on the dangers and the anti-natural character of sovereignty. Like Manent, he traces the problem of sovereignty to Machiavelli and Hobbes, also adding the thinking of Jean Bodin. Also like Manent, he is interested in the importance of political form and makes that notion central to his thinking, as few other critics of the modern state do. Slade writes, "In contrast to words such as *kingdom*, or *republic*, *state* seems a neutral, faceless kind of term. *State* does not name any natural form of community in which human beings ordinarily live—which explains the ease with which we speak of a 'world-state.' It is the hallmark of the State that it is not natural; it does not have its origins in any natural impulse of human beings to associate."[35] This short passage distils several of Manent's important themes: the unnatural or anti-natural character of the modern state form; the state's vulnerability to, and even preference for, the dominance of an empire of law and rule by anonymous tribunes, bureaucracies, and judges; the attempt to bring all of humanity under a global rule; and the moral neutrality of the state. As we saw earlier, Slade helps us understand that the modern "political form is the creation of political philosophers," which comes about with the conceptualization of sovereignty.[36] Slade confirms the divisions brought about by the modern form that Manent identifies as essential to representative democracy:

---

35 Francis Slade, "Rule as Sovereignty: The Universal and Homogenous State," in *The Truthful and the Good: Essays in Honor of Robert Sokolowski*, ed. John J. Drummond and James G. Hart (Dordrecht: Kluwer, 1996), 160. The subtitle of this essay, "Universal and Homogenous State," refers to a term introduced by Alexander Kojève and "appropriated" here by Slade. His appropriation highlights the way in which Hegel's understanding of the modern, sometimes referred to by Manent, is a reflection or even inversion of Manent's and Slade's very different interpretation. This way in which Hegel is both useful and wrong in Manent's thinking calls for greater scrutiny and further research. The homogeneity of the modern state is, as we have seen, a problem that Manent identifies in his call for a return to a science of the heterogeneity of human action in politics.

36 "Rule and Sovereignty," 161.

"Sovereignty is a name for rule considered in itself independently of rulers, of what Aristotle calls *politeuma*, the man or the men who rule in a political community. Rule detached from its natural embodiment is the core of modern political philosophy for whom rulers are never able to be persons in the ordinary, or natural, sense."[37] That philosophy seeks to enshrine reason itself (and thus exclude faith), not reason as a natural feature of embodied man, extending what Manent claims about the elevation of reason in the modern mind: "[R]ule understood as sovereignty does not belong to human beings whatever their kind. Sovereignty is the exercise of rule in the name of reason. Sovereignty . . . not only separates the rule from the ruled, it separates rule from the rulers."[38] Slade also confirms Manent's understanding of the effect of the state on the homogeneity of its people via the central mechanism of human rights:

> For the State what is paramount are the "rights" it confers upon its subjects, not the protection and promotion of virtue and vice in human beings. In becoming a citizen everyone exchanges whatever diverse social identities they had possessed for the identity conferred by the common status of State membership. The civil laws emancipate individuals from all forms of social definition and dependence. . . . The content of citizenship is universal, egalitarian "human rights."[39]

The modern subject is reduced simply and brutally to a bearer of rights. Manent's analysis of the defining equality and the universal ambitions of the modern state, then, receives an important validation in Slade's work. Slade synopsizes and complements conclusions that Manent reached about the modern form after the latter's extensive history of modernity and its predecessor forms.

Like Slade, Sokolowski confirms Manent's broad, formal conclusions about the modern state. He writes,

> The modern state . . . is something that arose through modern political philosophy. It claims to be something radically new and radically different from earlier forms of government. It is meant to be the definitive solution to the human political problem, not a solution for this time and place. It was initially

---

37 "Rule and Sovereignty," 163.
38 "Rule and Sovereignty," 170.
39 "Rule and Sovereignty," 175.

visualized by Machiavelli and baptized by Jean Bodin with
the name sovereignty. It was comprehensively described by
Hobbes, and worked out and adjusted by subsequent thinkers
like Locke, Rousseau, Kant, and Hegel. . . . To the extent that the
word *democracy* means the modern state, the one described by
Hobbes and glorified by Hegel, it presents a great human problem and an ominous threat to the human person. It is a formula
for organizing deracinated human beings.[40]

Sokolowski makes three claims that accord with Manent's. First, in the
classical view, "Men can think and express themselves. . . . [R]eason is
exercised in the founding of the city, in the deliberations that go on to
determine courses of action, and in specifying the laws of the city and adju-
dicating the application of the laws."[41] In the modern state, by contrast,
reason becomes merely a tool of the will. It is used to exclude faith and to
deny "the domain of truth. . . . The modern state is constituted as a new
reality, as the sovereign, by an act of sheer will by men in the state of
nature. . . . The sovereign state is separate from the people and it lords over
them."[42] The divisions of democracy and the enthronement of human will
that Manent identifies in the modern are evident here. Second, "modern
political thought considers the state to be an inevitable development in the
history of humanity. . . . No further prudential and philosophical reflection
is necessary concerning political society, because the final answer has
been reached in the evolution of world history."[43] Sokolowski rejects the
historicism that Manent found "*almost* irresistibly plausible." Finally, "the
Leviathan levels all prepolitical communities and authorities. It makes a
clean sweep. . . . Instead of assuming prepolitical societies and bringing
them to a higher perfection, the modern state is related to individuals,
which it takes out of the state of nature and transforms into a human
condition."[44] The modern form is that of equal individuals, with all other
Aristotelian natural relationships and distinctions of virtue erased. As
in Manent's science, the modern state in Sokolowski's estimation is
anti-natural and flattening; as such, it is inhuman.

---

40 Robert Sokolowski, "The Human Person and Political Life," *The Thomist* 65, no. 4
(2001): 516.

41 "Human Person," 518.

42 "Human Person," 519.

43 "Human Person," 521.

44 "Human Person," 523.

Sokolowski's view on the modern state, much in accord with Manent's, is especially interesting in light of a potentially powerful complementarity between these two thinkers' work. Manent writes of true human action as "resisting the world" or "negotiation with the world." These phrases resonate with Sokolowski's language of human action as "creasing the world." Manent provides an ontology of political form that modern philosophy proposed to replace with historicism; he restores Being to political thought as the antidote to History. In so doing, he claims that the political community is where man is at his most human, where his actions comprise human action par excellence. But while Manent considers particular episodes of human action from Achilles to Cato to Mother Teresa, he rarely approaches the question of the "what is" of human action itself.[45] Sokolowski, on the other hand, in his works *Moral Action: A Phenomenological Study* and *Phenomenology of the Human Person*, offers a comprehensive study of what it is to be human and to act in human ways. Like Manent, Sokolowski is both phenomenological and formal in his approach. In *Moral Action*, he seeks to "display the identifications and differentiations whose presence is required if there is to be human action at all. . . . [I]t is to clarify the being of deliberate, moral human conduct."[46] As Manent offers an ontology of political association, Sokolowski provides an "ontology of human conduct."[47] He draws a relationship between individual and political action that would be very familiar to Manent: "[I]f we flourish as human in our gratitude and generosity to another person, how much more real can we be when we achieve and recognize a performance that is good for our community? . . . In a large-scale action we recognize the performance as being good for many others, for a community, perhaps for men living in the future, and as such we make it our good."[48] In *Phenomenology of the Human Person*, again taking a formal approach, Sokolowski's "purpose is to clarify, philosophically, what human persons are. It is our rationality that makes us persons, and I wish to describe such rationality

---

45 One place where he makes a foray into the topic is in the epilogue to *Seeing Things Politically*, which comes from a 2014 lecture at the School for Advanced Studies in Social Sciences in Paris.

46 Robert Sokolowski, *Moral Action: A Phenomenological Study* (Bloomington, IN: Indiana University Press, 1985), 4. A full rendering of the complementarity suggested here is obviously beyond the scope of this book; I hope here only to open the possibility of such an investigation.

47 *Moral Action*, 6.

48 *Moral Action*, 73.

in action, to show how it is made manifest."[49] To do so, he introduces the term "agent of truth." Sokolowski thus provides the ontology of the Aristotelian rational man and the action of that man that is needed—and, in a sense, presumed—in Manent's science and ontology of political association and form.

Manent writes, "We no longer know what it means to act. We have lost the sense of action, and we understand action only as the application of the rule, or conformity to the rule."[50] Sokolowski's account of human action and what it is to be human performs an important service to Manent's own account: it explains in great depth and with great subtlety what is lost in the modern, what it is exactly that the modern state represses and how the state harms the human soul by removing the knowledge and the possibility of human action in all of its heterogeneity. By explaining what it is to be human and to act as a human, Sokolowski explains how the anti-natural state form is inhuman and thus exposes the cost of our reduction to beings who are merely bearers of rights. Read together, these thinkers give us a description of rational, moral, political man and the forms of his action and his associations that grasps the full reality of the human "what is." Both accept that this human reality comes from and is pointed toward something that transcends it, even as the human domain has truths and forms proper to it. Manent and Sokolowski join to provide a philosophy of man in the earthly city and in the intermixed zone between that city and the City of God that promises to be far more in accord with nature than its modern counterparts.

MANENT'S FULL ACHIEVEMENT

Manent writes,

> A work that satisfactorily brings together fidelity to human experience and commitment to religious perspective is rare. . . . [T]here is only one work, one text in which the two are strangely, paradoxically reconciled. No surprise here: . . . the Bible, especially the Old Testament, in which we find at once, directly and immediately, human experience in its greatest ignorance of God and, mysteriously, a presence of God that does not impinge upon, that does not cover up, the authenticity of experience. The

---

49 Sokolowski, *Phenomenology of the Human Person*, 7.
50 Manent, *Seeing Things Politically*, 156.

text of *Psalms* is particularly overwhelming because, in a chaotic and popular language, it maintains a balance that the greatest religious minds have not been able to maintain so perfectly.[51]

Manent points to the full range of human experiences and emotions contained in the Psalms. But perhaps one verse from the Douay-Rheims translation of Psalm 113 of captures Manent's work most fully: "Blessed be you of the Lord, who made heaven and earth. The heaven of heaven is the Lord's; but the earth he has given to the children of men."[52]

Manent brings European political movement under the Aristotelian principle that man is a political, rational animal by nature. In fulfilling that charge, he uses the more than two thousand years of events and thought since Aristotle to show us a political science that fills the philosophical void of the Ciceronian moment, indicts and condemns modern political philosophy, and exhibits the political and moral nature according to which man must seek the truth and act according to it. This is a nature in which God governs all things providentially but commands man, in God's image, to use his reason and freedom in order to choose and to act. He does not ignore us in his "heaven of heaven," but he has created a human domain in which man is the principle of action and God is man's telos. Manent's science is not a closed system walled off from heaven, nor is it a list of divinely revealed rules of conduct and procedure. It opens up, or perhaps reopens, the possibility of authentically being human by being political, a task of great difficulty and great reward. It is not a science for the City of God, where faith is unnecessary and knowledge of ourselves and of God is as perfect as the love of God. Nor is it for the earthly city of those who would ignore God and his proper claims in order to savor their own autonomy. This politics takes place where the City of God and the earthly city are intermixed, where man must negotiate his way and crease the world, pulled by pagan pride, striving for natural virtue, and attempting to follow the injunctions to love one's neighbor and forgive one's enemies. That is the human condition, and Manent points us toward a political science that will endure for as long as that condition prevails, until St. Augustine's philosophy of history comes to the fullness of time. "It is up to us to discern that we are carried and given life by what we think we have long since left behind. . . . Thus, today as in the past, and today much more than in the past, the question of actions to be done lies before

---

51 *Seeing Things Politically*, 63.
52 This is Psalm 115 in other translations such as the Revised Standard Version.

us, and political or practical science is always, or is now again, the first of the human sciences."[53]

53 Manent, *Seeing Things Politically*, 192 and 211.

BIBLIOGRAPHY

Aristotle. *Metaphysics*. Translated by Hugh Tredennick. Cambridge, MA: Harvard University Press, 1933.

———. *The Constitution of Athens*. Translated by J. M. Moore. Berkeley: University of California Press, 1986.

———. *Nicomachean Ethics*. Translated by David Ross. Oxford: Oxford University Press, 2009.

———. *Aristotle's Politics*. Translated by Carnes Lord. 2nd ed. Chicago: University of Chicago Press, 2013.

Augustine. *Confessions*. Translated by Henry Chadwick. Oxford: Oxford University Press, 1991.

———. *On Free Choice of the Will*. Translated by Thomas Williams. Indianapolis, IN: Hackett Publishing, 1993.

———. *The City of God against the Pagans*. Translated by R. W. Dyson. Cambridge: Cambridge University Press, 1998.

Baechler, Jean. "Dépérissement de la nation." In *Contrepoints et commentaires*, 104–13. Paris: Calmann-Lévy, 1996.

Bush, George W. "Second Inaugural Address." January 20, 2005. *NPR*. Transcript. https://www.npr.org/templates/story/story. php?storyId=4460172.

Cicero. *De Legibus*. Translated by Clinton Walker Keyes. Cambridge, MA: Harvard University Press, 1928.

———. *De Officiis*. Translated by Walter Miller. Cambridge, MA: Harvard University Press, 1913.

———. *De Re Publica*. Translated by Clinton Walker Keyes. Cambridge, MA: Harvard University Press, 1928.

Craiutu, Aurelian. "The Virtues of Political Moderation." *Political Theory: An International Journal of Political Philosophy* 29, no. 3 (2001): 449–68.

Couture, Yves. "Strauss face aux deux infinis modernes." *Archives Philosophie* 79, no. 3 (2016): 499–512.

De Ligio, Giulio, Jean-Vincent Holeindre, and Daniel Mahoney, eds. *La politique et l'âme: Autour de Pierre Manent*. Paris: CNRS Editions, 2014.

Descartes, René. *Meditations on First Philosophy*. In *The Philosophical Writings of Descartes*. Translated by John Cottingham, Robert Stoothoff, and Dugald Murdoch. Cambridge: Cambridge University Press, 1984.

Dougherty, Jude P. Review of *Democracy Without Nations?: The Fate of Self-Government in Europe*, by Pierre Manent. *Review of Metaphysics* 61, no. 4 (2008): 849–50.

———. Review of *Seeing Things Politically*, by Pierre Manent. *Review of Metaphysics* 69, no.2 (2015): 398–400.

———. "We Are Modern and Want to Be Modern." *Gilsonia: A Journal of Classical Philosophy* 4, no. 3 (2015): 241–49.

Gallagher, David M. Review of *An Intellectual History of Liberalism*, by Pierre Manent. *Review of Metaphysics* 49, no. 4 (1996): 933–34.

Geneens, Raf. "The Emergence of Supranational Politics: A New Breath of Life for the Nation-State?" *Telos: A Quarterly Journal of Critical Thought*, no. 156 (Fall 2011): 24–46.

Gilson, Étienne. *Les métamorphoses de la cité de Dieu*. Louvain: Publications Universitaires de Louvain, 1952.

Guerra, Marc. "Pierre Manent and the Dialectics of Augustine's City of God." In *Freedom and the Moral Law: Proceedings from the 36th Annual Convention of the Fellowship of Catholic Scholars*, edited by Elizabeth Shaw, 45–56. Notre Dame, IN: Fellowship of Catholic Scholars, 2013.

Haché, Étienne. "Penser le sens d'une humanité européenne à rebours du paganisme nationale et des incantations humanitaires." *Laval Théologique et Philosophique* 62, no. 3 (2006): 569–87.

Hancock, Ralph C. "Pierre Manent: Between Nature and History." In *Reason, Revelation, and the Civic Order: Political Philosophy and the Claims of Faith*, edited by Paul R. DeHart and Carson Holloway, 119–33. Dekalb, IL: Northern Illinois University Press, 2014.

———. "Conservatism, Aesthetic and Active: Reflections on Roger Scruton and Pierre Manent." *Perspectives on Political Science* 45, no. 4 (2016): 272–80.

Hittinger, Russell. "The Three Necessary Societies." *First Things* (June 2017). Accessed June 15, 2023. https://www.firstthings.com/article/2017/06/the-three-necessary-societies.

Janssens, David. "La part d'Athènes: L'Europe et la Loi." *Revue de réflexion interdisciplinaire* 24, no. 2 (2002): 5–19.

Keating, James F. Review of *Metamorphoses of the City: On the Western Dynamic*, by Pierre Manent. *Review of Politics* 76, no. 4 (2014): 679–84.

Lawler, Peter Augustine. "Nature, History, and the Human Individual: On Pierre Manent's Modern Liberty and Its Discontents." Review of *Modern Liberty and Its Discontents*, by Pierre Manent. *Interpretation: A Journal of Philosophy* 27, no. 1 (1999): 81–87.

Mahoney, Daniel. "Modern Man and Man '*Tout Court*': The Flight from Nature and the Modern Difference, Review Essay on *La cité de l'homme*." Review of *La cité de l'homme*, by Pierre Manent. *Interpretation: A Journal of Philosophy* 22, no. 3 (1995): 417–38.

———. "Modern Liberty and Its Discontents: An Introduction to the Political Reflection of Pierre Manent." In Manent, *Modern Liberty and Its Discontents*, 1–29.

———. "Communion and Consent: Pierre Manent on the Wellsprings of Western Liberty." *Perspectives on Political Science* 41, no. 2 (2012): 93–99.

———. "A Liberal and a Classic: Pierre Manent's Neo-Aristotelian Reading of Raymond Aron." *Perspectives on Political Science* 45, no. 4 (2016): 230–36.

MacIntyre, Alasdair. "An Interview with Giovanna Borradori." In *The MacIntyre Reader*, edited by Kelvin Knight, 255–66. Notre Dame, IN: University of Notre Dame Press, 1998.

———. "Politics, Philosophy and the Common Good." In *The MacIntyre Reader*, edited by Kelvin Knight, 235–51. Notre Dame, IN: University of Notre Dame Press, 1998.

Manent, Pierre. *Naissance de la politique moderne: Machiavel, Hobbes, Rousseau*. Paris: Payot, 1977.

———. *Tocqueville et la nature de la démocratie*. Paris: Julliard, 1982. Translated by John Waggoner as *Tocqueville and the Nature of Democracy* (Lanham, MD: Rowman & Littlefield, 1996).

———. "The Modern State." In *New French Thought: Political Philosophy*, edited by Mark Lilla, 123–33. Princeton, NJ: Princeton University Press, 1983.

———. "Raymond Aron." In *European Liberty: Four Essays on the Occasion of the 25th Anniversary of the Erasmus Prize Foundation*, 1–23. The Hague: Nijhoff, 1983. This essay also appears (in two places) under a different title in an entry below.

———. *Les Libéraux*. 2 vols. Paris: Hachettes Littératures, 1986.

———. *Histoire intellectuelle du libéralisme. Dix leçons*. Paris: Calmann-Lévy, 1987. Translated by Rebecca Balinski as *An Intellectual History of Liberalism* (Princeton, NJ: Princeton University Press, 1995).

———. "Strauss et Nietzsche." *Revue de Métaphysique et de Morale* 94, no. 3 (1989): 337–45.

———. *La Cité de l'homme*. Paris: Fayard, 1994. Translated by Marc A. LePain as *The City of Man* (Princeton, NJ: Princeton University Press, 1998).

———. "Raymond Aron—Political Educator." In *In Defense of Political Reason: Essays by Raymond Aron*, edited by Daniel J. Mahoney, 1–23. Lanham, MD: Rowman & Littlefield, 1994. This essay also appears above with the same title in *Political Reason in the Age of Ideology: Essays in Honor of Raymond Aron*, edited by Bryan-Paul Frost and Daniel J. Mahoney, 11–30. New Brunswick, NJ: Transaction Publishers, 2007.

———. Introduction to *Aurel Kolnai: The Utopian Mind and Other Papers*, edited by Francis Dunlop, xiii-xxvi. London: Athlone Press, 1995.

———. *Modern Liberty and Its Discontents: Pierre Manent*. Edited and translated by Daniel J. Mahoney and Paul Seaton. Lanham, MD: Rowman & Littlefield, 1998.

———. "Christianity and Democracy: Some Remarks on the Political History of Religion, or, on the Religious History of Modern Politics." In *Modern Liberty and Its Discontents*, 97–115.

———. "Toward the Work and Toward the World: Claude Lefort's Machiavelli." In *Modern Liberty and Its Discontents*, 47–63.

———. "The Truth, Perhaps." In *Modern Liberty and Its Discontents*, 33–43.

———. *Cours familier de philosophie politique*. Paris: Fayard, 2004. Translated by Marc A. Le Pain as *A World beyond Politics? A Defense of the Nation-State* (Princeton, NJ: Princeton University Press, 2006).

———. *La Raison des nations: Réflexions sur la démocratie en Europe*. Paris: Gallimard, 2006. Translated by Paul Seaton as *Democracy without Nations? The Fate of Self-Government in Europe* (Wilmington, DE: ISI Books, 2007).

———. "Tocqueville, Political Philosopher." In *The Cambridge Companion to Tocqueville*, edited by Cheryl B. Welch, 108–20. Cambridge: Cambridge University Press, 2006.

———. *Enquête sur la démocratie. Études de philosophie politique*. Paris: Gallimard, 2007.

———. "The Transatlantic Predicament." In *America at Risk: Threats to Self-Government in an Age of Uncertainty*, edited by Robert Faulkner and Susan M. Shell, 15–28. Ann Arbor, MI: University of Michigan Press, 2009.

———. *Le Regard politique: entretiens avec Bénédicte Delorme-Montini*. Paris: Flammarion, 2010. Translated by Ralph C. Hancock as *Seeing Things Politically: Interviews with Bénédicte Delorme-Montini* (South Bend, IN: St. Augustine's Press, 2015).

———. *Les métamorphoses de la cité: essai sur la dynamique de l'Occident*. Paris: Flammarion, 2010. Translated by Marc LePain as *Metamorphoses of the City: On the Western Dynamic* (Cambridge, MA: Harvard University Press, 2013).

———. "The Return of Political Philosophy." In *The Great Lie: Classic and Recent Appraisals of Ideology and Totalitarianism*, edited by F. Flagg Taylor IV, 575–92. Wilmington, DE: ISI Books, 2011.

———. "Between Athens and Jerusalem." *First Things*, no. 220 (February 2012): 35–39.

———. "Montaigne and Rousseau: Some Reflections." In *The Challenge of Rousseau*, edited and translated by Eve Grace and Christopher Kelly, 312–23. Cambridge: Cambridge University Press, 2012.

———. "Retrouver l'intelligence de la loi." *Revue Thomiste* 114, no. 1 (2014): 143–54.

———. *Montaigne: la vie sans loi*. Paris: Flammarion, 2014.

——. "Raison et Révélation: Quelques remarques sur l'analyse straussian et la synthèse chrétienne." *Archives de Philosophie* 79, no. 3 (2016), 513–22.

——. *Situation de la France.* Paris: Desclée de Brouwer, 2015. Translated by Ralph C. Hancock as *Beyond Radical Secularism: How France and the Christian West Should Respond to the Islamic Challenge* (South Bend, IN: St. Augustine's Press, 2016).

——. "The Tragedy of the Republic." *First Things* (May 2017). Accessed April 19, 2017. https://www.firstthings.com/article/2017/05/the-tragedy-of-the-republic.

——. *La loi naturelle et les droits de l'homme.* Paris: Presses Universitaires de France, 2018.

Manent, Pierre, Marcel Gauchet, and Alain Finkielkraut. *La démocratie de notre temps.* Paris: Tricorne, 2003.

McCarthy, John C. Review of *Tocqueville and the Nature of Democracy*, by Pierre Manent. *Review of Metaphysics* 51, no. 4 (1998): 945–47.

——. Review of *The City of Man*, by Pierre Manent. *Telos: A Quarterly Journal of Critical Thought*, no. 116 (Summer 1999): 175–87.

McCoy, Charles N. R. *The Structure of Political Thought: A Study in the History of Political Ideas.* New York: McGraw-Hill Book Company, 1963.

McDougall, Walter. *Promised Land, Crusader State: The American Encounter with the World since 1776.* New York: Houghton Mifflin, 1997.

Melanćon, Jérôme. "Affirmation et indétermination: Les droits de l'homme chez C. Lafort and P. Manent." *Science et Esprit: Revue de philosophie et de théologie* 56, no. 3 (2004): 303–19.

Pappin, Gladden J. "Pierre Manent and the Politics of the Possible." *Perspectives on Political Science* 45, no. 4 (2016): 300–308.

Paris, Crystal Cordell. "L'inspiration aristotélicienne dans la pensée de Pierre Manent. Les phénomènes, la chose commune, l'action." In De Ligio, Holeindre, and Mahoney, *La politique et l'âme*, 189–203.

Plato. *Republic.* Translated by G. M. A. Grube. Revised by C. D. C. Reeve. Indianapolis, IN: Hackett, 1992.

——. *Gorgias.* Translated by James H. Nichols Jr. Ithaca, NY: Cornell University Press, 1998.

——. *Statesman.* Translated by Christopher J. Rowe. Indianapolis, IN: Hackett, 1999.

Rinderle, Peter. "Die Idee der Demokratie in der neueren französischen Sozialphilosophie." *Zeitschrift für philosophische Forschung* 53, no. 2 (1999): 278–99.

Roddy, Mary. "Democracy and Political Life—Are They Compatible in the Modern State?" *Ethics Education* 13, no. 1 (2007): 4–13.

Seaton, Paul. "Aristotelus Revivus: Pierre Manent's Reflections on the Contemporary Political World." In *Faith, Reason, and Political Life Today*, edited by Peter Augustine Lawler and Dale McConkey, 163–88. Lanham, MD: Lexington, an imprint of Rowan & Littlefield, 2001.

———. "The Healing Light: An Introduction to the Political Philosophizing of Pierre Manent." PhD diss., Fordham University, 2003.

———. Review of *A World Beyond Politics? A Defense of the Nation State*, by Pierre Manent. *Review of Politics* 69, no. 4 (2007): 700–705.

Shelley, Trevor. *Globalization and Liberalism: An Essay on Montesquieu, Tocqueville, and Manent*. South Bend, IN: St. Augustine's Press, 2016.

Slongo, Paulo. Review of *Montaigne: La vie sans loi*, by Pierre Manent. *Filosofia Politica* 29, no. 2 (2015): 347–50.

Slade, Francis. "Rule as Sovereignty: The Universal and Homogenous State." In *The Truthful and the Good: Essays in Honor of Robert Sokolowski*, edited by John J. Drummond and James G. Hart, 159–80. Dordrecht: Kluwer, 1996.

———. "Two Versions of Political Philosophy: Teleology and the Conceptual Genesis of the Modern State." In *Natural Moral Law in Contemporary Society*, edited by Holger Zaborowski, 235–63. Washington, DC: The Catholic University of America Press, 2010.

Sokolowski, Robert. *Moral Action: A Phenomenological Study*. Bloomington, IN: Indiana University Press, 1985.

———. "The Human Person and Political Life." *The Thomist* 65, no. 4 (2001): 505–27.

———. *Phenomenology of the Human Person*. Cambridge: Cambridge University Press, 2008.

Strauss, Leo. *Natural Right and History*. Chicago, IL: University of Chicago Press, 1953.

———. *The City and Man*. Chicago, IL: University of Chicago Press, 1964.

———. *On Tyranny*. Ithaca, NY: Cornell University Press, 1968.

———. "The Three Waves of Modernity." In *An Introduction to Political Philosophy: Ten Essays by Leo Strauss*, edited by Hilail Gildin, 81–98. Detroit, MI: Wayne State University Press, 1989.

Voegelin, Eric. *Order and History*. Baton Rouge: University of Louisiana Press, 1957. Quoted in Manent, *Metamorphoses*, 32.

INDEX

A

America: confidence and democratic empire, 73n7, 178–80; continued aspects of nation form, 179; revolution and founding, 177, 184; Rome as example for founders, 114

Aristotle, 3, 10, 13–14, 18–20, 23, 34n39, 59n104, 61, 65, 67, 230–31, 237, 239–41, 245, 249; empire, Rome and, 113–24; as influence on Manent, 38–55; modern state and, 169, 173, 181, 183, 187–88, 193, 201, 205, 212, 227; nation and, 128, 131, 145n44, 146; polis or city and, 71–73, 75, 78–84, 88, 91–92, 96–98, 102–4, 109–12

Aron, Raymond, 4, 23, 51; as influence on Manent, 52–65, 67, 232

Athens, 28, 49, 72, 76, 79, 91, 131, 136; contrast with modern, 216; contrast with Rome, 116–23; emergence of politics and city from pre-political Athens in Homer, 88, 95–98, 196; remaining city and never empire, 113–16. *See also* City

Augustine, St., 23, 61, 72, 76, 107n110, 119, 120n151, 134, 141; Christian City of God vs. modern efforts to perfect the earthly city, 169–72, 196; Cicero and, 52–53; importance of love in political community and Leo Strauss, 64–65; as influence on Manent, 37, 42–51; limits of Manent's understanding of the person and, 242; in Manent's *City of Man*, 212; in Manent's *Metamorphoses of the City*, 224; as source of Christian critique of pagan politics, and two cities, 35, 161–63; source of Manent's philosophy of history, 227, 237, 249; three waves of history and, 165–67. *See also* Universality, impossibility of universal political form

B

Bacon, Roger, 200n93; Gilson and, 171; as modern philosopher, 61

Baechler, Jean, 56, 128–29

Besançon, Alain, 56

Bible, 156, 185; as offering fidelity to both human experience and religious commitment, 8n26, 248–49

Bloom, Allan, 65

Boccaccio, Giovanni, 149

Bush, George W., 179n24

Byzantine Empire, 77

C

Campanella, Tommaso, 171

Casanova, Claude, 56

Cato, 247

Charlemagne, 150

Chateaubriand, Francis-René de: on condition of human soul in modern age, 224

Christianity, 4, 17, 20, 72, 76, 81n29, 94, 127n1, 128, 196, 230, 232, 240, 242; as agent in political development, 23; Church as universal and political form, 141–44, 149–51, 158, 159–64, 170–73; common good and, 142; Covenant as essential to good life, rejected by modern man, 131–33, 143, 236–37; incompetence in political realm, 49; indeterminacy of and political form, 12–13; liberalism, human rights and, 211, 234; modern state and, 170–74, 185–90; as one of three waves of history, 164–67; and political thought, 8–9; role in Ciceronian moment and emergence of nation, 127–67; as starting point of European political development and nation, 130–41, 148–59; tension with political realm as driving modern thought, 32–38; tensions with liberalism, 186–225; de Tocqueville and movement towards equality/democracy, 176; understanding of virtue vs. modern, 30. *See also* St. Augustine, St.; Jesus Christ; Manent, Pierre; Thomas Aquinas, St.

Church. *See* Christianity

Church as political form. *See* Christianity

Churchill, Winston, 7, 45

Cicero, 59n104; Ciceronian moment and development of the nation form, 134, 144–67; in fulfillment of Manent's project, 249; as influence on Manent, 51–58; Machiavelli as marking end of the Ciceronian moment, 187–88; modern state and, 170, 176, 181–83; on Rome and the form of empire, 121–25; separation of private and public in Manent's *Intellectual History of Liberalism*, 207

Ciceronian moment. *See* Cicero

City or Polis: Aristotelian natural relationships and, 14; Aristotle' study of, 39–41; Raymond Aron and, 58, 59n104; Augustine and, 44–51;

common good and, 11; defined and limited, 19–20, 73–77; emergence of nation from city, retaining principle of city, 127–37; MacIntyre, Manent and, 19–21; modern differences with, 199–202, 213–14; modern escape from traditional relationship of city, 31; modern tension with nature, Christian "two cities" understanding, 33–37; as natural and tragic, 81–84, 108, 139; as original political form, 78; phenomenology and, 67–68; as political form, 68–125; political virtue in, 110; Leo Strauss and, 61; virtue of Athens and, 28. *See also* Athens; Rome

Claudel, Paul, 4

Common good or operation or thing, 11–12, 41–42, 51, 72, 102–12, 117–19, 145n44, 229–31, 233, 235, 237–41; Aristotle and, 14, 119, 131, 191; St. Augustine and, 45; Cicero and, 124; Church and, 142, 195; Hobbes and, 191, 195; Machiavelli and, 189; Alasdair MacIntyre and, 18–20; modern man and state as lacking, 215–17, 221, 223–25, 227; in pre-political Athens, 96–97; Rousseau and, 207–8. *See also* Man; Motion

Comte, Auguste, Étienne Gilson and, 171

Constant, Benjamin, 63, 79, 210, 213

Cyclopes, 104–6

D

Dante Alighieri, 149, 171; challenging papacy and in favor of empire, 187; Machiavelli and, 188; Manent's opposing Dante's support for universal form, 225; *Monarchy* and Europe's search for form to overcome divisions induced by Christianity, 139

Descartes, René, as discarding Aristotelian final cause, 4, 34n40, 61

E

Empire, 37, 172–73, 187, 221, 231; St. Augustine and, 45; and Ciceronian moment, breakdown and failure, 144–59; defined and compared to city, 72–78, 80, 99; emergence of nation and, 130–43; as epic, 83–84; modern democratic empire, 178–80; modern form as different, universalist empire, 220; as one of Manent's political forms, 68, 71; as political form, 112–25; in three waves of history, 165–66. *See also specific historical empires (e.g., Byzantine)*

English Civil War, 190

English Revolution, 203

Enlightenment, 19, 25, 186

European democratic empire, 178–80

F

Frederick II, 150

French Empire, 236

French Revolution, 62, 79, 129, 177, 185, 209–11, 214

Freud, Sigmund, 45

Fumet, Stanislaus and Aniouta, 4

G

Gilson, Étienne, 220; Hobbes and, 194; impossibility of humanity as
   universal political form, 224; loss of God in modern state as loss of
   politics, 227, 236; Manent's lectures at Catholic Institute of Paris and,
   226n169; as opposing modern effort to create universal political form
   and supporting St. Augustine's "two cities," 169–80

Guelphs and Ghibellines, as representing conflict between city and empire,
   137, 149

Guizot, Francois, 210

H

Hegel, George Wilhelm Friedrich, 25, 45, 61, 181, 246; Kojève and, 244n35

Heidegger, Martin, 15, 25, 62, 63n115, 66

Hesiod, 86

History and historicism, 3, 8, 14–18, 21, 23–31, 36–38, 40, 51, 59, 86–87, 105,
   130, 133, 210–25, 229–32, 239–41, 249; Manent's philosophy of history,
   182–83, 227; nation and kings and, 154; replacing metaphysics and
   nature, 174–76; Robert Sokolowski on, 246–47; Leo Strauss and, 63;
   three waves of history, 164–67

Hittinger, Russell, three necessary societies for man, 242–43

Hobbes, Thomas, 97, 107; in conception of modern state, 178; "democratic
   vector" of Europe and, 35; elements of his political thought in
   Intellectual History of Liberalism, 190–211; liberal denationalization
   and, 185; liberalism and, 39, 182, 185–86; modern political cycle,
   theologico-political question and, 223–24; Francis Slade and, 244;
   Robert Sokolowski and, 246; Leo Strauss's three waves of modern
   thinking and, 165n94

Homer, 100, 103–4, 122, 136; epic and tragic origin of city (and Achilles,
   Hector, Agamemnon, Paris, Briseis, Helen, Troy), 83–95; in Manent's
   account of origin of the city, 72; mediation in Plato and, 165; as national

poet, 136; reference in *City of Man*, 45; Weil's understanding of Iliad, 88. *See also* Athens

Human Nature. *See* Man

Human Rights, 6, 124–25, 180; Christianity and, 234; as insufficient for political life, 237–38; man as bearer of rights, 125, 166, 175, (vs. ancient citizen) 184, 216, 238; mediation and, 166–67, 232; modern state and, 191–93, (and Locke) 198, 200, 211, 220, 222, 226; Francis Slade and, 245; Robert Sokolowski and, 248; universal political form and, 232

J

Jesus Christ, 93–94, 140, 172

Jugnet, Louis, 55

K

Kant, Immanuel, 4, 19, 45, 53, 58, 60, 246

Kierkegaard, Søren, 25

King, 133–34, 141, 186, 231; compared to Hobbesian State, 194; effects of absence of king in modern state, 211, 222, 244; in emergence of nation form, 148–59; as man of motion, 153; Montesquieu and, 203. *See also* Nation

Kratos, 180

L

Lefort, Claude, 10, 62, 66

Leibniz, Gottfried Wilhelm, 171

Locke, John: elements of political thought in *Intellectual History of Liberalism*, 197–207; *homo oeconomicus* and, 215; as liberal thinker, 39; Robert Sokolowski and, 246

Luther, Martin, 156–58. *See also* Reformation, Protestant

M

Machiavelli, Niccolò, 182, 211; as beginning of modern project in Leo Strauss, 62; critique of Christianity and "democratic vector," 35, 43, 46, 149; elements of thought in *Intellectual History of Liberalism*, 185–90; elimination of claims of good, 196; as modern political philosopher, 17, 155; Robert Sokolowski and, 246; as Leo Strauss's first wave of modern thinking, 165n94

MacIntyre, Alasdair, comparison with Manent, politics and the human person, 18–21, 242–43

Mahoney, Daniel, on Manent and Raymond Aron, 57–58

Man: St. Augustine's understanding of man, 42–51; becoming political as becoming rational, 11, 87–89, 96, 154, 196, 102, (Hobbes's difference) 196; Christianity's effect on ("double vision"), 164; Cicero's understanding of man, 123–24; city and empire as natural forms for man, 72–78; importance of mortality in change to political and rational, 91–93; Alasdair MacIntyre on, 18–21, 242–43; modern man as different, restless, in opposition to nature, 24–38, 205–11, 213–20, (as rejecting metaphysics) 216; modern state's repression of human soul, 223; as political animal and Aristotle's understanding of human nature as political, rational, 14, 17, 38–42, 72, 79, 82–83, 87–89, 95, 107, 110, 112, (and Church) 139–41, 154, 182, 221, 230, 239, 241, 249; politics and political form and, 1–3, 9–13, 71, 250; pre-political understanding, 87; as principle of politics and political development, 3, 14, 16–18, 49, 88, 110, 132, 140, 183, 229, 231, 235, 249; Robert Sokolowski and, 246–48; Leo Strauss's types of philosophical vs. religious and, 63–65; three necessary societies for flourishing, 242–43; understanding man as Manent's project, 6

Manent, Pierre: classical/ancient philosophy and, 9–14; critique of liberalism and its view of man as basis of modern state in *Intellectual History of Liberalism*, 183–211; critique of modern state and its divisions of the human person in *A World Beyond Politics?*, 217–21; critique of modern state and its understanding of man in *City of Man*, 212–17; critique of modern state and loss of politics in *Metamorphoses of the City*, 221–25; critique of modern thinking on human rights in *La loi naturelle et les droits de l'homme*, 225–26; focus on political form and human person, 1–3, 5–7; "grand project" under Aristotle's "man as political animal" and, 230–32; on happiness, friendship, and non-political communities, 239–43; modern difference and, 24–32; political form and three waves of history, 164–67; preference for nation of Christian mark, 232–40; two paths of inquiry, history and philosophy, 14–18. *See also* Theologico-political question; Triangle of Politics, Philosophy, Religion

Maritain, Jacques, 4, 58

Marsilius of Padua, 149, 187; Machiavelli and, 188

Marx, Karl, 15, 25, 45, 97, 177, 182, 184

McCoy, Charles, common good and, 145n44

Mediation, 96, 123, 222; Christianity and, 133–34, 173; nation, Church and, 156–58; in three waves of European history, 165–67

Milton, John, 45

Modern Difference, 24–32, 40–43, 46, 52, 96, 101, 174, 191, 212–13, 230, 238; political form as revealing, 71; Leo Strauss and, 61–65. *See also* Man, Modern State

Modern State, 19–20, 27, 31, 39, 43–45, 58, 61, 68, 83, 100–104, 123–25, 127–29, 133–35, 139, 159, 166–67, 169–227; critique of liberalism and its view of man as basis of modern state in *Intellectual History of Liberalism*, 183–211; critique of modern state and its divisions of the human person and human nature in *A World Beyond Politics?* 217–21; critique of modern state and its understanding of man in *City of Man*, 212–17; critique of modern state and loss of politics in *Metamorphoses of the City*, 221–25; nation and, 144–47, 180; nation of Christian mark and, 232–39; Reformation and, 160; rejection of nature, 174; Francis Slade and Robert Sokolowski on, 243–48

Montaigne, Michel de, 17, 147

Montesquieu, 17, 35, 47, 63, 106, 174, 178, 213; Christianity and, 164; elements of political thought in *Intellectual History of Liberalism*, 202–6; modern difference and, 26–30

Motion (or Movement), 230; Raymond Aron and, 58; as ceasing in the modern, 227, 232, 237; Christianity as stimulation of modern motion, 35–38; in city, 82, 83; in empire, 78; human movement towards common good, 11, 45, 108–10, 112; in king and nation, 130–34, (and Church) 140–43, 153–54; in modern politics/state, 35, 47, 180, 188, 199, 207, 213; modern state's repression of movements of human soul, 223; Montesquieu and, 26, 205; passage from city to empire as source, 73; passage in Athens from pre-political to political, 73, 90, 98–99, 110–12, 114–15; of political form, 9, 14–17, 21, 49, 69, 71–72, 86, 88, 123, 127–28, 132, 182–83, 212, 224–25, 239; pre-political tribe and, 68; success of Manent's project and, 249; teleological basis for in Aristotle and St. Augustine, 51; in three waves of history, 176; towards God, 140; towards modern formlessness, 223. *See also* Man

Movement. *See* Motion

N

Napoleon, 45

Nation, 2, 20, 37, 49, 99, 125, 193, 231; as concluding the Ciceronian moment, 54; denationalization of modern state, 180, 184–86, 221–23; emergence, nation as political form, and Christianity, 127–67; emergence of modern state from, 176–80, 210–11; nation of Christian mark, 232–40; in opposition to universal political form, 170–73; in succession of European political form, 68; as whole or political form, 71

Nature. *See* Aristotle; City; History/Historicism; Man; Modern State; Nation

Nietzsche, Friedrich, 15, 25, 62, 63n115, 165

P

Paris, Crystal Cordell, 38, 66

Pascal, Blaise, 8

Péguy, Charles, 67

Peloponnesian War. *See* Sparta

Persian Empire, 72, 77

Person. *See* Man

Phenomenology, 17, 66–68; Robert Sokolowski and, 247

Plato, 10, 13–14, 39–40, 59n104, 82, 88, 91–92, 92n65, 96, 103–4, 183, 212; Raymond Aron and, 60–61; three waves of history and, 165–66

Polis. *See* City

Political form: defined, 1–3; summarized in Manent's thought, 12–13, 68–69. *See also major chapter headings and forms of* City; Empire; Modern State; Nation

Psalms, overcoming conflict between human experience and religious commitment, 8n26, 248–49

R

Reformation, Protestant, 133–34, 147–48, 153–59, 160, 167, 178, 233; denationalization and, 185

Renaissance, 144, 147–48, 159

Rome, 10, 183, 231; Cicero and, 53; exceptional as transforming from city to empire, 113–16. *See also* Cicero; Empire

Rousseau, Jean-Jacques, 11, 17, 29–30, 62, 63n115, 106–12, 165n94; elements of thought in *Intellectual History of Liberalism*, 205–11; Robert Sokolowski and, 246

S

Shakespeare, William, 121n153, 136; *Hamlet*, 45

Slade, Francis, 2, 71, 229; human rights and, 245; modern state and, 181–82, 243–45

Socrates, 7, 86, 88, 92n65, 93–94, 165

Sokolowski, Robert, 41n56, 68, 229; on classical view and modern state, 243–48; human rights and, 248

Sparta, 79, 85, 91, 97, 98, 113–14, 123, 209

Strauss, Leo, 7, 10n30, 23, 51, 75, 78, 212; choice/conflict between philosophy and religion and, 53, 62, (Bible as overcoming) 248; definition of polis or city and, 19–20, 73, 79–81; as influence on Manent especially on theologico-political question and modern difference, 55–65; Manent's break with Strauss on Caesarism and tyranny and, 116–20; phenomenology and, 66; three waves of modern thinking and, 165

T

Teresa of Calcutta, St., 247

Theologico-political question, 23, 32–37, 46, 50, 71, 75, 121n152, 127, 134, 143; in emergence of the nation, 149–60; Hobbes and, 194, 224; liberalism and, 211; Machiavelli and, 186–89; Leo Strauss and, 64

Thomas Aquinas, St., 7, 45, 131, 187–88; as influence on Manent, 51–55

Three necessary societies for man, 242–43

Three waves of history, 164–67

Thucydides, 10, 59, 61, 82, 91–92, 212

Tocqueville, Alexis de, 17, 35, 39, 41; movement towards equality and democracy, 176–77, 210

Triangle of Politics, Philosophy, Religion, 7–9, 18, 25, 36, 43, 45, 47, 51, 53, 59, 64, 94, 106, 120, 140, 143, 146, 152, 172, 182, 232, 236–37; modern state and, 224, 239

U

Universality, impossibility of universal political form, 100, 122, 124, 127n1, 148, 169–74, 179–81, (Hobbes and) 194, 215, 220–24, 227, 229, 232, 235, 244n35, 245. *See also* Christianity; Church

V

Vico, 104–8
Voegelin, Eric, 86, 116–17

W

Weber, Max, 158, 217
Weil, Simone, 88–89, 94